Remapping the History of Catholicism in the United States

Remapping the History of Catholicism in the United States:

Essays from the *U.S. Catholic Historian*

EDITED BY DAVID J. ENDRES

The Catholic University of America Press
Washington, DC

Selection Copyright © 2017 The Catholic University of America Press

All rights reserved

The paper used in this publication meets the minimum requirements
of American National Standards for Information Science -
Permanence of Paper for Printed Library Materials, ANSI
Z39.48-1984.

Cataloging-in-Publication Data available from the Library of Congress

ISBN 978-0-8132-2969-0

Table of Contents

Preface
 David J. Endres vii

Remapping American Catholicism
 Timothy Matovina 1

"Organized Catholic Womanhood": Suffrage, Citizenship
 and the National Council of Catholic Women
 Jeanne Petit 49

Mother Katharine Drexel's Benevolent Empire:
 The Bureau of Catholic Indian Missions and the
 Education of Native Americans, 1885–1935
 Amanda Bresie 71

The Daughters of Charity as Cultural Intermediaries:
 Women, Religion, and Race in Early Twentieth-Century
 Los Angeles
 Kristine Ashton Gunnell 95

Dorothy Day and César Chávez: American Catholic Lives
 in Nonviolence
 Anne Klejment 119

Black Power, Vatican II, and the Emergence of
 Black Catholic Liturgies
 Matthew J. Cressler 145

The Cold War, the Council, and American Catholicism
 in a Global World
 Joseph P. Chinnici, OFM 167

Preface

In 2010 Timothy Matovina encouraged the readers of the *U.S. Catholic Historian* to forge ahead in "remapping American Catholicism" by addressing the need to tell the story of often forgotten American Catholics, including women, African Americans, Latinos, Asian Americans, and those on the frontier and U.S. borderlands. By investigating their stories, Matovina proposed that these studies might inform and even demand a remapping of the "general narratives" of U.S. Catholic history to "more adequately encompasses the various peoples, places, and events that formed it."[1]

For more than three decades, the *U.S. Catholic Historian* has attempted to further this goal: remapping the history of Catholicism in the United States, particularly aware of lesser explored subjects. Beginning in 1984, the journal, under long-time editor Christopher J. Kauffman, adopted its signature "thematic" approach, assembling essays according to topics ranging from war and peace to the Catholic intellectual tradition to spirituality and devotion. Issues were also devoted to racial, ethnic, and gender identities, giving voice to American Catholics often seen as "separate" if not inferior.[2]

This assembly of essays from the *U.S. Catholic Historian*, including seven of the most popular and path-breaking contributions of recent years, may serve as a model for the historians engaged in the effort of charting the complexity and diversity of American Catholicism.

Timothy Matovina is professor of theology at the University of Notre Dame and co-director of the university's Institute for Latino Studies. Matovina has written extensively on Latino Catholicism and here provides a call to reexamine our relating of Catholic America's past to include not only European immigrants and their descendants but other ethnic and racial groups.

---

1. Timothy Matovina, "Remapping American Catholicism," *U.S. Catholic Historian* 28, no. 4 (Fall 2010): 31–72; quote at 32.
2. For the history of the journal and an assessment of its unique thematic approach, see James T. Fisher, "Christopher Kauffman, the *U.S. Catholic Historian*, and the Future of American Catholic History," *U.S. Catholic Historian* 24, no. 2 (Spring 2006): 19–26.

Jeanne Petit, professor of history at Hope College in Holland, Michigan, explores Catholic womanhood's strength and organizational zeal in the post–World War I era, noting the obstacles and successes of women's attempts to be recognized fully as American citizens and members of the Church.

Anne Klejment, professor of history at the University of St. Thomas in St. Paul, Minnesota, weaves together the lives of Dorothy Day and César Chávez to illustrate their use of nonviolence and "weapons of the spirit" to respond to societal injustice.

Amanda Bresie, chair of the history department at Greenhill School in Dallas, Texas, provides a window into the life of Mother Katharine Drexel, noting the generosity of the millionaire heiress, but also her meticulous record keeping and close supervision of the recipients of her aid. What emerges is the portrait of a saint who successfully employed money and mission to educate and evangelize countless Native and African Americans.

Kristine Ashton Gunnell, research affiliate at the UCLA Center for the Study of Women, analyzes the ways in which a community of women religious, the Daughters of Charity, crossed cultural boundaries to offer charitable assistance to Mexican and Japanese communities in Los Angeles, furthering their process of Americanization. Her essay was the 2014 winner of the Arrington-Prucha Prize of the Western History Association for the best essay of the year on religious history in the West.

Matthew J. Cressler, assistant professor of religious studies at the College of Charleston in Charleston, South Carolina, explores the intersection of Black Power and distinctive African American-inspired liturgies, arguing that the liturgy became a "site of struggle" as black self-determination and nationalism impacted worship and black Catholic identity.

Joseph P. Chinnici, OFM, president emeritus of the Franciscan School of Theology, Oceanside, California, in affiliation with the University of San Diego, offers an important essay on reenvisioning post-conciliar U.S. Catholicism in its global context, offering a new approach to how we consider the American Catholic narrative and write its history.

It is our hope that these essays may inspire historians to continue to engage in the cartographic task of remapping the U.S. Catholic experience.

DAVID J. ENDRES
Editor, *U.S. Catholic Historian*

Remapping American Catholicism

Timothy Matovina*

Histories of Catholicism in the United States tend to depict Catholics as progressing from disestablishment in a Protestant nation to struggling immigrants to successful American Catholics, or Catholic Americans. But today the U.S. Catholic Church is no longer an overwhelmingly European immigrant church, as it was a century ago, nor is it solely an "Americanized" church. Rather, it is a church largely of middle-class, European-descent Catholics with sizeable contingents of African Americans, Asian, and African immigrants, some Native Americans, and especially an expanding numbers of Latinos whose ancestors were the first major group of Catholics in what is now the United States. The growing Latino presence necessitates sharper attention to the international dimensions of Catholicism in the United States, particularly the hemispheric intersections of U.S. and Latin American history. This growing presence also underscores that the present and future of ecclesial life and mission is best addressed with a clearer view of the part Latinos—and their fellow Catholics—have played in our collective past.

Father José Antonio Díaz de León, the last Franciscan priest serving in Texas when it was still part of Mexico, died mysteriously in 1834 near the east Texas town of Nacogdoches. A judge exonerated an Anglo American accused of murdering Díaz de León amidst rumors that the priest's death of a gunshot wound was a suicide. Mexican Catholics decried this decision as a sham. How could their pastor, who had served faithfully on the Texas frontier for nearly all his years as a priest, have committed such a desperate act?[1]

---

*This essay originally appeared in *U.S. Catholic Historian* 28, no. 4 (Fall 2010): 31–72. Many thanks to Gilberto M. Hinojosa, Robert Wright, O.M.I., and other colleagues of CEHILA USA who offered critical comments on an earlier draft of this essay presented at the organization's 2009 annual meeting. Most especially, thanks to Moises Sandoval for his scholarship and dedication which launched the historical study of Latino Christians in the United States and made possible a remapping project such as this essay.

1. Primary sources and a fuller account of the incidents recorded in this and the following paragraph are in Timothy Matovina, "Lay Initiatives in Worship on the Texas *Frontera*, 1830–1860," *U.S. Catholic Historian* 12, no. 4 (Fall 1994): 108–111; Robert E. Wright, "Father

Seven years later Vincentian priests John Timon and Jean Marie Odin made a pastoral visit to Nacogdoches. They deplored the conditions of Mexican Catholics, whom they said Anglo Americans had indiscriminately killed, driven away, and robbed of their lands. Father Odin also reported that Anglo Americans had burned the local Catholic church building to the ground. Yet these and other visitors observed that Mexican Catholic laity continued to gather in private homes for feast days and weekly worship services and celebrated rituals like funerals. Catholicism in Nacogdoches remained almost entirely a lay-led effort until 1847 when (by then) Bishop Odin was finally able to appoint two priests to replace Father Díaz de León. Parishioners' eager reception of the sacraments from their new pastors testified to their enduring faith amidst a tumultuous period of social upheaval.

These largely forgotten events occurred simultaneously with more widely known episodes in U.S. Catholic history. General histories and survey courses of U.S. Catholicism inevitably examine the atrocities of the anti-Catholic mob that burned the Ursuline convent to the ground at Charlestown, Massachusetts (across the river from Boston) in 1834, the same year of Father Díaz de León's assassination and concurrent with the burning of the Nacogdoches parish church. Historical overviews also explore the saga of European Catholic immigrants, such as the Irish and the Germans, whose migration flows increased significantly during the very same decades that Mexican Catholics at Nacogdoches struggled in faith for their very survival as a community. Irish-born John Hughes became bishop (later archbishop) of New York in 1842, the same year that Odin, the first bishop of Texas (and later archbishop of New Orleans), was ordained to the episcopacy, but Odin's two decades of endeavor to advance the Catholic Church and faith in Texas are far less recognized than Hughes' simultaneous labors in New York.

U.S. Catholic historians' strong foci on the eastern seaboard and European settlers and immigrants mirror longstanding emphases in the broader scholarship of North American religious history. Studies in recent decades have addressed lacunae in this historiography, such as the role of regionalism, the frontier, women, African Americans, and Asian Americans, to name but a few.[2] Collectively these studies reveal that, while documenting "for-

---

Refugio de la Garza: Controverted Religious Leader," in *Tejano Leadership in Mexican and Revolutionary Texas*, ed. Jesús F. de la Teja (College Station: Texas A&M University Press, 2010), 83, 96–97, n. 50.

2. Thomas A. Tweed, ed., *Retelling U.S. Religious History* (Berkeley: University of California Press, 1997); Catherine A. Brekus, ed., *The Religious History of American Women: Reimagining the Past* (Chapel Hill: University of North Carolina Press, 2007). See also the book series American Catholic Identities: A Documentary History, gen. ed. Christopher J. Kauffman (9 vols., Maryknoll, NY: Orbis, 1999–2004); Religion by Region, gen. ed. Mark Silk (8 vols., Walnut Creek, CA: AltaMira Press, 2004–2006).

gotten" peoples, histories, and regions is an essential intellectual endeavor, it is only a first step toward the more long-range goal of investigating how to remap general narratives of the past in a manner that more adequately encompasses the various peoples, places, and events that formed it. Building on the groundbreaking work of Moises Sandoval, this essay is part of that larger effort to rethink such narratives in U.S. religious history, and U.S. Catholicism in particular, in this case through the lens of Latino Catholic experience.[3]

Interpreting the past is never a neutral endeavor, of course. A basic truism of historical studies is that those who control the present construct the past in order to shape the future. With this challenge in mind, how can we understand the past in a way that sheds light on the tragedies of Father Díaz de León and the Ursulines at Charlestown, Catholicism in Nacogdoches and in New York, the contributions of Bishops Odin and Hughes, and the experiences of Mexican, Irish, German, and other Catholics? More broadly, what are the basic themes of U.S. Catholic history? What gradual trends or dramatic turning points mark it into distinct time periods? How do Latinos fit into and shape the overall narrative? Obviously the answers to all these questions are matters of interpretation and no single response is unilaterally comprehensive. But how one responds is decisive for a number of the issues and topics that are fundamental to understanding the Hispanic presence and the future of Catholics in the United States.

It is no surprise that for Latinos the most contentious renderings of the U.S. Catholic past are those that obscure their contributions, sometimes to the point of near invisibility. While the strongest expressions of this critique are usually directed at more dated scholarly works, as recently as 2008 James O'Toole's *The Faithful: A History of Catholics in America* encompasses only two brief references to Hispanics from the origins of U.S. Catholicism to the dawn of the twenty-first century. The final chapter of O'Toole's examination of U.S. Catholic history from the perspective of the lay faithful depicts Latinos as an important component of Catholicism's ongoing evolution in the United States in the new century, but unfortunately this leaves the impression that only now are Hispanics becoming a noteworthy element of the U.S. Catholic story.[4]

---

3. Moises Sandoval, ed., *Fronteras: A History of the Latin American Church in the USA Since 1513* (San Antonio: Mexican American Cultural Center Press, 1983); Sandoval, *On the Move: A History of the Hispanic Church in the United States* (1990; 2nd ed., Maryknoll, NY: Orbis, 2006).

4. James M. O'Toole, *The Faithful: A History of Catholics in America* (Cambridge: Belknap Press of Harvard University Press, 2008), 100, 226, chap. 6, "The Church in the Twenty-first Century."

To varying degrees other recent general histories of U.S. Catholicism address the Hispanic Catholic presence and contribution more adequately. A number of historians begin their rendering of the U.S. Catholic story with the Spanish colonial era rather than with the establishment of the later and overwhelmingly Protestant British colonies. Woven into the narrative of general works like those of James Hennesey, Jay Dolan, Charles Morris, and James Fisher are discussions of immigration patterns, demographic shifts, and Latino Catholic leaders, organizations, movements, religious traditions, political involvement, and social activism. But these historical treatments often subsume Hispanics into an Americanization paradigm presumed to hold true for all Catholics in the United States. Morris concluded his acclaimed 1997 work with the assertion that there is a "standoff between the tradition of Rome and the tradition of America [the United States]." His claim is based on an understanding of U.S. Catholicism as, in the words of Dolan, a fledgling "republican" church after U.S. independence that expanded into an "immigrant church" in the nineteenth- and early twentieth-centuries and after World War II had "come of age" as "American," a process often depicted as culminating in John F. Kennedy's election as president which signaled for numerous Catholics the authentication of their full acceptance in U.S. society.[5]

Even those who protest Americanization as a detriment to Catholicism divide the U.S. Catholic past into a similar series of historical eras. Distancing himself from previous authors he deemed "one-sided in a progressivist [*sic*] direction," Joseph Varacalli presented his 2006 work *The Catholic Experience in America* as "one of many more balanced and orthodox pieces of scholarship that . . . should be viewed, partly at least, as a result of the intellectual legacy of Pope John Paul II." Yet Varacalli follows the same basic pattern of historical periods as the predecessors he critiques, albeit with his own interpretive slant. He depicts Catholicism in the United States as evolving from modest beginnings as a "minority church" in the first decades of the new republic to a period of nearly a century and a half in which mass immigration and effective episcopal leadership enabled Catholics to forge a subculture that "successfully propagated" the faith. In his view the zenith of Catholic subculture and its defense against "a then Protestant and a mostly unsympathetic civilization" was the period following World War II. But upward

---

5. James Hennesey, *American Catholics: A History of the Roman Catholic Community in the United States* (New York: Oxford, 1981); Jay P. Dolan, *The American Catholic Experience: A History from Colonial Times to the Present* (1985; reprint, Notre Dame, IN: University of Notre Dame Press, 1992), 125, 417; Charles R. Morris, *American Catholic: The Saints and Sinners Who Built America's Most Powerful Church* (New York: Times Books, 1997), 431; James T. Fisher, *Communion of Immigrants: A History of Catholics in America* (2000; new ed., New York: Oxford, 2008).

mobility, progressive interpretations of the Second Vatican Council, and secularization in society at large significantly diminished the countercultural edge of the subculture and the vitality of Catholic faith. While Varacalli diverges from previous authors in his addition of a fourth historical era he deems the Catholic "restorationist" movement under the pontificates of Popes John Paul II and Benedict XVI, he does not depart from the dominant schema. Instead he critiques the process of Americanization that others depict in a more positive light.[6]

Some scholars question whether the immigrant to Americanization paradigm is the best lens through which to examine the U.S. Catholic experience, even for the experience of European Catholic immigrants and their descendants. Others critique the language of "coming of age," noting that, whatever their level of formal education and status, European immigrants did not sojourn in a perpetual state of childhood immaturity, nor did adopting the English language and U.S. social norms indicate their descendants had advanced to the age of adulthood.[7] Nonetheless, the contention that U.S. Catholics have become "Americanized" to a significant degree remains an important interpretive lens through which most scholars, pastoral leaders, and other observers examine Catholicism in the United States.

The core question about the Americanization paradigm is, in the long view will the undeniably profound assimilation that transpired in the period roughly from 1920 to 1980 end up appearing more as an anomaly in U.S. Catholic history, or as the norm? Are there interpretive lenses that illuminate important alternative understandings of the historical trajectories of U.S. Catholicism? From the perspective of many ecclesial leaders, for example, a more pressing concern is the loosening of attachment to the institutional church in recent decades as reflected in data such as the relatively fewer vocations to the priesthood and religious life and the lower rates of Catholic school enrollment and Sunday Mass attendance, trends evident to varying but significant degrees among both immigrant and U.S.-born "Americanized" Catholics. How will future historians assess trends such as these, their interrelation with the Americanization paradigm, and the relative explanatory significance of each for understanding Catholicism in the United States? Are

---

6. Joseph A. Varacalli, *The Catholic Experience in America* (Westport, CT: Greenwood, 2006), xx, 23–24, part II, "Catholicism and Civilization in the United States: A Chronological Overview."

7. See, e.g., Michael J. Baxter, "Writing History in a World Without Ends: An Evangelical Catholic Critique of United States Catholic History," *Pro Ecclesia* 5 (Fall 1996): 440–469; William L. Portier, "Americanism and Inculturation, 1899–1999," *Communio* 27 (Spring 2000): 139–160; Peter R. D'Agostino, *Rome in America: Transnational Catholic Ideology from the Risorgimento to Fascism* (Chapel Hill: University of North Carolina Press, 2004).

there other interpretive lenses no one has yet articulated that will rise to the fore in analyses of the U.S. Catholic past? At this juncture the most tenable conclusion about the Americanization paradigm is that it offers considerable insight into the experience of European immigrants' descendants from the interwar period until the two decades following the Second Vatican Council, as well as into the subsequent contentious debates about the stance Catholics should take vis-à-vis the wider U.S. society. To presume that the Americanization paradigm is the best or even the sole organizational schema for U.S. Catholic history, and in particular for examining the place of groups like African Americans and Latinos within that history, remains unsubstantiated.

Thus a decisive challenge is to construct a history of U.S. Catholicism that incorporates Latinos, and other non-European groups, but is not modeled exclusively on European Catholic immigrants and their descendants' societal ascent and assimilation during the middle six decades of the twentieth century. Indeed, in broad strokes the history of Latino Catholics inverts the standard depiction of their counterparts from nations like Ireland, Germany, Poland, and Italy. While Catholics were a small minority in the British colonies, in lands from Florida to California they comprised a more substantial population under Catholic Spain. While the first mass group of Catholics to settle in the United States was nineteenth-century European immigrants, the first large group of Hispanic Catholics became part of the nation during that same era without ever leaving home, as they were incorporated into its boundaries during U.S. territorial expansion into Florida and then westward. Just as European immigration diminished to relatively miniscule numbers as a result of restrictive immigration legislation in the 1920s, Hispanic immigration began in earnest with the Mexican Revolution. The counter trajectory of Latino Catholic history in the United States vis-à-vis that of their European-descent coreligionists necessitates a reanalysis of each epoch delineated in the standard historiography, particularly the period since World War II as waves of Hispanic immigrants have comprised an increasingly significant portion of what was purportedly an established, Americanized, post-immigrant church.

A Latino perspective on U.S. Catholic history also necessitates sharper attention to its international dimensions, especially the intersections of U.S. and Latin American history. Following the Spanish colonial presence in lands now part of the United States, U.S. political and economic expansionism led to the conquest of nearly half of Mexico's national territory at the midpoint of the nineteenth century, consolidated U.S. occupation of Puerto Rico five decades later, helped create the economic conditions for the origins of late nineteenth and early twentieth-century immigration from Mexico, resulted in a U.S. presence throughout the Caribbean and Central America that facilitated migrations from those regions, and has driven the globalization process that fed an immigration explosion from throughout Latin America since World War II. This latter process blurred the border between Latin and North America, accelerating the development of previous links between Catholicism in the United States and Catholicism in the rest of the Americas. It also produced an unprecedented diversification of national origin groups among Latinos in U.S. Catholicism. Examining the U.S. Catholic past through the lens of this diverse Hispanic experience—as well as through the experience of Europeans and other groups—expands on a unilateral Americanization paradigm with a hemispheric perspective that is essential for understanding the current demographic Hispanicization of Catholicism in the United States.

Colonial Origins

Jay Dolan's introduction to the U.S. history survey course exemplifies a fundamental revision many contemporary scholars have adopted for U.S. Catholic historiography. Dolan's custom on the first day of class was to ask his students the significance of three years in American history: 1607, 1608, and 1610. At least one student is always able to recognize 1607 as the date for the founding of the first British colony, Jamestown. But rarely can anyone identify 1608 as the founding date for Québec, and 1610 for Santa Fe. Dolan attests that "the reasoning behind my pedagogical cunning is to impress upon the students the French and Spanish dimension of American history as well as the more familiar English aspect." Colonial U.S. historians like Alan Taylor have expanded on Dolan's treatment, noting even less-acknowledged arrivals within territories that later became part of the United States, such as Dutch colonies, Russian settlement in Alaska, and British incursions into Hawaii.[8] Implicitly, this approach answers an essential question for any overview of U.S. history: does the subject matter encompass solely the British colonists and other peoples and territories *only when* they become part of the U.S. nation, or does it encompass the inhabitants of regions now part of the United States both *before and after* their incorporation? Rather than a story of thirteen original colonies and their westward expansion, the latter perspective accentuates the encounter and conflict of peoples, primarily the southward moving French, the northward moving Spanish, the westward moving British, the natives who already occupied the land, and the slaves and immigrants who settled among them. Given that both the French and Spanish colonists were from Catholic countries, any comprehensive analysis of U.S.

---

8. Jay P. Dolan and Allan Figueroa Deck, eds., *Hispanic Catholic Culture in the U.S.: Issues and Concerns* (Notre Dame, IN: University of Notre Dame Press, 1994), 440; Alan Taylor, *American Colonies* (New York: Viking, 2001).

Catholic history must examine their foundational presence and the extent of their influence on subsequent developments.

Spanish-speaking Catholics have lived in what is now the United States for twice as long as the nation has existed. The first diocese in the New World was established in 1511 at San Juan, Puerto Rico, now a commonwealth associated with the United States. Subjects of the Spanish crown founded the first permanent European settlement within the current borders of the fifty states at St. Augustine, Florida in 1565, four decades before the establishment of Jamestown, and in 1620 established at that settlement the first Marian shrine in what is now the continental United States, *Nuestra Señora de la Leche y Buen Parto* (Our Nursing Mother of Happy Delivery). Before the end of the sixteenth century, Spanish Jesuits and Franciscans initiated missionary activities in present-day Georgia and even as far north as Virginia. In 1598 Spanish subjects traversed present-day El Paso, Texas and proceeded north to establish the permanent foundation of Catholicism in what is now the Southwest.

Catholics in the thirteen British colonies were a repressed minority in a Protestant land, eventually even losing the elective franchise in Maryland, the only British colony that Catholics founded. They comprised scarcely one percent of the population at the signing of the Declaration of Independence. Meanwhile, in Hispanic settlements from Florida to California, Catholicism was the established religion under Spain and, in the Southwest, under Mexico after it won independence in 1821. This prescription led newcomers to the region such as escaped slaves from Georgia who were granted freedom in Spanish Florida, famed Alamo defender James Bowie in Texas, and renowned scout Kit Carson in New Mexico to accept Catholic baptism and at least nominal practice of the faith. From the standpoints of original settlement, societal influence, and institutional presence, the origins of Catholicism in what is now the United States were decidedly Hispanic.

Contemporary Latinos acclaim their ancestors' foundational role in various ways. El Paso residents contend that members of the Juan de Oñate expedition celebrated the "first Thanksgiving" in the United States on April 30, 1598 in gratitude for surviving their trek across the Chihuahuan Desert. The Oñate expedition festivities included a Catholic Mass and a meal for which the Spaniards provided game and natives from the region supplied fish. Since 1989 the El Paso Mission Trail Association has commemorated the event annually with a community picnic and festivities and Mass in historic sites like the San Elizario Presidio Chapel. Costumed participants and members of the local Tigua Indians reenact the Oñate expedition's day of thanks. In 1991, a delegation from El Paso visited Plymouth Rock dressed as Spanish conquistadores and, according to an El Paso Mission Trail Association press release, was amicably "arrested and charged with blasphemy and spreading malicious rumors for stating that the real First Thanksgiving took place in Texas." Though this staged confrontation was aimed at drawing publicity to both parties involved, the same press release also proudly noted that "the Plymouth trial judge ordered a delegation of Pilgrims to travel to El Paso the following year to observe the Texas Thanksgiving."[9]

Yet on the whole popular perceptions have frequently relegated the historical significance of Hispanic Catholicism in the colonial period to a romanticized and bygone day of the Spanish missions. Such depictions appeared in print immediately after the U.S. takeover of northern Mexico in the Mexican American War (1846–1848), such as Francis Baylies' eyewitness account of the U.S. army's overland advance from San Antonio down to the heart of Mexico, which encompassed his laudatory observations about the missionary efforts of Spanish friars among the native peoples of Texas. Although he incorrectly identified the missioners as Jesuits rather than Franciscans, Baylies marveled at the "magnificent traces" of their labors during the Spanish colonial era noteworthy in the ruins of the mission compounds near San Antonio. He also bemoaned the general decline in local conditions since Mexican independence, including the deterioration of the "magnificent churches [and] monasteries" which "once the outposts of christianity [sic], were now moss-covered ruins." According to Baylies, after Mexico won independence "everything went to decay. Agriculture, learning, the mechanic arts, shared the common fate; and when the banners of the United States were unfurled in these distant and desolate places, the descendants of the noble and chivalric Castilians had sunk to the level, perhaps beneath it, of the aboriginal savages."[10]

Baylies' justification of the U.S. conquest as a redemption of Mexican backwardness and corruption induced his sharp, Eurocentric contrast between the decline of the missions under Mexico and the previous "golden age" of the missions in which Spanish friars selflessly taught Christianity, Spanish culture, and European civilization to native peoples. Writer Helen

---

9. "The First Thanksgiving?," in *The Texas Almanac* at http://www.texasalmanac.com/history/highlights/thanksgiving/; El Paso Mission Trail Association, Inc., "First Documented Thanksgiving Was Held 23 Years Before the Pilgrims' Celebration" (press release), April 3, 1995 (copy in possession of author). Though El Paso and Juárez were a single settlement until the mid-nineteenth century when the new international border between the United States and Mexico separated them, the celebration of this first Mass of Thanksgiving actually occurred on what today is the Mexican side of the river, across from San Elizario Presidio.

10. Francis Baylies, *A Narrative of Major General Wool's Campaign in Mexico* (Albany, NY: Little, 1851), 11.

Hunt Jackson extended this view to a national audience through a series of 1883 *Century Magazine* articles on Fray Junípero Serra, the founder of the California missions. Though the daughter of a strict Massachusetts Congregationalist family, Jackson found spiritual inspiration in her hagiographic perception of Serra and his fellow Franciscans, even deeming their labors superior to those of the Puritans, whom she claimed "drove the Indians farther and farther into the wilderness every year, fighting and killing them," while the Spanish friars "were gathering the Indians by thousands into communities and feeding and teaching them." Jackson's bestselling novel *Ramona*, first published in 1884, solidified this idealized view of the missions in the popular mindset. A love story set against her presentation of the social upheaval after the passing of the missions, Jackson's literary success cast a long shadow of "Ramonamania": rail tours of the California missions, a 1919 D.W. Griffin film starring Mary Pickford as Ramona, an annual Ramona theatrical pageant that continues to this day, initiatives to restore Spanish missions, and, most conspicuously, the development of Mission and Spanish Revival architectural styles that mark the landscape of towns and cities across the Southwest and beyond.[11]

A number of scholars and other commentators have noted that many restored missions and writings about them fail to account for indigenous perspectives on the mission system, including the cultural shock, harsh treatment, and death from European diseases that many Native Americans experienced in mission communities. Yet even professional historians often fall into the false presumptions that the missions were the only Catholic religious institutions in the Spanish colonies and Mexican territories and that *all* the missions underwent a period of abandonment and decline.[12] In fact, parishes, military chapels, private shrines, and some missions have been the homes of Catholic faith communities from colonial times until the present day.

The "arrival" of Christianity in lands now part of the continental United States began with Spanish expeditions into the area, such as Juan Ponce de León's famous excursions into Florida and the fated Pánfilo de Narváez expedition, from which only Alvar Núñez Cabeza de Vaca and a handful of companions survived after an eight-year ordeal of hunger, captivity, and an

---

11. Roberto Lint Sagarena, "Building California's Past: Mission Revival Architecture and Regional Identity," *Journal of Urban History* 28 (May 2002): 432–434; Helen Hunt Jackson, *Ramona: A Story* (Boston: Roberts Brothers, 1884). The quotation is cited from Sagarena, originally in Helen Hunt Jackson, "Father Junípero and His Work (pt. 2)," *The Century Magazine* 26 (June 1883): 201.

12. Timothy Matovina, "Beyond the Missions: The Diocesan Church in the Hispanic Southwest," *American Catholic Studies* 117 (Fall 2006): 1–15.

overland trek from Florida to New Spain (present-day Mexico).[13] Later, Spanish subjects established settlements to stake territorial claims for the Spanish Crown, pursue economic gain, and propagate Catholicism among native populations. *Villas* (towns) with formal civil and church institutions, military garrisons, and missions provided historically tested structures around which Hispanic frontier communities emerged.[14]

Catholic missionaries, usually Franciscan friars with the major exception being Eusebio Kino and his fellow Jesuits in Arizona, accompanied exploratory expeditions and then were an integral part of Spanish efforts to establish settlements. Sometimes the friars founded missions within or near settled indigenous communities. In other cases, they induced nomadic peoples to settle down at newly established missions, usually in the vicinity of Spanish towns and military garrisons. Since they typically had but a single or small group of friars and perhaps a few Spanish military personnel, the mission settlements were in effect missionary-led Indian towns. While initially the prospect of entering the missions to stave off enemies, starvation, and harsh winters seemed attractive to some Native Americans, a number of them eventually found mission life too alien and coercive. Not only were they not accustomed to the Spanish work routines and religious lifestyles, they also found unacceptable the friars' demands that they shed their traditional ways. Many became resentful and left the missions. In some cases outright rebellion ensued, most famously in 1680 when New Mexico's Pueblo Indians exploded into open violence under the leadership of a shaman or spiritual leader named Popé, driving the Spaniards and their loyal indigenous subjects from the region and purging their communities of Catholic symbols and everything Spanish.[15] Though the Spanish reconquered them beginning in 1692 and Franciscan missionary efforts resumed, the revolt illuminated the potential clash of civilizations in mission life.

On the other hand, a number of Native Americans remained within the world of the missions, accepted Christianity, and took on Hispanic and Catholic identities. In various locales the native peoples revered missionaries for their faith, dedication, and willingness to advocate for them within the Spanish colonial system. Julio César, who identified himself as a "pure-blooded Indian" of California, recalled with fondness that as a resident of

---

13. Andrés Reséndez, *A Land So Strange: The Epic Journey of Cabeza de Vaca* (New York: Basic, 2007).
14. The best overview of Spanish settlement in what is now the Southwest United States is David J. Weber, *The Spanish Frontier in North America* (New Haven, CT: Yale University Press, 1992).
15. David J. Weber, ed., *What Caused the Pueblo Revolt of 1680?* (Boston: Bedford/St. Martin's, 1999).

Mission San Luís Rey (near San Diego) during his youth a Padre Francisco was the priest in charge of the mission and "the Indians called him 'Tequedeuma,' an Indian word which signified that the padre was very sympathetic and considerate toward the Indians; in fact, he was very loving and good."[16] For the missionaries, Hispanicizing the natives entailed creating living spaces for their charges around impressive churches that became the center of everyday life. The missionaries worked diligently inculcating Catholicism, defining work regimes, establishing predictable daily life routines, teaching the Spanish language, overseeing social interactions, enforcing Christian-appropriate gender relations, and striving to modify cultural practices among the natives they deemed contrary to Christianity.

At the same time, even as natives were incorporated into Catholicism and Hispanic society, to varying degrees they exerted their own cultural influence on the Hispanic newcomers. For example, archeological research reveals the presence of Coahuiltecan artifacts such as pottery, tools, and blankets in San Antonio's Hispanic households during the colonial period. Coahuiltecans and other native peoples also brought to Catholic rituals some of the spirit and elements of their *mitote* celebrations, which included singing, dancing, and feasting to mark occasions like the summer harvest, hunting or fishing expeditions, or the return of the full moon.[17]

The Spanish Crown viewed the missions as temporary institutions whose role was to prepare Native Americans to become good Spanish subjects. Officially, from their inception the missions were destined for secularization, that is, transference from missionary to civil authorities and diocesan clergy once the friars completed the work of Hispanicizing the natives. But in fact secularization varied from region to region, depending on socioeconomic realities, central government policies, the level of cooperation among Native Americans, and the often competing interests of missionaries and local officials.

In theory, the indigenous converts at the missions were to receive individual land allotments and other assets in the secularization process to aid them in their transition to a new status as Hispanicized Catholics. But in numerous cases this did not occur: the Native Americans simply lost every-

---

16. Julio César, "Recollections of my Youth at San Luís Rey Mission," in *Spanish Borderlands Sourcebook: Native American Perspectives on the Hispanic Colonization of Alta California*, ed. Edward D. Castillo (New York: Garland, 1991), 13–15, at 13.

17. Gilberto M. Hinojosa, "Friars and Indians: Towards a Perspective of Cultural Interaction in the San Antonio Mission," *U.S. Catholic Historian* 9, nos. 1–2 (Winter/Spring 1990): 7–26; Gilberto M. Hinojosa and Anne A. Fox, "Indians and Their Culture in San Fernando de Béxar," in *Tejano Origins in Eighteenth-Century San Antonio*, ed. Gerald E. Poyo and Gilberto M. Hinojosa (Austin: University of Texas Press, 1991), 105–120.

thing to unscrupulous officials or other Hispanic residents, often moving into Hispanic towns where they occupied the bottom of the social structure. However the mission residents fared, the secularization process transformed their communities from corporate entities under the authority and protection of specific missionary orders to independent communities that became another element of Hispanic civil society. In the process the majority of missions no longer had resident clergy. A large number fell into disrepair, many of them later rebuilt. Nonetheless, the church structures at locales like Santa Barbara, California; Ysleta, Texas (near El Paso); and San Xavier del Bac south of Tucson, Arizona, among others, continued to function as Catholic houses of worship down to the present day.

Male friars produced the vast majority of extant mission records, which consequently tend to accentuate their perspectives, accomplishments, and struggles. Nonetheless, the missions reveal a longstanding, significant element of Latino Catholicism: the faith and leadership of women like Eulalia Pérez, who became a prominent figure at Mission San Gabriel (near Los Angeles). A native of Loreto, Baja California, Pérez moved to the mission in the early nineteenth century with her husband, who was assigned there as a guard. After her husband's death, Pérez lived at the mission with her son and five daughters, where she became the head housekeeper, a leadership position in the mission community that grew increasingly significant as the number of friars decreased. Her duties included managing supplies and their distribution, as well as supervising Native American workers. As the elderly Eulalia noted somewhat modestly in a memoir she dictated to an interviewer, as the "mistress of the keys" (*llavera*) at the mission she "was responsible for a variety of duties." In fact she was the lay overseer of the mission community's daily life.[18]

Though missions were numerically the predominant Catholic institution in the northern stretches of New Spain, parishes, military chaplaincies, and private chapels also played a crucial role in establishing and maintaining Catholicism. Unlike the missions in which the population consisted exclusively of Native Americans save for a few friars and Hispanic military personnel, these other religious foundations provided for the spiritual welfare of Hispanic civilian and military settlers and their descendants, as well for some natives who eventually joined their communities. Parishes first appeared with the establishment of formal towns and grew in number as some missions were secularized and became ordinary parishes. Local resi-

---

18. "Eulalia Pérez: Una vieja y sus recuerdos," in *Nineteenth Century Californio Testimonials*, ed. Rosaura Sánchez, Beatrice Pita, and Bárbara Reyes (San Diego: University of California at San Diego Ethnic Studies/Third World Studies, 1994), 32–44, at 36.

dents built the churches and sought to obtain the services of priests, either religious order priests like the Franciscans or diocesan priests, who were primarily trained to serve existing Spanish-speaking Catholic communities rather than to work for the conversion of Native Americans. In Spanish colonial times, Hispanic Catholics established parishes in places like St. Augustine, San Antonio, Laredo, Santa Fe, Albuquerque, and Los Angeles, along with military chapels in other locales, such as Santa Barbara and Monterey, California, where the current Catholic cathedral has its origins in a colonial military chapel.

The construction of the first church edifice in San José, California illuminates local initiative in establishing parishes. In 1802 settlers at San José, which had been founded in 1777, petitioned for permission to build a chapel. From its foundation the community had relied on mission Santa Clara about four miles away for their spiritual needs. When they received the required permission the 217 settlers immediately began work building their church. In 1804 an earthquake destroyed their newly-completed chapel, but the community persisted and rebuilt it, at one juncture receiving help from the military commander at nearby Monterey, who sent individuals under judicial sanction to work on the church building. Once built, the settlers took it upon themselves to negotiate with the Franciscans at Mission Santa Clara for their spiritual services.[19]

Private chapels and pilgrimage sites also reveal local initiative and the origins of contemporary Hispanic Catholicism in the colonial past, most famously the sanctuary of Chimayó in New Mexico. Tewa Indians acclaimed the healing properties of Chimayó's sacred earth long before Catholic settlers arrived at this locale on the western side of the Sangre de Cristo Mountains. Spanish subjects completed the first chapel at the site in 1816 and dedicated the Santuario de Chimayó to Nuestro Señor de Esquipulas (Our Lord of Esquipulas), a Guatemalan representation of the crucifixion associated with a Mayan sacred place of healing earth. During the 1850s, however, devotees of the Santuario de Chimayó added a statue of the Santo Niño de Atocha (Holy Child of Atocha) in response to a new local shrine dedicated to the Santo Niño. Subsequently the Santo Niño and the miraculous dirt became the focal points for most Santuario devotees. They remain so today for thousands of pilgrims who visit Chimayó annually.[20]

---

19. Gilbert R. Cruz, *Let There Be Towns: Spanish Municipal Origins in the American Southwest, 1610–1810* (College Station: Texas A&M University Press, 1988), 111, 124–125.
20. Ramón A. Gutiérrez, "El Santuario de Chimayó: A Syncretic Shrine in New Mexico," in *Feasts and Celebrations in North American Ethnic Communities*, ed. Ramón A. Gutiérrez and Geneviève Fabre (Albuquerque: University of New Mexico Press. 1995), 71–86.

Though Louisiana was under Spanish control from 1766 to 1803 and Spain controlled Florida for well over two centuries until 1821 (with one hiatus of British rule from 1763 to 1783), most Hispanic Catholics in what is now the United States resided in the Southwest. During the Spanish colonial era and the subsequent period after Mexican independence in 1821, New Mexico was the most populous territory and thus the one with the largest number of Catholics. By the beginning of the nineteenth century, the diocesan clergy in New Mexico had begun the process of slowly displacing the Franciscan missionaries who had served in the region since the late sixteenth century. This was, of course, a natural and predictable course of events since the missions had always been viewed as temporary institutions dedicated to preparing the indigenous communities for parish life as Hispanic citizens. In 1798 the Diocese of Durango, which encompassed New Mexico, introduced the first diocesan pastors to the region, one for the parish at Santa Fe and the other at Santa Cruz. As the Franciscan numbers declined, particularly after Mexican independence when many Spanish friars were forcibly exiled or left the new republic out of loyalty to their native Spain, the diocesan priests increased thanks to recruitment of local youth who went to seminary in Durango. Between 1823 and 1826, four New Mexicans completed their training and returned home to begin their ministries. By the end of the 1840s, the Franciscans had all left or died and some seventeen or eighteen diocesan priests, most of them recruited locally, served the spiritual needs of New Mexico's parish communities. In the end, the church's viability in New Mexico depended on the communities themselves, including their ability to recruit their youth into the priesthood.[21]

One such local vocation, Father Ramón Ortiz (1814–1896), was born in Santa Fe, attended seminary at Durango, and was ordained there in 1837. Within a matter of months he began a parochial assignment in the El Paso district that lasted nearly sixty years. An activist priest, Ortiz was a staunch defender of Mexican sovereignty. As U.S. troops prepared to occupy his local area during the U.S.-Mexican War of 1846–1848, Ortiz wrote his bishop, vowing that the local populace would defend their nation at all costs. Subsequently the curate served as an elected delegate to the national congress in Mexico City, where he opposed the 1848 Treaty of Guadalupe Hidalgo, which ended the war and ceded nearly half of Mexico's territory to the United States. When New Mexican territorial governor William Carr Lane

---

21. Robert E. Wright, "How Many Are 'A Few'? Catholic Clergy in Central and Northern New Mexico, 1780–1851," in *Seeds of Struggle/Harvest of Faith: The Papers of the Archdiocese of Santa Fe Catholic Cuarto Centennial Conference on the History of the Catholic Church in New Mexico*, ed. Thomas J. Steele, Paul Rhetts, and Barbe Awalt (Albuquerque: LPD, 1998), 219–261.

sought to occupy Mexican territory in 1853 (land later ceded to the United States through the 1854 Gadsden Purchase), Ortiz rode out to confront the governor. The curate then returned to El Paso and alerted local authorities, who mounted a force of 800 men to defend their borders. Subsequently Ortiz offered dedicated pastoral service on both sides of the river that formed the new international boundary between Mexico and the United States until his death in 1896.[22]

Priests and their lay parishioners enacted cultural ways and traditions that included Catholic religious expressions. Communities drew on rituals, devotions, and celebrations of their ancestors such as the celebration of saint days and other feasts, processions, Mass, initiation rites, *compadrazgo* (godparentage), and dramatic proclamations of Christ's death and removal from the cross, among others. One ritual practiced during the Spanish colonial era at the parish church of San Francisco de Asís in Santa Fe was a Good Friday service in which devotees' removed Jesus' body from the cross, placed it in the arms of his grieving mother, and then accompanied the corpse through the streets in a solemn procession. The church sanctuary served as the hill of Calvary for this occasion, with the statue of Our Lady of Solitude placed prominently to depict Mary at the foot of the cross. A priest's *Sermón de la Soledad* (Sermon of Solitude) accompanied the ritual, inviting congregants to "travel by meditation and contemplation to Golgatha, also called Mount Calvary" and then dramatizing in great detail what "our eyes see in this sad, ill-fated, and mournful place."[23]

The intensity of Catholic devotion and commitment is difficult to assess precisely, but undoubtedly varied from place to place, from household to household, and from person to person. Michael Carroll has noted the unfortunate tendency of commentators' "taking the sort of Hispano Catholicism that existed in New Mexico during the late nineteenth and early twentieth centuries and projecting it onto the colonial past." At the same time, Carroll's contention that colonial New Mexicans were only nominally Catholic is unconvincing. He alleges that widely documented religious practices in colonial New Mexico such as feast days, initiation rites, and the like primarily reflected social norms and not religious sensibilities, basing his conclusion on the argument that extant sources do not reveal New Mexicans engaged extensively in practices evident in other locales of Latin America and Spain: apparitions, cults for sacred images, painted ex-votos, and the ecclesial

---

22. Mary D. Taylor, "Cura de la Frontera, Ramón Ortiz," *U.S. Catholic Historian* 9, nos. 1–2 (Winter/Spring 1990): 67–85.

23. Manuel Antonio García del Valle, Good Friday sermon, April 20, 1821, in *New Mexican Spanish Religious Oratory, 1800–1900*, ed. and trans. Thomas J. Steele (Albuquerque: University of New Mexico Press, 1997), 19–39, at 23.

reforms that church leaders promoted after the Council of Trent such as increased Mass attendance and knowledge of doctrine. Yet Carroll did not consider that difficult economic conditions, lower population density, and isolation mitigated against a broad manifestation of these particular religious expressions in New Mexico, as well as against the influence of ecclesial authority more prevalent elsewhere among Spanish-speaking populations. Nor does Carroll offer comparisons to settlements in Texas, California, and other areas of New Spain's northern frontier, which in fact evidenced patterns of religious practice similar to those in New Mexico. In the end he does not offer compelling evidence to sustain his argument that widespread Catholic practices constituted an overwhelmingly social phenomenon largely devoid of religious significance. Nonetheless, Carroll's cautionary note about not presuming a uniformly fervent Hispanic Catholicism is well taken. The Hispanic colonial enterprise differs from subsequent eras in that Catholicism was the prescribed religion, but romanticized views of a pristine and unvarying Catholic faith among all residents are unfounded.[24]

Latino Catholicism in places from St. Augustine, Florida to Sonoma, California originated with communities planted during the sixteenth through the nineteenth centuries. As the United States expanded from the original thirteen colonies to span the North American continent during the first half of the nineteenth century, Hispanic Catholic places of worship and some 80,000 Spanish-speaking Catholics were incorporated into the growing nation. Extant faith communities, religious traditions, and clergy in various locales belie presuppositions of a radical break with the Spanish colonial past that dismiss Hispanic foundations of Catholicism in what became the United States.

Enduring Communities of Faith

Famine in Ireland and revolution in Germany accelerated Catholic immigration during the mid-nineteenth century, making Catholicism the largest single denomination in the United States by the 1850 census. Commenting on these and subsequent waves of immigrants, Pulitzer Prize winner Oscar Handlin would later famously remark, "Once I thought to write a history of the immigrants in America. Then I discovered that the immigrants *were* American history."[25] His sweeping thesis does not account for the experience

---

24. Michael P. Carroll, *The Penitente Brotherhood: Patriarchy and Hispano-Catholicism in New Mexico* (Baltimore: Johns Hopkins University Press, 2002), 41, chap. 2, "The Golden Age That Wasn't: Hispano Piety before 1800."

25. Oscar Handlin, *The Uprooted: The Epic Story of the Great Migration that Made the American People* (Boston: Little, Brown, 1951), 3.

of mid-nineteenth-century Mexican Catholics in the Southwest who, as a common quip puts it, did not cross the border but had the border cross them during U.S. territorial expansion. Unlike the saga of their contemporary European coreligionists, who as émigrés sought haven in a new land, the story of the first large group of Hispanic Catholics in the United States is primarily a tale of faith, struggle, and endurance in places where their Spanish and Mexican forebears had already created a homeland. In one often-repeated phrase they were "foreigners in our native land" who survived the U.S. takeover of northern Mexico.[26] For generations German immigrants recalled 1848 as a year of revolution and the Irish as a moment at the height of the potato famine, but the same date is etched in the consciousness of Mexicans and Mexican Americans as the pivotal juncture when military defeat led Mexico's president to cede nearly half his nation's territory to the United States. While historians, immigrant descendants, and national symbols like the Statue of Liberty enshrine immigrant ascendancy as a quintessential American story, Hispanics incorporated into the United States underwent the disestablishment of their religion along with widespread loss of their lands, economic wellbeing, political clout, and cultural hegemony. Their *aguante* (unyielding endurance) and faith during this time of social upheaval is one of the most frequently overlooked chapters in U.S. Catholic history.

The conquest of northern Mexico began with the war between Texas and Mexico (1835–1836), which resulted in the establishment of an independent Texas Republic. Nine years later the United States annexed Texas and another war erupted in disputed territory along the Rio Grande River near present-day Brownsville, Texas. The 1848 Treaty of Guadalupe Hidalgo brought an official end to this war, established new borders between Mexico and the United States, and purportedly guaranteed the citizenship, property, and religious rights of Mexican citizens who chose to remain in the conquered territories. Mexico lost the present-day states of Texas, Nevada, California, Utah, and parts of New Mexico, Arizona, Colorado, and Wyoming. Six years later the Gadsen Purchase or, as Mexicans call it, the *Tratado de Mesilla* (Treaty of Mesilla), completed the U.S. takeover of former Mexican territories. With the threat of another U.S. invasion as the backdrop for negotiations, James Gadsen "purchased" the southern sections of present-day Arizona and New Mexico for $10 million. This land acquisition enabled U.S. entrepreneurs to expropriate the profits from this terri-

---

26. Juan N. Seguín, *Personal Memoirs of John N. Seguín from the Year 1834 to the Retreat of General Woll from the City of San Antonio in 1842* (San Antonio: Ledger Book and Job Office, 1858), iv; Pablo de la Guerra, Speech to the California legislature, April 26, 1856, reprinted in *El Grito: A Journal of Contemporary Mexican-American Thought* 5 (Fall 1971): 19. Seguín's memoirs are reprinted in *A Revolution Remembered: The Memoirs and Selected Correspondence of Juan N. Seguín*, ed. Jesús F. de la Teja (Austin: State House, 1991).

tory's rich mine deposits and its suitability as a route for expanding rail transportation networks.

The futility of direct resistance to U.S. occupation was painfully evident in events like the 1847 Taos Rebellion, an uprising in which Hispanic and Native American allies attempted to overthrow U.S. rule established in New Mexico the previous year. Insurrectionists assassinated territorial governor Charles Bent and at least fifteen other Anglo Americans, but U.S. forces quickly suppressed the rebellion and publicly hanged its leaders. Military defeat merely initiated the process of U.S. conquest and expansion, as law enforcement personnel, judicial and political officials, occupying troops, and a growing Anglo-American populace imposed U.S. rule. Violence against Mexicans at times reached extreme proportions, but the judicial system afforded little if any protection for them despite their U.S. citizenship. The frequent lynching of Mexican residents even included the hanging of a woman. In California a vigilante mob of Anglo Americans condemned a woman named Josefa to avenge the death of their fellow miner, Fred Cannon, whom Josefa had killed with a knife after he broke down her door in a drunken rage. Anglo-American newcomers further consolidated the conquest by asserting their dominion over political and economic life. When Texas became a state in 1845, for example, Mexican San Antonians lost control of the city council their ancestors had established and led for more than a century. They also lost most of their land holdings, often in biased legal proceedings and in some cases through outright criminal removal from their homes and property. Increasingly Mexicans became a working underclass.[27] Demographic shifts facilitated the diminishment of their political and economic influence. Nowhere was this shift more dramatic than in northern California, where the Gold Rush altered the demographic profile almost overnight.

Hispanic hegemony in religious life and public celebrations also dissipated in the half century after the U.S. takeover of the Southwest. By 1890 in the formerly "Catholic" town of Los Angeles there were seventy-eight religious organizations, including groups such as Congregationalists, Jews, Buddhists, Baptists, Unitarians, and an African Methodist Episcopal congregation. In various locales, Anglo Americans promoted the participation of Mexican-descent residents in the parades and ceremonies of newly-organized U.S. holidays like the Fourth of July. As one report of an 1851 celebration

---

27. Juan Romero, "Begetting the Mexican American: Padre Martínez and the 1847 Rebellion," in *Seeds of Struggle/Harvest of Faith*, ed. Steele, Rhetts, and Awalt, 345–371; Rodolfo Acuña, *Occupied America: A History of Chicanos* (1972; 3rd ed., New York: Harper & Row, 1988), 118–121; Timothy Matovina, *Tejano Religion and Ethnicity: San Antonio, 1821–1860* (Austin: University of Texas Press, 1995), 51–52, 68.

in San Antonio stated: "We have many foreigners [*sic*] among us who know nothing of our government, who have no national feeling in common with us.... Let us induce them to partake with us in our festivities, they will soon partake our feelings, and when so, they will be citizens indeed."[28]

Parishes and other elements of Catholic life were not immune to change during the turbulent period of transition. Dioceses were established at places like Galveston (1847), Santa Fe (1853), San Francisco (1853), Denver (1887), and Tucson (1897). European clergy served in many areas of the Southwest, with the French predominating in Texas, New Mexico, and Arizona, the Irish in northern California, and the Spanish in southern California. During the second half of the nineteenth century, Catholic bishops' appointments in the region reflected this same pattern, with the exception of a Spaniard in northern California. Scores of religious sisters also crossed the Atlantic or came from the eastern United States and began schools, hospitals, orphanages, and other apostolic work in the Southwest.

Differences in culture and religious practice led some newly-arrived Catholic leaders to misunderstand and criticize their Mexican co-religionists in some respects. The first resident bishop of Los Angeles, Thaddeus Amat, oversaw an 1862 synod meeting that forbade Mexican Catholic faith expressions like *los pastores*, a festive proclamation of the shepherds who worshiped the newborn infant Jesus. Reflecting the nineteenth-century ultramontane posture that many European clergy brought with them to the United States, one that stressed loyalty to the pope and the standardization of Catholic ritual and devotion, Amat and the synod fathers repeatedly cited the decrees of the sixteenth-century Council of Trent as the authoritative source for their ecclesial legislation. They ordered priests to "carefully avoid introducing any practices or rites foreign to Roman [practices]" and bemoaned "the scandal which often arises" from Mexican traditions they found too boisterous and indecorous. Thus they demanded that public processions, funeral traditions, and religious feasts strictly adhere to the rubrics of the Roman Ritual and banned long-standing local practices like festive displays of devotion during processions, cannon salutes as a form of religious devotion, and the fiestas and entertainments that accompanied religious celebrations.[29]

---

28. Michael E. Engh, *Frontier Faiths: Church, Temple, and Synagogue in Los Angeles, 1846–1888* (Albuquerque: University of New Mexico Press, 1992), 189–190; *San Antonio Ledger*, July 10, 1851.

29. Michael E. Engh, "From *Frontera* Faith to Roman Rubrics: Altering Hispanic Religious Customs in Los Angeles, 1855–1880," *U.S. Catholic Historian* 12, no. 4 (Fall 1994): 90–95, at 92, 94. The cited passages are from *Constitutiones ... Synodo Dioecesana Prima* (San Francisco: Vicente Torras, 1862), 26.

A number of Protestants were utterly condemnatory in their assessment of Mexican Catholicism. After observing public devotion during the feast of the Mexican national patroness, Our Lady of Guadalupe, at Monterey, California, Congregationalist minister Walter Colton mockingly quipped that Guadalupe probably knew or cared little about such religious exhibitions. Baptist minister Lewis Smith wrote from Santa Fe that, along with various other rituals, Mexicans reenacted the "farce" of Jesus' crucifixion. Undoubtedly the most renowned of the attacks on Hispanic traditions was directed at the brotherhoods of *Los Hermanos de Nuestro Padre Jesús Nazareno* (Brothers of Our Father Jesus the Nazarene), or *Penitentes*, in northern New Mexico and southern Colorado. Local residents frequently deemed outside observers of their rites "Penitente hunters" because of their intrusive presence and the sensationalistic reports they wrote about the brotherhoods' religious practices.[30]

Protestant leaders attributed U.S. expansion to divine providence and adopted a view of religious "manifest destiny." They saw Hispanic Catholicism as inherently inferior and Protestantism as a force that would inevitably conquer all of the Americas. One minister wrote that the Anglo-American takeover of Texas was "an indication of Providence in relation to the propagation of divine truth in other parts of the Mexican dominions[,] . . . Guatemala and all South America" as well as "the beginning of the downfall of [the] Antichrist, and the spread of the Savior's power of the gospel." Three years before the outbreak of war with Mexico, William Hickling Prescott published his best-selling *History of the Conquest of Mexico*, a romanticized portrayal of Hernán Cortés and the sixteenth-century Spanish invasion of the Aztec empire. In the judgment of historian Jenny Franchot, this influential treatise "subtly modulates into a critique of the vitiated Hispanic civilization that results from the conquest, thus providing an ancestor narrative justifying Mexican subordination to an expansionist Protestant United States."[31]

Explicitly or not, the presumed superiority of civilization and Christianity in the United States has been the most consistent justification for the nation's history of expansionism. Willa Cather's bestselling 1927 novel *Death Comes for the Archbishop* played a large part in popularizing this justification. Set in

---

30. Walter Colton, *Three Years in California* (Stanford, CA: Stanford University Press, 1949), 224; Steele, ed., *New Mexican Spanish Religious Oratory*, 94. One of the earliest and most infamous depictions of the Penitentes was Charles F. Lummis, *The Land of Poco Tiempo* (New York: C. Scribner's Sons, 1893), 79–108.

31. A.B. Lawrence, "Introduction," in *Texas in 1840* (New York: William W. Allen, 1840), xviii–xix; William Hickling Prescott, *History of the Conquest of Mexico* (New York: Harper, 1843); Jenny Franchot, *Roads to Rome: The Antebellum Protestant Encounter with Catholicism* (Berkeley: University of California Press, 1994), 38–62, at 40.

nineteenth-century New Mexico, the novel juxtaposes the life of Jean Baptiste Lamy (1814–1888), a French priest who became the first bishop (and later archbishop) of Santa Fe, with the native New Mexican priest Antonio José Martínez (1793–1867). Fictionalized as Bishop Latour, Lamy is idealized as a saintly and civilizing force whose heroic efforts rescued deluded New Mexican Catholics from his antagonist, the allegedly decadent and despotic Martínez. Even Cather's physical description of Martínez—"his mouth was the very assertion of violent, uncurbed passions and tyrannical self-will; the full lips thrust out and taut, like the flesh of animals distended by fear or desire"—evokes disdain and repulsion. Her plot line leaves no doubt that the imposition of U.S. rule and new religious leadership in New Mexico and the greater Southwest was both a sacred duty and a moral imperative.[32]

Cather's depiction of Father Martínez parallels the vitriol of earlier anti-Catholic literature such as Maria Monk's *Awful Disclosures of the Hotel Dieu Nunnery in Montreal* (1836), a slanderous and unfounded account of convent life that became the best-selling literary work of its day. Yet numerous European-descent Catholics were effusive in their praise of *Death Comes for the Archbishop*. Their acclamation of Cather, who was raised Baptist and became an Episcopalian, coincided with a period of rising influence of the Ku Klux Klan and anti-Catholic nativism. Focusing on the laudatory depiction of Lamy as a holy priest and as an Americanizing influence, rather than the derogatory figure of Martínez, a number of priests and nuns wrote Cather congratulatory letters. The editor of *Catholic Library World* regarded Cather "the outstanding American woman novelist of the day" and *Death Comes for the Archbishop* "her greatest book." A columnist in the national lay Catholic opinion journal *Commonweal* extolled the book's depiction of Lamy and his French clerical companions, who gave "all their powers, their endurance, their courage, their strength, their culture, their riches of European experience" to the task of "saving souls" among Native Americans and "the scanty and static Mexican population." This writer went so far as to deem it "the duty of Catholics to buy and read and spread Willa Cather's masterpiece."[33] Cather's sharp delineation between a normative Euro-American Catholicism and its deficient Hispanic counterpart clearly struck a chord with European-descent Catholics struggling to cast aside their stigmatization as foreigners and achieve social acceptability in the United States.

---

32. Willa Cather, *Death Comes for the Archbishop* (New York: Alfred A. Knopf, 1927), 141. I am indebted to Roberto Lint Sagarena for his insightful work on *Death Comes for the Archbishop* and its role in shaping the historiography of the Southwest and perceptions of the region's Mexican inhabitants.

33. "Willa Cather," *Catholic Library World* (January 15, 1932): 30; Michael Williams, "Willa Cather's Masterpiece," *Commonweal* (September 28, 1927): 491–492.

As renowned historian of the Southwest David Weber has noted, "even scholarly writers must reckon with Cather's imagination." Robert Wright and Gilberto Hinojosa concur that historians of the Southwest—both historians of religion and those who study other topics—have generally "adhered to the basic outline of the received historiographical tradition" reflected in Cather's novel. In his 1981 work *American Catholics*, the distinguished U.S. Catholic historian James Hennesey states that in nineteenth-century New Mexico, the church under Mexican leadership was "decadent" and "sacramental life was virtually non-existent." He contends that "Padre José Antonio [*sic*] Martínez of Taos, depicted under his own name in Willa Cather's *Death Comes for the Archbishop*, was a classic case" of corrupt native priests who "extorted exorbitant fees" and neglected their pastoral duties, leaving local religious culture plagued by "ignorance, neglect, and permissiveness." Regarding Lamy, Hennesey concludes that "the diocese and then the archdiocese of Santa Fe stand as a monument to [his] energy and organizing genius." Though subsequently he offers a more sympathetic overview of Mexican Catholic leaders in California, in his initial treatment of their legacy Hennesey contends that after the secularization of the California missions in 1834 "religion declined" and the Californios were "innocent of cultural influence" and spent their days in "a free and lazy life, riding madly about the countryside, enjoying brutal blood sports."[34]

Mexican Catholics have contested such scandalously deprecating portrayals from the first years of their incorporation into the United States. In December 1848 Bishop John Hughes of New York wrote José de la Guerra y Noriega of Santa Barbara seeking information about conditions in California for the Provincial Council of Baltimore held the following May. Hughes' inquiry included the assertion that all Mexican clergy had abandoned California, leaving Catholics there "destitute of all spiritual aid." In his response, de la Guerra stated that "with due respect to the Mexican priests, that the information which has been given to Your Illustrious Lordship regarding their conduct [abandoning their parishioners] during these latter times does not correspond with the facts." He reported that there were still sixteen priests in California.[35]

---

34. David Weber, *On the Edge of Empire: The Taos Hacienda of los Martínez* (Santa Fe: Museum of New Mexico Press, 1996), 78; Robert E. Wright, "Local Church Emergence and Mission Decline: The Historiography of the Catholic Church in the Southwest during the Spanish and Mexican Periods," *U.S. Catholic Historian* 9, nos. 1–2 (Winter/Spring 1990): 27–48, at 44; Gilberto M. Hinojosa, "The Enduring Hispanic Faith Communities: Spanish and Texas Church Historiography," *Journal of Texas Catholic History and Culture* 1 (March 1990): 20–41; Hennesey, *American Catholics*, 21, 137–138, 140–141.

35. Cited correspondence is from the transcription in Joseph A. Thompson, *El Gran Capitán, José de la Guerra: A Historical Biographical Study* (Los Angeles: Cabrera & Sons, 1961), 219–225, at 220, 223.

Mexican residents employed various strategies to accommodate the new regime. In many locales where ethnic Mexicans remained the majority, Anglo Americans consolidated control by means of a "peace structure," a "post-war arrangement that allows the victors to maintain law and order without the constant use of force." The peace structure entailed an arrangement between Anglo-American newcomers and the elites of Mexican communities that did not alter traditional authority structures but placed Anglo Americans atop the existing hierarchy. Often marriages between Anglo-American men and daughters from the elite families of a locale played a key role in this arrangement. These marriages offered Anglo Americans the advantages of land, inherited wealth, and social status. At the same time, they offered Mexican residents allies to help protect familial interests and land holdings within the new political and economic structures. After the U.S. takeover, such allies were particularly useful as many Mexicans did not speak English, were unfamiliar with the legal system, and were vulnerable to accusations of disloyalty toward the United States. It is not surprising, then, that during the time of transition, in places like San Antonio "at least one daughter from almost every *rico* [rich] family . . . married an Anglo."[36]

Some residents of the former Mexican territories survived the effects of the U.S. takeover through isolation. In places like northern New Mexico, some degree of autonomy was possible because of the physical distance from U.S. institutions and influence. While this isolation was often the result of circumstance as much as design, Hispanic communities embraced the opportunities for cultural continuity. Nonetheless, in the end, even the most isolated settlements did not fully escape U.S. influence. In the towns and the urban areas that expanded with the arrival of the railroads in the 1870s and 1880s, Mexican *barrios* (neighborhoods) resulted from forced segregation as well as the desire for separation from Anglo-American society. As an ethnic enclave, the barrio mediated a sense of split existence between the familiarity of Mexican home and neighborhood and the alienation of the Anglo-American world where barrio residents often worked and sometimes went to school. At the same time, however, the barrio provided a strong base for group survival, cultural retention, and ethnic pride. In this way it was a structure that enabled Mexicans to sustain themselves despite the social changes they endured.[37]

---

36. David Montejano, *Anglos and Mexicans in the Making of Texas, 1836–1986* (Austin: University of Texas Press. 1987), 34; Jane Dysart, "Mexican Women in San Antonio, 1830–1860: The Assimilation Process," *Western Historical Quarterly* 7 (October 1976): 365–375, at 370.

37. Albert Camarillo, *Chicanos in a Changing Society: From Mexican Pueblos to American Barrios in Santa Barbara and Southern California, 1848–1930* (Cambridge: Harvard University Press, 1979); Richard Griswold del Castillo, *The Los Angeles Barrio, 1850–1890: A Social History* (Berkeley: University of California Press, 1979); Matovina, *Tejano Religion and Ethnicity*, 49–82.

Hispanic residents like New Mexican Rafael Romero drew on their heritage as natives of the region to defend themselves more directly against what they perceived as the impositions of newcomers. When the territorial governor blocked Jesuit attempts to establish the tax-exempt and degree-granting status of their new school in Las Vegas, New Mexico in 1878, Romero made a spirited defense of Catholics' rights. His public address during festivities for the close of the school's first academic year acclaimed his hearers as native New Mexicans whose "ancestors penetrated into these deserted and dangerous regions many years before the Mayflower floated over the dancing waves that washed Plymouth Rock." He went on to remind his audience that Jesus was also "tormented by a provincial governor," claiming that the oppressive actions of their current territorial governor were worse than the misdeeds of Pontius Pilate, whose sin, according to Romero, was one of omission rather than direct persecution of the innocent. Defending himself against possible retorts that he spoke too harshly, he went on to ask rhetorically:

> Am I not a Catholic citizen of a Catholic land, New Mexico? And have I not, as a New Mexican Catholic, been grossly insulted by a pathetic public official? What does it mean when a man sent to be the governor of a Catholic land, in an official message directed to Catholic legislators and to our Catholic people, piles insult upon insult against a religious order of the Catholic Church?[38]

Mexican resistance to the consolidation of U.S. rule was not limited to rhetoric. During the war between Mexico and the United States, some offered military resistance to the foreign invaders, such as Californians who defeated U.S. forces at battles in the Los Angeles area and at the hamlet of San Pasqual before peaceably coming to terms with their more numerous and heavily-armed foes. Violent resistance erupted in various locales even after the U.S. conquest. In the decades following the U.S. Civil War, guerrilla leaders like Tiburcio Vásquez in California and Juan Cortina in Texas led retaliatory movements protesting the endemic violence and injustice their people suffered at the hands of Anglo Americans. Mexican residents also defended their rights in the political arena, as at the 1845 Texas Constitutional Convention when delegate José Antonio Navarro was able to prevent passage of a law that restricted voting rights to Anglo-American residents.[39]

---

38. Steele, ed., *New Mexican Spanish Religious Oratory*, 148–159, at 153, 155.
39. Leonard Pitt, *The Decline of the Californios: A Social History of the Spanish-Speaking Californians, 1846–1890* (Berkeley: University of California Press, 1966), 33–35; Acuña, *Occupied America*, 43–47, 124–125; José Antonio Navarro, *Defending Mexican Valor in Texas: José Antonio Navarro's Historical Writings, 1853–1857*, ed. David R. McDonald and Timothy Matovina (Austin: State House, 1995), 19–20.

Conflicts between Mexicans and Catholic leaders at times resulted in public controversy and even open resistance, as in the infamous and frequently-cited conflict between Padre Martínez and (Arch)bishop Lamy. In 1875 Bishop Dominic Manucy of Brownsville rejected a request that twenty-two exiled Mexican sisters reside in the area and serve Mexican-descent Catholics. Local Spanish-speaking Catholics were incensed at Manucy's decision, particularly since they offered to pay the living costs for the sisters. On the day the women religious were to board the train and depart from Brownsville, an angry crowd removed their train from its tracks and refused to let authorities replace it.[40]

But a number of foreign Catholic clergy and religious became beloved among the Mexican Catholics they served and energetically supported and enhanced their people's faith life and religious practices. Bishop Jean Marie Odin offered ministrations in Spanish and insisted that other priests coming to Texas do the same. He participated in Mexican religious feasts like local celebrations in honor of Our Lady of Guadalupe and spoke enthusiastically of the religious zeal demonstrated in these celebrations. San Francisco's first archbishop, Joseph Alemany, enjoyed a similar rapport with Spanish-speaking Catholics under his care. Women religious led Catholic initiatives in numerous locales, such as Los Angeles, where the Daughters of Charity of St. Vincent de Paul arrived in 1856 to establish a school and orphanage, but soon expanded their ministries to meet other needs such as health care, disaster relief, catechetical instruction, and job placement for women. Most of the sisters who served during the nineteenth century were of Irish descent, but their numbers included women from Mexico and Spain as well as several local Hispanic women who joined the order after receiving their education from the sisters. In Colorado, New Mexico, and the El Paso district, exiled Italian Jesuits served in parishes and as circuit-riders to scores of mission stations. They also founded a college at Las Vegas, New Mexico, which they later moved to its current locale in Denver and eventually renamed Regis University, and established *La Revista Católica*, the first Spanish-language Catholic newspaper in the United States.[41]

---

40. José Roberto Juárez, "La iglesia Católica y el Chicano en sud Texas, 1836–1911," *Aztlán* 4 (Fall 1973): 230–232. For the conflict between Martínez and Lamy, see e.g. Juan Romero, with Moises Sandoval, *Reluctant Dawn: Historia del Padre A. J. Martínez, Cura de Taos* (San Antonio: Mexican American Cultural Center Press, 1976); Angélico Chávez, *But Time and Chance: The Story of Padre Martínez of Taos, 1793–1867* (Santa Fe: Sunstone, 1981).

41. Jean Marie Odin to Jean-Baptiste Étienne, February 7, 1842, in *The United States Catholic Magazine and Monthly Review* 3 (October 1844): 727–730, at 729; Odin to Anthony Blanc, December 12, 1852, Catholic Archives of Texas, Austin; Jeffrey M. Burns, "The Mexican Catholic Community in California," in *Mexican Americans and the Catholic Church, 1900–1965*, ed. Jay P. Dolan and Gilberto M. Hinojosa (Notre Dame, IN: University of Notre Dame Press, 1994), 129–233, at 134–135; Engh, *Frontier Faiths*, chap. 7 "Soldiers of Christ, Angels of Mercy"; Gerald McKevitt, *Brokers of Culture: Italian Jesuits in the American West, 1848–1919* (Stanford, CA: Stanford University Press, 2007), chap. 8, "'The Darkest Part of the U.S.A.': The Southwest."

Our Lady of Guadalupe procession flowing out of San Fernando Cathedral in San Antonio, Texas, 1933 (Courtesy of San Antonio Light Collection, University of Texas Institute of Texan Cultures, San Antonio, Texas, #0140-F).

A number of local communities asserted their Mexican Catholic heritage in the public spaces of civic life through their long-standing rituals and devotions, sometimes on their own as in the case of Nacogdoches after Father Díaz de León's murder or Los Angeles after Bishop Amat's restrictive decrees, at other times with the support of sympathetic priests and religious. From Texas to California, various communities continued to enthusiastically celebrate established local traditions such as pilgrimages, los pastores, Holy Week, Corpus Christi, and established patronal feast days like that of Our Lady of Guadalupe. The persistence of religious traditions is particularly striking in light of some Protestant leaders' attempts to ban, replace, and condemn them. In the face of such initiatives, as well as military conquest and occupation, violence and lawlessness, political and economic displacement, rapid demographic change, and the erosion of cultural hegemony, Spanish-speaking Catholic feasts and devotions had a heightened significance. These religious traditions provided an ongoing means of public communal expression, affirmation, faith, and resistance to newcomers who criticized or attempted to suppress Mexican-descent residents' heritage. Undoubtedly fear and anger at their subjugation intensified religious fervor among many devotees.

The most renowned lay group that served as the protectors of treasured local traditions was the aforementioned Penitentes of northern New Mexico and southern Colorado. Penitente brotherhoods evolved in towns and villages well before the U.S. takeover of the area. Their most noticeable function was to commemorate Christ's passion and death, although they also provided community leadership and fostered social integration. Organized as separate local entities, Penitente brotherhoods had a leader named the *Hermano Mayor* (literally "older brother") and a *morada* (literally "habitation") or chapter house where they held meetings and religious devotions. Despite the sharp criticism they often received from outsiders, the Penitentes continued providing leadership for prayer and social life in numerous local communities.[42]

In more urban areas, which tended to have a greater presence of priests and religious, activist Mexican lay women and men continued traditional feast days and faith expressions in Catholic parishes. The annual series of celebrations for Tucson's original patron saint, St. Augustine, lasted for an entire month at San Agustín parish. Similarly, San Fernando parishioners in San Antonio organized public rituals and festivities for Our Lady of Guadalupe, Christmas, San Fernando, San Antonio, San Juan, San Pedro, and other feasts. Most conspicuous among these rites was the annual Guadalupe feast, celebrated with a colorful outdoor procession, elaborate decorations adorning the Guadalupe image and their parish church, gun and cannon salutes, extended ringing of the church bells, and large crowds for services conducted in Spanish.[43]

Women frequently played a key leadership role in public worship and devotion. Doña María Cornelia Salazar and Señora Juana Epifanía de Jesús Valdéz were *madrinas* (godmothers) for the solemn blessing of a new statue for the 1874 Guadalupe feast day at Our Lady of Guadalupe parish in Conejos, Colorado. Throughout the region young women served in processions as the immediate attendants for the Guadalupe image in her annual feast-day celebration.[44] They occupied similar places of prominence in processions for

---

42. J. Manuel Espinosa, "The Origins of the Penitentes of New Mexico: Separating Fact from Fiction," *Catholic Historical Review* 79 (July 1993): 454–477; Alberto López Pulido, *The Sacred World of the Penitentes* (Washington, DC: Smithsonian Institution Press, 2000).

43. Federico José María Ronstadt, *Borderman: Memoirs of Federico José María Ronstadt*, ed. Edward F. Ronstadt (Albuquerque: University of New Mexico Press, 1993), 92; Timothy Matovina, *Guadalupe and Her Faithful: Latino Catholics in San Antonio, from Colonial Origins to the Present* (Baltimore: Johns Hopkins University Press, 2005), chap. 3, "Defender of Dignidad, 1836–1900."

44. Salvatore Personè, Letter of March 1875, as cited in Marianne L. Stoller and Thomas J. Steele, SJ, eds., *Diary of the Jesuit Residence of Our Lady of Guadalupe Parish, Conejos, Colorado: December 1871–December 1875* (Colorado Springs: Colorado College Press, 1982), 185–186; Rena Maverick Green, ed., *Memoirs of Mary A. Maverick* (San Antonio: Alamo,

other Marian feast days like the Assumption.[45] Even when male Penitentes provided significant leadership for communal worship, women played vital roles in local traditions like the annual procession for the feast of St. John the Baptist.[46] Often these leadership roles did not significantly alter restrictions on women in other public functions, reinforced the notion that women were naturally more pious than men, and symbolically linked the purity of young girls dressed in white with icons like the Virgin Mary, a communal accentuation of feminine chastity that lacked a corresponding association between young boys and Jesus. Yet Mexican-descent women extended their familial efforts to transmit cultural and devotional traditions into a public role of community leadership that shaped Mexican Catholics' ritual expressions. Their leadership illuminates what Ana María Díaz-Stevens calls the "matriarchal core" of Latino Catholicism, that is, women's exercise of autonomous authority in communal devotions despite the ongoing patriarchal limitations of institutional Catholicism and Latin American societies.[47]

A number of communities in the Southwest struggled for their very survival. In the process their observance of long-standing traditions often abated or even ceased. Nonetheless, as Bishop Henry Granjon of Tucson noted in 1902 during his first pastoral visit to Las Cruces, New Mexico, many Mexican-descent Catholics in the Southwest continued to practice their own customs and traditions decades after the U.S. takeover of their lands. According to Bishop Granjon, in the Southwest these traditions served to "maintain the unity of the Mexican population and permit them to resist, to a certain extent, the invasions of the Anglo-Saxon race."[48] The waves of newly-arrived women religious and clergy like Granjon vastly increased the Catholic institutional presence and support structures in the region, enhancing leadership initiatives among Mexican Catholics that enabled a number of local populations to adapt and continue their traditional expressions of faith, defend their sense of dignity, collectively respond to the effects of conquest, and express their own ethnic legitimation.

1921), 53–54; Odin to Étienne, February 7, 1842; Abbe [Emanuel] Domenech, *Missionary Adventures in Texas and Mexico* (London: Longman, Brown, Green, Longmans, and Roberts, 1858), 357–359.

45. *Los Angeles Star*, August 22, 1857.

46. Cleofas M. Jaramillo, *Shadows of the Past (Sombras del Pasado)* (Santa Fe: Seton Village Press, 1941), 85–86.

47. Ana María Díaz-Stevens, "The Saving Grace: The Matriarchal Core of Latino Catholicism," *Latino Studies Journal* 4 (September 1993): 60–78.

48. Henry Granjon, *Along the Rio Grande: A Pastoral Visit to Southwest New Mexico in 1902*, ed. Michael Romero Taylor, trans. Mary W. de López (Albuquerque: University of New Mexico Press, 1986), 39.

New Immigrants

Israel Zangwill's play *The Melting-Pot* opened on Broadway in 1908 and extended into popular parlance the term "melting pot," a concept first articulated in a famous passage of French-American writer Hector St. John de Crèvecoeur's 1782 book *Letters from an American Farmer*. The success of *The Melting-Pot* was rooted in an assimilationist perspective many Americans endorsed, including President Theodore Roosevelt, who at the conclusion of the opening performance in the nation's capital leaned over the edge of his box and shouted, "That's a great play, Mr. Zangwill, that's a great play." In one of the play's most memorable lines its hero, a Russian Jewish immigrant named David Quixano, deems the United States "the great Melting-Pot" in which the "blood hatreds and rivalries" of Europe dissolve in the "fires of God," the crucible through which "God is making the American." As scholars like Philip Gleason have shown, even more than the dissipation of one's native language and customs, at its core the ideology of the melting pot entailed the acceptance that the U.S. experiment in democracy represented a decisive break with the past and a new order and model for the future.[49] Zangwill's success was somewhat ironic, given its bold proclamation of the power of a U.S. melting pot to assimilate newcomers and the national sentiment to restrict European immigration that arose concurrently with his play. By the 1920s new legislation severely curtailed the flow of European émigrés that had continued almost unabated over the previous century.

The waning numbers of first-generation Catholics from Europe hastened their transition to monolingual English and the acceptance of U.S. cultural norms. John Tracy Ellis, widely regarded as the premier historian of U.S. Catholicism, observed in his influential general history of American Catholics that the 1920s immigration laws "made a direct contribution to the maturity of the Church in the sense that during the [following] generation its faithful for the first time had an opportunity to become more or less stabilized." Assessing Ellis' scholarly achievement, Daniel J. Boorstin, the editor of the Chicago History of American Civilization book series in which the Ellis volume appeared, wrote in his 1969 editor's preface to the second edition of the book that recent American Catholic history "is a peculiarly significant and inspiring chapter in the growth and fulfillment of American institutions." More recently, Charles Morris has concluded that "except for the newest waves of Hispanic immigrants, American Catholics have long since made it in America. As much as any other religious body, they are middle-

---

49. Israel Zangwill, *The Melting-Pot: Drama in Four Acts* (New York: Macmillan, 1909), 37; Philip Gleason, "American Identity and Americanization," in *Harvard Encyclopedia of American Ethnic Groups* (Cambridge: Harvard University Press, 1980), 31–34.

class, suburban, educated, affluent. They exercise control over their own lives in ways that their grandparents never did."[50]

U.S. Catholics had long argued that Boorstin's and Morris' affirmation was true: they were no less American than their counterparts of other faiths. In a 1948 *New York Times* interview, Archbishop John T. McNicholas of Cincinnati, chairman of the administrative board of the National Catholic Welfare Conference, contested accusations of Catholic disloyalty from the newly-formed organization Protestants and Other Americans United for Separation of Church and State. McNicholas stated that he and his fellow bishops "deny absolutely and without any qualification that the Catholic bishops of the United States are seeking a union of church and state by any endeavors whatsoever" and that Catholics would not do so even if one day they constituted a majority in the country. Catholic political candidates also vigorously protested accusations that they were unable to uphold the Constitution because their first loyalty was to the Vatican, such as the 1960 indictment of Dr. Ramsey Pollard, President of the Southern Baptist Convention: "No matter what [John F.] Kennedy might say, he cannot separate himself from his church if he is a true Catholic. . . . All we ask is that Roman Catholicism lift its bloody hand from the throats of those that want to worship in the church of their choice." Kennedy and the only previous Catholic national party candidate for president, Alfred E. Smith, famously stated their support for the separation of church and state and all other articles of the Constitution, Smith in a 1927 article in the *Atlantic Monthly* and Kennedy in a speech to the Greater Houston Ministerial Association. Kennedy's election was a watershed moment for Catholics, an electoral victory that, in the words of journalist William Shannon "wiped away the bitterness and disappointment of Al Smith's defeat in 1928; it removed any lingering sense of social inferiority and insecurity."[51]

Hispanics were a small part of the nineteenth-century immigration that gave rise to the Americanizing process of the twentieth century. Though an open border between the United States and Mexico allowed Mexican citizens to migrate even after the Treaty of Guadalupe Hidalgo, their numbers were relatively low until the last three decades of the nineteenth century, when gradually a larger group of immigrants and refugees began to arrive.

---

50. John Tracy Ellis, *American Catholicism* (1956; 2nd ed., Chicago: University of Chicago Press, 1969), ix, 129; Morris, *American Catholic*, 431.

51. "Denies Catholics Oppose Separation: Archbishop McNicholas Says Protestant Group Erred in Recent Manifesto," *New York Times*, January 26, 1948; Theodore C. Sorensen, *Kennedy* (New York: Harper & Row, 1965), 194; Alfred E. Smith, "Catholic and Patriotic: Governor Smith Replies," *Atlantic Monthly* 39 (May 1927): 721–728; John F. Kennedy, Speech to the Greater Houston Ministerial Association, September 12, 1960, at http://www.presidency.ucsb.edu/ws/?pid=25773; William V. Shannon, *The American Irish* (New York: Macmillan, 1963), 393.

After the U.S. Civil War ended in 1865, railroad construction, mining, and agriculture in the regions from Texas to California, and then in Mexico itself, linked the regions economically, creating migration flows of Mexican labor north. The Porfirio Díaz regime (1876–1911) in Mexico promoted economic growth linked to foreign interests, leading to prosperity for some but displacement and migration for others who went to the United States looking for work. U.S. interests in Caribbean products, particularly sugar and tobacco, also encouraged the movement of Puerto Ricans and Cubans to the United States. Intermittent struggles for independence in both Puerto Rico and Cuba led some political activists into U.S. exile. While many political exiles were skeptical if not antagonistic toward the Catholic Church and its leaders, who in their native lands consisted largely of Spaniards and others who supported Spanish colonial rule, Caribbean newcomers augmented the diversity of Hispanic Catholics in the United States.[52]

Like European Catholic émigrés, many Hispanics advocated for national or ethnic parishes as a means to retain their language, cultural practices, sense of group identity, and Catholic faith. As early as 1871, Catholics at San Francisco proposed a national parish to serve the Spanish-speaking population in their growing city. Although most Spanish-speaking residents were of Mexican descent, representatives from the consulates of Chile, Peru, Nicaragua, Colombia, Bolivia, Costa Rica, and Spain were among the leaders in this effort, making it one of if not the first pan-Hispanic Catholic initiative in the United States. Four years later, San Francisco archbishop Joseph Alemany established the national parish of Our Lady of Guadalupe. In 1879, Cuban lay Catholics in Key West, Florida worked with church officials to establish a chapel named after *Nuestra Señora de la Caridad del Cobre* (Our Lady of Charity of El Cobre), the most prominent Marian icon and devotional tradition in Cuban Catholicism. Worshipers at the chapel organized the Caridad del Cobre feast, other Marian devotions, Christmas pageants, and even a celebrated pastoral visit from the archbishop of Santiago, Cuba.[53]

---

52. David G. Gutiérrez, *Walls and Mirrors: Mexican Americans, Mexican Immigrants, and the Politics of Ethnicity* (Berkeley: University of California Press, 1995), chap. 2, "Economic Development and Immigration"; Gerald E. Poyo, *"With All, and for the Good of All": The Emergence of Popular Nationalism in the Cuban Communities of the United States, 1848–1898* (Durham, NC: Duke University Press, 1989); Lisandro Pérez, "Cuban Catholics in the United States," in *Puerto Rican and Cuban Catholics in the U.S., 1900–1965*, ed. Jay P. Dolan and Jaime R. Vidal (Notre Dame, IN: University of Notre Dame Press, 1994), 158–173.

53. Spaniards and Hispanic Americans of San Francisco, *Lo que puede y necesita la raza española en San Francisco* (circular letter printed in San Francisco), 1871, copy in Bancroft Library, University of California, Berkeley; *A History of St. Mary Star of the Sea Catholic Church: The Oldest Roman Catholic Parish in the Diocese of Miami* (Key West: n.p., 1996); "Chronicles of the Sisters of the Holy Names of Jesus and Mary—Key West, Florida" (typescript), n.d., records of the Sisters of the Holy Names of Jesus and Mary, Albany, New York.

One of the earliest Cuban exiles was the influential priest, Venerable Félix Varela (1788–1853), who fled to New York in 1823 after the Spanish regime he opposed as a Cuban delegate to the Spanish Cortes (parliament) condemned him to death. In exile, Varela worked as a parish priest and eventually rose to the position of vicar general for the diocese of New York. But even in the midst of a busy pastoral life among Irish and other New York Catholics, he continued to advocate for Cuban independence from Spain and the abolition of the slave trade, along with writing and thinking about politics, philosophy, and religion. He published an important exile newspaper, *El Habanero*, in which he promoted Cuban independence, and maintained active correspondence and intellectual exchange with his compatriots on the island. Although the Spanish government pardoned him in 1833, Varela refused to acknowledge that his support for constitutional rule represented criminal activity. He remained in exile and never returned to Cuba. Now a candidate for official canonization as a Catholic saint and the only Catholic priest to receive the honor of being imprinted on a U.S. postage stamp, Varela is also recognized as a precursor of Cuban pro-independence thought. Cubans often describe him as "the one who first taught us to think."[54]

As European immigration declined and the process of their incorporation into American life quickened over the course of the twentieth century, nascent Hispanic immigration accelerated. The expansion of cities and agribusiness in the Southwest, the enticement of railroad and industrial jobs in the Midwest, and exemption from the exclusionary 1920s legislation that curtailed European immigration were key factors attracting Mexican émigrés. Massive Mexican immigration began after the outbreak of the Mexican Revolution in 1910, expanding the population of existing ethnic Mexican communities in the Southwest and establishing scores of new populations in that region and beyond. Intermittent periods of relative calm followed the enactment of the 1917 Mexican Constitution, but violence erupted once again in central and western Mexico when President Plutarco Elías Calles (1924–1928) vigorously enforced anticlerical articles of that constitution. The resulting guerrilla war, known as the Cristero Rebellion (1926–1929), drove even more émigrés north to the United States, many fleeing religious persecution. During the Depression era of the 1930s Mexican migration all but came to a halt and a wave of nativist fever led to the repatriation of numerous Mexicans and the illegal deportation of many native-born Mexican American citizens. But the northward flow resumed with growing work opportunities during

---

54. Antonio Hernández Travieso, *El Padre Varela: Biografía del Forjador de la Conciencia Cubana* (2nd ed., Miami: Ediciones Universal, 1984); Félix Varela, *Letters to Elpidio*, ed. Felipe J. Estévez (Mahwah, NJ: Paulist, 1989); Juan M. Navia, *An Apostle for the Immigrants: The Exile Years of Father Félix Varela y Morales, 1823–1853* (Salisbury, MD: Factor Press, 2002).

Children share in the joyful anticipation of receiving candies and other surprises from a piñata in a Chicago archdiocesan celebration to honor the patron saint of Puerto Rico, St. John the Baptist, ca. 1955 (Courtesy of Claretian Publications, Chicago, Illinois).

World War II. The infamous guest worker or Bracero Program (1942–1964) brought some five million contracted workers north from Mexico, a number of whom stayed or eventually returned to establish homes in the United States. A number of undocumented migrants also crossed into the United States. Many of them stayed permanently. After the Bracero Program ended, the number of undocumented workers increased dramatically, a trend that continues into the twenty-first century. Today ethnic Mexicans in the United States comprise about two thirds of the more than 45 million Latinos in the country. Though the Latino population is widely dispersed across the nation, half of Latinos live in California or Texas due primarily to the heavy concentration of ethnic Mexicans in those two states.[55]

---

55. Michael J. Gonzales, *The Mexican Revolution, 1910–1940* (Albuquerque: University of New Mexico Press, 2002); Gutiérrez, *Walls and Mirrors*; Roberto R. Treviño, *The Church in the Barrio: Mexican American Ethno-Catholicism in Houston* (Chapel Hill: University of

The Puerto Rican case illustrates economic dynamics that led migrants from the Caribbean and Latin America northward. Following the U.S. occupation of the island in 1898 after the Spanish American War, Puerto Rico's subsistence farming and primarily agricultural economy increasingly became a single, cash crop enterprise. During the last decade of Spanish rule, the island produced 57,000 tons of sugar a year. Five years after the U.S. takeover that rate had increased to 200,000 tons per year. By 1930 it was 900,000 tons a year. This transition to a single export commodity subject to price fluctuations on international markets placed a great deal of pressure on the traditional subsistence economy. As owners concentrated their landholdings to facilitate productivity and growth, Puerto Rican farmers were displaced. Also problematic was the nature of sugar production that only provided work part of the year during the harvests, leaving workers unemployed or underemployed the rest of the year. Puerto Ricans left home in increasing numbers, searching for a more stable livelihood. The number of Puerto Ricans living on the mainland increased from 1,513 in 1910 to nearly 53,000 in 1930. Migratory pressures became even more dramatic after World War II when policymakers introduced incentives to create a manufacturing base, a program known as Operation Bootstrap. Industrialization initiated a new era in the island's economic history, producing a nascent middle class. At the same time, the urbanization of a primarily rural people and the uneven participation in the economic benefits of industrialization caused many more to leave home in an unprecedented migration to the mainland. The first great waves of Puerto Rican migrants after World War II went to New York City, where more than eighty percent of the Puerto Rican population on the mainland lived in 1950. But over time Puerto Ricans increasingly moved beyond New York to other locales, including a growing number who gained higher education during the transformations of Puerto Rico's economy. Today approximately ten percent of the Latino population on the mainland is Puerto Rican.[56]

Thousands of Cubans also left their homeland, in their case largely as a result of Fidel Castro's 1959 rise to power in the Cuban Revolution, a strug-

---

North Carolina Press, 2006); Edwin Hernández with Rebecca Burwell and Jeffrey Smith, "A Study of Hispanic Catholics: Why Are They Leaving the Church: Implications for the New Evangelization," in *The New Evangelization: Overcoming the Obstacles*, ed. Steven Boguslawski and Ralph Martin (Mahwah, NJ: Paulist, 2008), 112.

56. Joseph P. Fitzpatrick, *Puerto Rican Americans: The Meaning of Migration to the Mainland* (1971; 2nd ed., Englewood Cliffs, NJ: Prentice-Hall, 1987), 10, 17, 33–36; Ana María Díaz-Stevens, *Oxcart Catholicism on Fifth Avenue: The Impact of the Puerto Rican Migration upon the Archdiocese of New York* (Notre Dame, IN: University of Notre Dame Press, 1993); Jaime R. Vidal, "Citizens Yet Strangers: The Puerto Rican Experience," in *Puerto Rican and Cuban Catholics in the U.S.*, ed. Dolan and Vidal, 9–143; Hernández, "A Study of Hispanic Catholics," 112.

gle that a number of Catholics initially supported. Castro's radicalizing of the revolution led to confrontations between his government and Catholic Church leaders. In November 1959 they convened a National Catholic Congress that drew some one million supporters to Havana's Plaza Cívica, or Plaza de la Revolución as it later became known, to reaffirm their Catholic allegiance and, implicitly, protest the country's political direction. The following year Cuban Catholic bishops and lay leaders publicly acknowledged the need for reforms to advance the wellbeing of the poor, but also called for human rights for all citizens and expressed alarm at the government's growing relations with Communist bloc nations. Subsequently thousands of Catholics fled the island, some joining exile counter-revolutionary groups such as those that conducted the failed 1961 Bay of Pigs invasion. Castro cited such actions as a rationale to repress church leaders. By 1963, some 200,000 Cubans had arrived in the United States, including the core of Cuba's Catholic militant laity and leadership. The majority of Cubans initially established themselves in the Miami area, but the federally-run Cuban Refugee Program settled others in locales across the country. While many of these first exiles were educated, professional, and Catholic, over the following decades as Castro's stance shifted back and forth between restrictive and more open immigration policies those who abandoned the island encompassed a wider spectrum of Cuban society. The largest group after the initial exodus came in 1980 when the Cuban government opened the port of Mariel for exiles wishing to pick up family members. As the boats arrived from Florida, authorities filled them with people who wanted to leave but also with others who were forcibly deported, about 125,000 Cubans in all. All told over a million Cubans arrived in the United States in the half century since the Cuban Revolution.[57]

Countries from throughout the Western hemisphere were represented in the U.S. immigration flows by the 1990s, making the U.S. Latino population more complex and diverse than ever. Civil wars during the 1970s and 1980s in Central America, especially in El Salvador, Guatemala, and Nicaragua, were the catalyst for growing numbers of refugees from that region. In El Salvador, for example, a civil war ravaged between 1979 and 1992, claiming the lives of over 75,000 victims until a 1992 peace accord brought some alleviation to hostilities. Refugees numbering in the hundreds of thousands fled the country. Economic dynamics, urbanization, increases in birth rates and life expectancies, growing expectations for better lives among the people, improved transportation, ties with family members

---

57. Gerald E. Poyo, *Cuban Catholics in the United States, 1960–1980: Exile and Integration* (Notre Dame, IN: University of Notre Dame Press, 2007), 50–84; Pérez, "Cuban Catholics in the United States," 189–207.

already in the United States, and the communications revolution led people from across Latin America and the Caribbean to immigrate. The Dominican presence in the United States was fairly limited until the last years of dictator General Rafael Leónidas Trujillo, who ruled the Dominican Republic from 1930 to 1961 and severely restricted international migration. After Trujillo's 1961 assassination the migrant flow accelerated, the majority of émigrés settling in New York and the environs. By 1990, Dominicans in New York numbered some 700,000 and rivaled the local Puerto Rican population in size. Though South Americans comprise a relatively small minority of U.S. Hispanics, in recent decades their numbers have also increased, with Colombians, Peruvians, and Ecuadorians predominating, but with additional émigrés from nations such as Argentina, Chile, and Brazil. Given the distance involved in their migration, those able to make it to the United States tend to have a higher income and level of education. Consequently they are disproportionately represented among the clergy and lay leaders in dioceses and parishes, exercising an influence beyond their numbers.[58]

Over the past half century immigration from at least twenty countries where Spanish is a primary language has made the United States the fifth largest and the most diverse Spanish-speaking country in the world. Besides the usual immigrant challenge of accommodating themselves to U.S. church and society, many émigrés must incorporate themselves into Hispanic communities in which another national group predominates, such as the first Cubans to settle in Puerto Rican enclaves in New York, Nicaraguans who joined previous Cuban exiles in Miami, and Central and South Americans in ethnic Mexican strongholds throughout the Southwest.[59] Yet to varying degrees an Iberian Catholic heritage, as well as indigenous and African roots, exerts a common influence on Latin Americans from distinct national backgrounds. In the Caribbean, where Spanish colonizers decimated native populations and forcibly resettled numerous African slaves, the African influence remains particularly strong. In places like Peru, Guatemala, and Mexico where elements of the Inca, Maya, and Aztec civilizations continued to exert influence even after the Spanish conquest, these and other ancient indige-

---

58. David M. Reimers, *Still the Golden Door: The Third World Comes to America* (1985; 2nd ed., New York: Columbia University Press, 1992); María Cristina García, *Seeking Refuge: Central American Immigration to Mexico, the United States, and Canada* (Berkeley: University of California Press, 2006); Silvio Torres-Saillant and Ramona Hernández, *The Dominican Americans* (Westport, CT: Greenwood, 1998); Fanny Tabares, "Pastoral Care of Catholic South Americans Living in the United States," *Chicago Studies* 36 (December 1997): 269–281.

59. For a history of twentieth-century Latino Catholicism in San Antonio, Chicago, New York, and Miami that examines relations between Latinos of different backgrounds, see David A. Badillo, *Latinos and the New Immigrant Church* (Baltimore: Johns Hopkins University Press, 2006).

nous cultures shape contemporary life. The mixing or *mestizaje* of Iberian, African, and indigenous cultures is a shared but also complex process with numerous local, regional, and national variations.

Latin America's most direct influence on Catholicism in the United States is the cultures and formative experiences that immigrants raised in their respective homelands carry with them. Nicaraguan refugee Sara García fled the civil war in her country with her husband and three children in 1984. Resettled as an undocumented resident in Newark, García noted in an interview that her fear of deportation to a native country where she would be punished or even killed led to a deepening of her trust in God: "All we can do is commend ourselves to God whenever we leave the house and, when we return, thank the Lord we made it safe and sound." But she also stated that her Catholic faith was rooted in her childhood experiences in rural Nicaragua. García only received a first-grade education, but remembered the nuns who came to offer the catechesis that prepared her for her first communion. Though her family's poverty was so acute that her mother worked day and night and had little time to take her children to church, the influence of her mother's example and the Catholic culture of her childhood were lasting. Regarding her faith, García echoed the sentiments of many Hispanic Catholics, "I was born a Catholic and, God willing, I will die a Catholic."[60]

The profound but vastly diverse formative experiences of émigrés from the Caribbean, Mexico, and Central and South America defy easy generalization. Church-state relations have a long history, as evidenced in the acrimonious episodes of conflict in Mexico and, in more recent decades, in the elections of a Catholic priest and bishop as presidents of Haiti and Paraguay, respectively, in both cases leading these clergy to desist from exercising their priestly functions at the behest of Vatican officials. Historically, the number of available clergy is another key factor shaping Catholic impact, in some cases sufficient priests to wield significant influence but usually less than enough to address large and dispersed Catholic populations. Devotional expressions of faith are widely practiced in a Catholicism that values direct— what theologians call sacramental—encounters with God, Mary, and the saints in everyday life. Every country in Latin America has at least one shrine dedicated to a Marian apparition that is a center of national veneration and identity. Yet the faith stance among local populations ranges from those who engage Catholicism as primarily a heritage of devotional traditions, as a means to struggle for justice, or as an institution with a defined body of doc-

---

60. Archdiocese of Newark, Office of Research and Planning, *Presencia Nueva: Knowledge for Service and Hope: A Study of Hispanics in the Archdiocese of Newark* (Newark, NJ: Archdiocese of Newark, 1988), 158–163, at 158, 163.

trines and teachings. Not surprisingly, many Latin Americans perceive Catholicism entails some combination of these or other elements, though a substantial number are involved with Catholicism only nominally or not at all. Protestantism, especially in its Pentecostal and evangelical forms, has expanded rapidly though unevenly throughout the continent. Mexico remains one of the most staunchly Catholic nations in terms of the preferred denominational allegiance of its population, while Puerto Rico, where the U.S. government and churches conducted an energetic program of Americanization and Protestant proselytizing after annexing the island in 1898, is among the most Protestant. Such historical and religious legacies mark in myriad ways the perceptions of any Latino émigré who spent formative years at home before arriving in the United States.[61]

Catholic ministries to Hispanic newcomers expanded with the rising tide of immigration. Émigré clergy, women religious, and lay leaders ministered among their compatriots, as during the Mexican Revolution, the Cristero Rebellion, and their aftermath, when Mexican Catholics collaborated with U.S. church officials to establish new parishes in such diverse places as Los Angeles, Houston, Dallas, Kansas City, Milwaukee, St. Paul, and Toledo. Twelve Mexican parishes opened in Los Angeles alone between 1923 and 1928, with the total number of predominantly Mexican parishes in the archdiocese increasing to sixty-four by 1947. In other instances U.S. Catholics engaged in outreach to the newcomers, such as the visionary lay apostolic endeavors of Mary Julia Workman in settlement house ministry in Los Angeles and Veronica Miriam Spellmire in establishing and fostering the phenomenal growth of the Confraternity of Christian Doctrine in San Antonio, as well as the response of the New York archdiocese to Puerto Rican migration under the leadership of Cardinal Francis Spellman and priests like Joseph Fitzpatrick, SJ, Robert Fox, Ivan Illich, and Robert Stern. U.S.-born Hispanics also engaged in dedicated ecclesial service to their own communities, such as the Missionary Catechists of Divine Providence (MCDPs), the first and only religious order of Mexican American women founded in the United States, who have provided leadership in evangelization and catechesis in the Southwest and beyond for more than eighty years.[62]

---

61. Enrique Düssel, ed. *The Church in Latin America, 1492–1992* (Maryknoll, NY: Orbis, 1992); Anna L. Peterson and Manuel A. Vásquez, *Latin American Religions: Histories and Documents in Context* (New York: New York University Press, 2008); Díaz-Stevens, *Oxcart Catholicism*, 52–59.

62. *Mexican Americans and the Catholic Church*, ed. Dolan and Hinojosa, 74, 163, 248, 266, 281–282; Michael E. Engh, "From the City of Angels to the Parishes of San Antonio: Catholic Organization, Women Activists, and Racial Intersections, 1900–1950," in *Catholicism in the American West: A Rosary of Hidden Voices*, ed. Roberto R. Treviño and Richard V. Francaviglio (College Station: Texas A&M University Press, 2008), 42–71; Díaz-Stevens,

Like European Catholic immigrants before them, each group of Latino newcomers fostered ministries and church structures that served the needs of their compatriots. None illustrate such initiatives more clearly than Cuban exiles. Historically, Catholicism had a relatively minor role in Cuban society. The church hierarchy never wielded the political influence it did in Latin American locales such as Mexico. Practice of the faith was far stronger among the elite and more nominal among the masses of the working class, especially in the island's predominantly rural areas. Yet a Catholic renaissance gradually emerged during the first half of the twentieth century which, while still largely focused on the middle and upper classes, led to an array of schools, lay movements, and social action initiatives that helped form strong cohorts of Catholic leaders. The strength and public activism of this leadership was sufficient that, under Castro, all foreign priests and a significant portion of Cuban priests were deported or left the island under duress. Proportionally these clergy provided exile communities with substantially more priests of their own than any other Latino group. Since the first exiles were drawn heavily from Cuba's middle and upper classes, lay Catholic leaders who had received substantial faith formation in Cuba were also well prepared to play a key role in organizing educational and pastoral initiatives once they arrived in the United States.[63]

Cuban Catholics in Miami wasted little time creating a formal presence. Catholic schools opened to accommodate the demand among Cubans, including the continuation in exile of several academies that the Castro government had closed in Cuba, such as the highly regarded Belén and La Salle. These schools offered an English-language Catholic education within a Cuban cultural environment that promoted the Spanish language, Cuban identity, and an exile consciousness. By 1962 sixteen parishes in the Miami area had Spanish-speaking priests on staff. A year later a predominantly Cuban congregation, San Juan Bosco, was established in Miami's Little Havana district. Substantial numbers of Cuban Catholics helped found or participated in other parishes. Shortly after the 1965 closing of the Second Vatican Council and the enactment of its decrees that led to the celebration of the Eucharist in vernacular languages rather than Latin, Miami-area parishes had a combined total of thirty weekly Masses in Spanish. Nearly one hundred Cuban priests were serving in the Miami archdiocese by 1975.[64]

Oxcart Catholicism; Vidal, "Citizens Yet Strangers," chap. 6 "Implementing the Vision"; Anita de Luna, "*Evangelizadoras del barrio*: The Rise of the Missionary Catechists of Divine Providence," *U.S. Catholic Historian* 21, no. 1 (Winter 2003): 53–71.
    63. Poyo, *Cuban Catholics in the United States*, 11–32.
    64. Ibid., 93–96, 102–103.

A Cuban rafter prays for safe arrival off the coast of Florida, 1994 (Courtesy of *The Miami Herald*/Charles Trainor).

Though Cubans found U.S. Catholicism more parish-based than had been the case in their homeland, where lay apostolic movements played a central role in their practice of the faith, Cuban lay initiatives helped nurture their Catholicism in exile. The "transplanting" of the Agrupación Católica Universitaria (ACU) exemplifies the dynamism of lay organizations. Spanish Jesuit Felipe Rey de Castro founded the ACU in 1931 to form select university students and professional men as Catholic leaders through the spiritual exercises of St. Ignatius of Loyola. On the eve of the Cuban Revolution, the sodality had nearly 600 members or *agrupados*, as they refer to themselves. They had fostered from among their numbers the vocations of over two dozen Jesuits and four diocesan priests, including Bishop Eduardo Boza Masvidal, who became the most influential Cuban bishop in exile. The ACU also engaged extensively in charitable works and in social reform efforts like its influential 1958 report on rural workers, *¿Por qué reforma agraria?* (*Why Agrarian Reform?*). Father Rey de Castro's successor as ACU spiritual director, his fellow Jesuit Amando Llorente, gathered ACU members for a retreat within a month of his exile to Miami. Shortly thereafter exiled ACU members began to publish the organization's newspaper, *Esto Vir*, and by 1963 they had convened an international ACU convention in Atlanta. These efforts enabled Cubans who had not settled in Miami to remain involved, as did Father Llorente's pastoral visits to dispersed ACU members and the distribution of his taped weekly homilies. Adapting to their new circumstances, by 1966 the ACU had accepted non-Cubans as members, a decision that enabled the group to grow in numbers and remain viable into the twenty-first century.[65]

Cuba's Nuestra Señora de la Caridad del Cobre was the most important symbol of Cuban exile Catholicism. Devotees had venerated her since the seventeenth century and she became the official patroness of Cuba in 1916. Though the original image of the patroness resides in the church of Cobre in eastern Cuba, a replica from a parish church in Guanabo Beach just east of Havana arrived in Miami for the Virgin's feast day celebration on September 8, 1961. Subsequently Cuban exiles continued to fervently commemorate the annual feast of their patroness. Their 1966 celebration inspired Miami bishop (later archbishop) Coleman Carroll to call for the construction of a sanctuary dedicated to her. At Bishop Carroll's invitation the leader for this initiative was Msgr. Agustín Román, a highly-regarded priest who later became the first Cuban named a bishop in the United States. Over the next seven years exiles helped fund the construction of the sanctuary that Carroll consecrated upon its completion in 1973. The shrine quickly became a place of pilgrimage for Cubans who linked la Caridad to their sense of Cuban nationality.[66]

Cuban Catholics expressed deep gratitude for Carroll's endorsement of la Caridad shrine and for the Miami diocese's outreach efforts to exiles through its Centro Hispano Católico. Monsignor Bryan Walsh was a tireless advocate for Cubans during their resettlement and led the famous "Operation Peter Pan" that found accommodations for young Cubans whose parents sent them ahead out of fear they would be conscripted into Communist-led schools or military service. But there were also tensions between Cubans and U.S. church leaders. ACU members accused Archbishop Carroll and his assistants of being heavy handed in their imposition of an assimilationist agenda on Cubans, contending that the U.S. clergy "feared the cultural expression of Catholicism that Cubans brought with them would disrupt the ecclesial unity of the diocese of Miami." Agrupados bemoaned what they perceived as "a thorough attempt to force Cubans to adhere to American patterns and to swiftly transform themselves into American Catholics." Whether intended or not, many Cubans perceived that Miami church officials sought to purge their intense exile consciousness and anti-Communism, as when Archbishop Carroll prohibited popular Cuban priest Father Ramón

---

65. José M. Hernández, "The ACU: Transplanting a Cuban Lay Organization to the United States," *U.S. Catholic Historian* 21, no. 1 (Winter 2003): 99–114.

66. Thomas A. Tweed, *Our Lady of the Exile: Diasporic Religion at a Cuban Catholic Shrine in Miami* (New York: Oxford, 1997), chap. 1, "The Virgin's Exile: The Cuban Patroness and the Diaspora in Miami."

O'Farrill from delivering an invocation at the 1972 Republican National Convention. A report in the Spanish-language Miami newspaper *Alerta* outlined the situation of Cuban priests like O'Farrill, concluding that "the Cuban Catholic priests of Miami are the object of a severe and unprecedented discrimination on the part of this city's archbishop." Not surprisingly, Archbishop Carroll disagreed with such charges, citing his considerable effort to welcome Cuban exiles in the archdiocese and make them part of its structures and life of faith. He contended that Cuban initiatives conducted without diocesan approval and oversight weakened episcopal authority and ecclesial unity.[67]

The Cuban case illustrates two parallel forces in motion within U.S. Catholicism since World War II. Latino Catholics, previously a largely Mexican and Puerto Rican population concentrated in New York, the Southwest, and various Midwestern cities and towns, now encompass contingents from every nation of Latin America and the Caribbean and extend from Seattle to Boston, from Miami to Alaska. The growth of their population—more than 35 percent of Catholics according to estimates from the United States Conference of Catholic Bishops (USCCB)[68]—occurred contiguously with European-descent Catholics' rise to respectability as full-fledged Americans. Many Euro-American Catholics have only vague memories of their immigrant heritage. Today there are more Catholic millionaires and more Catholics in Congress than any other denomination. Six of nine justices on the Supreme Court are Catholic. As Allan Figueroa Deck has noted, the Hispanic "second wave" of Catholic immigration to the United States has occurred just as "U.S. Catholics have become comfortable with their hard-earned [American] identity" and "achieved acceptance in a predominantly Protestant and rather anti-Catholic country."[69] The relations between early Cuban exiles and officials of the Miami (arch)diocese—a mix of compassionate outreach, misunderstanding, frustration, and collaboration—illustrates the varied exchanges occurring between Latinos and their coreligionists in parishes and dioceses throughout the country.

Catholicism in America

The Cuban exile experience is but one example of the myriad ways that, for good and for ill, Catholics in the American hemisphere mutually influ-

---

67. Hernández, "The ACU," 104; *Alerta* (Miami), 1 September 1972; Poyo, *Cuban Catholics in the United States*, 190–9.
68. "Demographics," http://www.usccb.org/issues-and-action/cultural-diversity/hispanic-latino/demographics/.
69. Allan Figueroa Deck, *The Second Wave: Hispanic Ministry and the Evangelization of Cultures* (Mahwah, NJ: Paulist, 1989), 1.

ence their fellow Catholics in other locales. Recognizing this reality, contemporary church officials have promoted vital links they deem conducive to stronger Catholic faith and evangelization in the hemisphere. The Latin American episcopal conferences at Medellín, Puebla, Santo Domingo, and Aparecida, as well as the 1997 Synod on America, have increasingly taken a more hemispheric focus. In a homily at Yankee Stadium on his first visit to the United States, Pope John Paul II boldly likened the split between the richer and more powerful nations and the more economically impoverished nations of the world to the rich man and Lazarus of Luke 16. He avowed that one of the great challenges in the American hemisphere and in our world today is to see that the destinies of the richer northern and poorer southern halves of the planet are intimately conjoined. Significantly, in subsequent teachings John Paul did not speak of "America" in the plural, but in the singular. In his apostolic exhortation *Ecclesia in America*, the title of which itself denotes the interconnectedness of the hemisphere, he noted explicitly that his "decision to speak of *America* in the singular was an attempt to express not only the unity which in some way already exists, but also to point to that closer bond that the peoples of the continent seek and that the church wishes to foster as part of her own mission."[70]

Interpreters of the past do well to adopt the vision of John Paul and the bishops of the hemisphere, reimagining national histories within the context of an international American Catholicism. In this approach the term "American" itself, usually employed in the United States to designate the national ethos, connotes historical links and the need for solidarity across international borders. Without discounting the interpretive contribution of the Americanization paradigm, particularly for understanding the experience of European-descent Catholics, a hemispheric American perspective enhances the effort to construct a narrative of the U.S. Catholic past that encompasses the struggles and contributions of Father Díaz de León, his Nacogdoches parishioners, and Bishop Odin, as well as their east coast contemporaries and numerous other Catholics.

One implication of this broader perspective is the need to articulate the multiple origins of Catholicism in what is now the United States. The first French Catholic settlement within the current U.S. borders was on Ste. Croix (De Monts) Island in Maine and, like early Hispanic settlements, also preceded the first British colony. Escaped slaves from the Carolinas and

---

70. John Paul II, "Do Not Leave to the Poor the Crumbs of Your Feast: Homily of Pope John Paul II at Yankee Stadium (October 2, 1979)," *The Pope Speaks* 24 (1979): 312–317; John Paul II, *Ecclesia in America*, no. 5 (emphasis original), English translation in *Origins* 28 (February 4, 1999): 565–592.

Georgia, whom Spanish officials in Florida welcomed as free persons on condition that they converted to Catholicism, were the first persons of African descent to establish a settlement in territories now part of the United States. They founded Gracia Real de Santa Teresa de Mose near St. Augustine in 1738. Afro-Latino Catholic influence was also evident in places like Los Angeles, where more than half of the *primer pobladores* (first settlers) in 1781 were at least partially African. Native peoples became Catholic in response to colonial missionary efforts, most notably Saint Kateri Tekakwitha (1656–1680), a child of Algonquin and Mohawk parents born in what is now Auriesville, New York. Tekakwitha was baptized when she was twenty and, though weakened with various physical complications from a bout with smallpox, inspired many through her life of prayer, fasting, and service.[71] Historical studies of the United States understandably focus on the British and then U.S. ascent over French, native, and Spanish rivals in the formation of a new nation. But the story of U.S. Catholicism must treat the various peoples who first lived the Catholic faith and established Catholic institutional presence in places now part of the United States, and then examine the contact and conflict between these groups as the European powers, the natives, and the nascent U.S. nation vied for territorial control.

The subsequent growth and development of Catholicism in the United States during the great century of European immigration (1820–1920) cannot be fully explicated without due attention to non-immigrant Catholics. Like Mexicans in the Southwest, Native Americans struggled to endure, some in communities that Spanish and French missioners had previously sought to evangelize, others within the new system of U.S. laws, Indian reservations, and government-sanctioned Christianization efforts. The travails of African Americans were no less traumatic. Catholic laity, priests, and religious orders had slaves, a number of whom were baptized Catholic and instructed in the faith. When President Abraham Lincoln signed into law a military draft to support the northern Civil War cause in 1863, New Yorkers, many of them immigrant Irish Catholics who vied with African Americans for unskilled labor jobs, assaulted black residents in one of the bloodiest riots in the history of the city. Servant of God Augustus Tolton, a former slave who became the first African American priest, had to study in Rome because segregated U.S. seminaries would not admit him. Yet both African American and Native American Catholics exhibited uncommon

---

71. Allan Greer, *Mohawk Saint: Catherine Tekakwitha and the Jesuits* (New York: Oxford University Press, 2005). On the history of African American Catholics, see Cyprian Davis, *The History of Black Catholics in the United States* (New York: Crossroad, 1990); Davis and Jamie Phelps, eds., *"Stamped with the Image of God": African Americans as God's Image in Black* (Maryknoll, NY: Orbis, 2003).

steadfastness in their faith against all odds. Venerable Pierre Toussaint (1766–1853), born a slave in the French colony of Santo Domingo (Haiti), resettled with his master in New York, where he became a successful hairdresser among the city's aristocratic women, obtained his freedom, and was renowned for his devotion to daily Mass and remarkable life of charity. Venerable Henriette Delille (c. 1813–1862) accomplished the amazing feat of founding an African American order of women religious in antebellum New Orleans and is acclaimed as a "servant of slaves" and "witness to the poor." Nicholas Black Elk (c. 1863–1950) was celebrated both as a medicine man among the Lakota Sioux of the Northern Plains and as a lay Catholic catechist.[72] The history of Catholics such as these cannot be subsumed into a saga of immigrants. Conquered, enslaved, and free peoples of color—along with the more numerous and influential immigrants—necessitate examining more deeply how the distinct experiences of entry into the United States shaped participation in church and society and thus to varying degrees the formation of U.S. Catholicism.

The Americanization of émigrés' descendants in the course of the twentieth century occurred simultaneously with another crucial historical trend: the significant new immigration of Catholics to the United States. Demographic growth in U.S. Catholicism over the past half century is heavily rooted in immigration from Asia, the Pacific Islands, Africa, and particularly Latin America. USCCB officials estimate that nearly half the Catholics in the United States are of non-European ancestry. In the Archdiocese of Los Angeles alone, the Eucharist is regularly celebrated in forty-two languages. The Catholic Church in the United States is the most ethnically and racially diverse national ecclesial body in the world. Historical analyses must explore the implications of this striking phenomenon.

Today the international and especially the hemispheric connections of Catholicism in the United States are more extensive than ever. Interactions between émigrés and their fellow U.S. residents is the most common means through which church and society in the United States and various other nations shape one another. Immigrants exert influence on their ancestral homelands, particularly Hispanics who live in greater proximity to their native countries. Certainly their major economic influence is the remittances

---

72. Arthur Jones, *Pierre Toussaint* (New York: Doubleday, 2003); Cyprian Davis, *Henriette Delille: Servant of Slaves, Witness to the Poor* (New Orleans: Archives of the Archdiocese of New Orleans, 2004); Damian Costello, *Black Elk: Colonialism and Lakota Catholicism* (Maryknoll, NY: Orbis, 2005). On the history of Native American Catholics, see Christopher Vecsey, *American Indian Catholics* (3 vols., Notre Dame, IN: University of Notre Dame Press, 1996–1999); Marie Therese Archambault, Mark G. Thiel, and Vecsey, eds., *The Crossing of Two Roads: Being Catholic and Native in the United States* (Maryknoll, NY: Orbis, 2003).

immigrant workers send home, which in some years has averaged as much as $2 billion per month to Mexico alone. Remittances support not only family members but also community projects such as the sponsorship of feast day celebrations and the construction and upkeep of churches, religious shrines, and schools. The conspicuous flow of fiscal resources reflects less often noted cultural and religious exchanges, like the experiences immigrants have in parishes, prayer groups, and church renewal movements in the United States that they carry with them when they return home to visit or resettle. Mexican parishioners from Nuestra Señora del Rosario parish in Coeneo, Michoacán illustrate the capacity of immigrants to transform religious practice in their native land. The numerous baptisms and marriages émigrés return home to celebrate, especially during the weeks surrounding the Christmas holiday, has notably shifted the ritual calendar of parish life from a cycle of traditional devotions and feast days to a cycle of sacraments and family gatherings that revolve around the schedules of returning immigrants. Hispanic Catholics in the United States have also initiated outreach efforts to Latin America, such as the Amor en Acción lay missionary community in the Archdiocese of Miami, which was formally established in 1976 under the inspiration of Alicia Marill and Adriano Garcia to foster ministerial collaboration in the Dominican Republic and Haiti.[73]

A hemispheric perspective on Catholicism requires attention to migratory flows in all directions, which in the last half century have encompassed a relatively small but significant group of U.S. Catholics who have visited Latin America or served in church ministries there. Often their experiences transform their understanding of Catholicism, as well as their attitudes toward the foreign policy of the United States. Catholics from the United States have received ministerial training at centers such as the Institute of Intercultural Communication, which Father Ivan Illich founded in Puerto Rico in 1957. During its fifteen years in operation the Institute staff trained numerous priests, seminarians, and other pastoral workers for the Archdiocese of New York. Women religious, priests, and lay missioners have also established significant and vital links between the United States and the rest of the Americas through missionary institutes, most notably Maryknoll. Other Latin American links include U.S. Catholics' awareness and involvement with liberation theology, the civil wars in Central America during the 1970s and 1980s, well-known incidents like the 1980 murders of Blessed Oscar Romero and four U.S. women serving in El Salvador, and the numer-

---

73. Luis E. Murillo, "Tamales on the Fourth of July: The Transnational Parish of Coeneo, Michoacán," *Religion and American Culture: A Journal of Interpretation* 19 (Summer 2009): 137–168; Amor en Acción, at http://www.amorenaccion.com. See also Badillo, *Latinos and the New Immigrant Church*, 125–141.

ous delegations of students, scholars, and church leaders who have visited and established contacts in Central and South America and the Caribbean.

The ambitious project of a hemispheric approach holds great promise for studies of U.S. Catholic history, first and foremost through placing those investigations within the broad context of one of the most momentous events of Christianity's second millennium: the encounter and clash of the Old and the New Worlds. Conquest, settlement, enslavement, immigration, and exile were the human—and too often inhuman—experiences that constituted this massive intermingling of diverse peoples. Wars to establish nation states independent of European rule and struggles to this day for life, dignity, and self-determination are part of the painful legacy of violence and conquest that gave birth to the hemisphere Europeans named America. Despite rampant injustices, Native Americans, Africans, Europeans, their mixed-race offspring, and to a lesser extent Asians have all contributed to the formation of new societies, cultures, and traditions. Interpreters of U.S. Catholic history need to address all these peoples and experiences within the current borders of the United States, but against the backdrop and comparative framework of the American continent. This entails the recognition that the U.S. Catholic Church was never exclusively an immigrant church, nor is it solely an "Americanized" church today. Rather, it is a church built on the founding faith of migratory, conquered, and enslaved peoples that currently is largely run by middle-class, European-descent Catholics with growing numbers of Latino, Asian, and African immigrants, along with sizeable contingents of U.S.-born Latinos, African Americans, and some Native Americans. Renderings of the U.S. Catholic story, as well as of the present and future of the Church's life and mission in the United States, are best addressed with a clearer view of the part Latinos and all our fellow Catholics have played in our collective past.

"Organized Catholic Womanhood": Suffrage, Citizenship, and the National Council of Catholic Women

Jeanne Petit*

As women in a male-led church and as Catholics in a Protestant-dominated country, Catholic laywomen in the United States had limited opportunities to create their own political identities. Yet the conditions of post-World War I America offered laywomen an opportunity to claim a role in public debates. Catholic clergy and laywomen formed the National Council of Catholic Women (NCCW) on the eve of the passage of the Nineteenth Amendment. Its leaders and members took advantage of social changes of the 1920s to claim their right as citizens and carve out a political niche for themselves as organized Catholic women. The NCCW defined their work in the post-suffrage era by partnering with women's groups who sought protective labor legislation while at the same time critiquing demands for equal rights, greater access to birth control, and new standards of dress and behavior for women. Overall, while the women of the NCCW faced many roadblocks from clergy and never achieved the degree of success for which they longed, they offered new ways for Catholic laywomen to understand their relationship to their church and nation.

In 1921, the laywomen of the newly-formed National Council of Catholic Women (NCCW) found themselves on the defensive. The *National Catholic Welfare Council Bulletin* had reprinted a speech by Sebastian G. Messmer, Archbishop of Milwaukee, in which he minimized

---

*This essay originally appeared in *U.S. Catholic Historian* 26, no. 1 (Winter 2008): 83–100. A version of this research was presented at the 2007 National Endowment for the Humanities Summer Seminar on "Religious Diversity and the Common Good," directed by Dr. Alan Wolfe of the Boisi Center at Boston College. Members of the seminar provided many helpful suggestions for improving this essay. The author would also like to thank Anita Specht, Janis Gibbs, Natalie Dykstra and John Hanson for their careful read and useful comments on this essay.

their work by declaring, "Man is made by God to fight the public battles, not the woman."[1] The NCCW, however, did not take this sitting down. An article in the *Bulletin's* next issue, titled "Organized Catholic Womanhood," did not mention Messmer's name but did challenge the central premise of his speech by claiming that it was essential that Catholic women take the lead in public debates. Pointing to the changes caused by the Nineteenth Amendment, the anonymous author insisted that Catholic women needed to organize on a national level in order to counteract Protestant and secular women in national debates dealing with "not only the industrial but the moral well-being of woman." Those who belittled or deemphasized the need for such an organization would achieve that "which the bigot and the anti-clerical so much desire—Catholic women as a united body are pushed into the background submerged in some secular so-called patriotic movement—divided among themselves." "But," the article continued, "the vision and wisdom of Catholic women will save us from that day . . . for we live our faith when we realize that we are all parts of the Body of Christ—The Church."[2] Catholic women, according to the author, had to exercise their rights as citizens in order to defend and live their faith.

A year later, the women of the NCCW again found themselves on the defensive, this time when their president, Gertrude Gavin, attended the 1922 Pan-American Women's Conference in Baltimore sponsored by the League of Women Voters. Gavin left outraged after one of the speakers, Carrie Chapman Catt, had implied that Catholics were ardent opponents of suffrage for women, and another, Lady Astor, referred to the United States as a Protestant country. The NCCW's executive committee quickly adopted resolutions stating that they deplored "the injection into the deliberations of the League of Women Voters statements concerning the attitude of Catholics toward suffrage which tend to sow dissention and misunderstanding among the members of the League, many of whom are Catholic women." The resolution also attacked statements "concerning America being a Protestant country, statements out of harmony with historic truth, including the Constitution of the United States, which guarantees freedom of religious belief to all."[3] So again, the women of the NCCW took action when their citizenship status was denigrated, this time by

---

1. "Archbishop (S.G.) Messmer's Forceful Appeal for the Men's Council: Catholic Clergy Urged to Support Movement in Milwaukee Archdiocese," *The National Catholic Welfare Council Bulletin* (June 1921): 23–24. In this speech, Messmer was promoting the newly-formed National Council of Catholic Men.
2. "Organized Catholic Womanhood," *NCWC Bulletin* (July 1921): 16.
3. "National Council of Catholic Women Newssheet to Organizations," May 22, 1922, Box 62, Collection 10, National Council of Catholic Women, American Catholic History Research Center and University Archives, Catholic University of America (hereafter ACUA).

Father John Burke, Executive Director of the National Catholic Welfare Council, with members of the NCCW (Courtesy of the American Catholic History Research Center and University Archives, Catholic University of America).

defending their right as Catholics to be respected as equals within national women's organizations.

Since the early nineteenth century, Catholic women had built orphanages, hospitals and schools and performed other forms of what became known as social work, but sisters in religious orders, not laywomen, did most of this work.[4] Moreover, most Americans, both Catholic and non-Catholic, did not see this work as political. The women of the NCCW saw themselves as doing something different. In creating a national, political organization for laywomen, they sought to define a civic identity for middle-class Catholic women, one where they would be full participants in the nation's political process. As the stories above illustrate, however, the Catholic laywomen of the NCCW fought a two-front battle to be taken seriously as political actors. In an era when Catholic immigrants were viewed as objects of protection and uplift by

---

4. There is also an extensive literature on the institutions built by women religious. See, for instance, Maureen Fitzgerald, *Habits of Compassion: Irish Catholic Nuns and the Origins of New York's Welfare System, 1830–1920* (Urbana, IL: University of Illinois Press, 2006); Suellen Hoy, *Good Hearts: Catholic Sisters in Chicago's Past* (Urbana, IL: University of Illinois Press, 2006); Carol E. Coburn and Martha Smith, *Spirited Lives: How Nuns Shaped Catholic Culture and American Life, 1836–1920* (Chapel Hill, NC: The University of North Carolina Press, 1999).

middle-class Protestant and secular activist women reformers, the middle-class, native-born women of the NCCW sought to prove that Catholic women should have some say in defining the "woman" agenda. At the same time, they had to justify their existence to an often hostile male clergy.

The marginalized position of Catholic laywomen in their church and as women activists has also made it difficult for them to be taken seriously by historians.[5] Historians of United States Catholicism have analyzed how the hierarchy in the Church proscribed for Catholic laywomen a decidedly submissive and domestic role; their first priorities, after adherence to their faith, were always to be their husbands, children, and homes.[6] As historian Leslie Tentler pointed out, most priests and bishops had opposed suffrage, and almost all "associated the truly feminine with modesty, domesticity, and a want of intellectualism."[7] Historians of women who study the suffrage era give almost no attention to the political identities of Catholic women, either pre- or post-suffrage, and instead emphasize the Catholic Church as a major force in opposition to feminism and women's rights.[8]

---

5. For work that focuses specifically on the activism of Catholic laywomen, see Kathleen Sprows Cummings, "'Not the New Woman?': Irish American Women and the Creation of a Visible Past, 1890–1900," *U.S. Catholic Historian* 19, no. 1 (Winter 2001): 37–52; Dierdre M. Moloney, "Divisions of Labor: The Roles of American Catholic Lay Women, Lay Men and Women Religious in Charity Provision," *U.S. Catholic Historian* 20, no. 1 (Winter 2002): 41–55.

6. In general, the study of the relationship between Catholic women and the creation of gender ideologies has fallen through the cracks of both American gender history and religious history. For works by historians of Catholicism that specifically deal with gender ideologies of both Catholic manhood, and particularly Catholic womanhood, see Paula Kane, "General Introduction" in Paula Kane, James Kenneally and Karen Kennelly, eds., *Gender Identities in American Catholicism*, American Catholic Identities: A Documentary History, Christopher Kauffman, general editor (Maryknoll, NY: Orbis Books, 2001), xix–xxxi; Penny Edgell Becker, "'Rational Amusement and Sound Instruction': Constructing the True Catholic Woman in the Ave Maria," in *Religion and American Culture* 8 (Winter 1998): 55–90; Colleen McDannell, "'True Men as We Need Them': Catholicism and the Irish-American Male," *American Studies* 27, no. 2 (1986): 19–36; Paula M. Kane, *Separatism and Subculture: Boston Catholicism, 1900–1920* (Chapel Hill, NC: University of North Carolina Press, 1994), 48–107; 200–252; and Robert Orsi, *Thank You Saint Jude: Women's Devotion to the Patron Saint of Hopeless Causes* (New Haven: Yale University Press, 1996); David Hackett, "Gender and Religion in American Culture, 1870–1930," *Religion and American Culture* 2 (Summer 1995): 127–145. Some significant works that focus on the actions and beliefs of Catholic women in United States history include James J. Kenneally, *The History of American Catholic Women* (New York: Crossroad, 1990); Karen Kennelly, CSJ, ed., *American Catholic Women: A Historical Exploration* (New York: Macmillan Publishing Company, 1989).

7. Leslie Woodcock Tentler, *Catholics and Contraception: An American History* (Ithaca: Cornell University Press, 2004), 56–57.

8. See, for instance, Susan Marilley, *Women's Suffrage and the Origins of Liberal Feminism in the United States, 1820–1920* (Cambridge, MA: Harvard University Press, 1996), 178–180; Jane Jerome Camhi, *Women Against Women: American Anti-Suffragism, 1880–1920* (Brooklyn: Carlson Publishing, Inc., 1994), 111–115; Eleanor Flexner and Ellen Fitzpatrick, *Century of Struggle: The Woman's Rights Movement in the United States* (Cambridge, MA: Belknap Press of Harvard University Press, 1996), 263–264.

It is true that as women within a hierarchical and patriarchal church and as Catholics in a largely Protestant country, U.S. Catholic laywomen had a limited scope to create their own political identities. Yet the conditions of the post-World War I United States offered Catholic women a unique opportunity to do just that. The leaders and members of the National Council of Catholic Women took advantage of a climate of anti-Catholicism and the splits within the former suffrage movement to claim their right as citizens, partake in public debates, and carve out a political niche for themselves as organized Catholic women. To make this argument, I begin by looking at how Catholic clergy and laywomen created the NCCW on the eve of the passage of the Nineteenth Amendment. Next, I examine how the women of the NCCW defined their work in the post-suffrage era by partnering with women's groups who sought protective labor legislation and critiquing women's groups who demanded equal rights. Finally, I examine the limits the Catholic hierarchy placed on the women of the NCCW, especially as women in general began to lose political influence in the nation. Overall, while the women of the NCCW faced many roadblocks from the clergy and never achieved the success they longed for, they offered new ways for Catholic laywomen to understand their relationship to their church and their nation.

The Formation of the National Council of Catholic Women

The American Catholic hierarchy first felt the need for a national and politically-active Catholic women's organization after the United States entered World War I. These were years of 100% Americanization campaigns, Red Scares and the rise of the Ku Klux Klan, and U.S. Catholics, whose membership was drawn largely from immigrants and their descendants, found their legitimacy as Americans under attack.[9] In 1918, bishops from around the country formed the National Catholic War Council to coordinate the American Catholic war effort both of clergy and laity, at home and abroad.[10] Soon after the War Council formed in 1918, its leaders started to

---

9. John Higham, *Strangers in the Land: Patterns of American Nativism, 1860–1925* (New Brunswick, NJ: Rutgers University Press, 1955, 1994), 291–299; John McGreevy, *Catholicism and American Freedom: A History* (New York: W.W. Norton and Company, 2003), 147; Lynn Dumenil, "The Tribal Twenties: 'Assimilated' Catholics' Response to Anti-Catholicism in the 1920's," *Journal of American Ethnic History* 11 (Fall 1991): 42.

10. For work on the creation and work of the National Catholic War Council, see Elizabeth McKeown, *War and Welfare: American Catholics and World War I* (New York: Garland, 1988) and Ronald Schaffer, *America in the Great War: The Rise of the War Welfare State* (New York: Oxford University Press, 1991), 64–74. For information on the creation and work of the National Catholic Welfare Council, see Jay Dolan, *The American Catholic Experience: A History From Colonial Times to the Present* (Garden City, NY: Image Books, 1987), 342–44; See also Douglas J. Slawson, *The Foundation and First Decades of the National Catholic Welfare Council* (Washington, DC: The Catholic University of America Press, 1992), 26–45; Eliza-

get letters from Catholic women across the country stating their desire for a national organization that could coordinate the work of local or diocesan Catholic women's groups.[11] These women had noticed how Protestant and secular women's groups had taken the lead on war bond drives, Red Cross campaigns and other work for the war effort, while Catholic women had little to no representation. And as the war ended in late 1918, supporters of a national Catholic women's group declared that the need for a national organization was even more acute.

The bishops and priests of the War Council were sufficiently alarmed by the lack of representation of Catholic women in national war work and in late 1918, they formed a Committee on Women's Activities.[12] In 1919, aided by a grant from the federal government for reconstruction work, the Women's Committee began a project of establishing a series of Community Houses, staffed mostly by native-born, middle-class Catholic laywomen, to provide safe housing and recreation to working women and "Americanize" southeastern European immigrants by teaching classes in English and civics. Overall, nineteen of these houses were established in mostly mid-sized cities in the Northeast and Midwest.[13]

Right from the beginning, the women who participated in the Women's Committee of the War Council had to face dismissive attitudes from both clergy and non-Catholic women reformers. In March of 1919, Margaret Long, the Director of Field Work for the National Catholic Community Houses, vented her frustration in a letter to her superior. She complained that bishops and priests in the dioceses where these houses were created offered little support, and it was "discouraging to go about the country talking to and stimulating our women" and then finding the clergy "most apa-

---

beth McKeown, "The National Bishop's Conference: An Analysis of Its Origins," *Catholic Historical Review* 66 (October 1980): 565–583.

11. See letters in file 6–20, Box 37, Box 37, Collection 10, National Catholic War Council Women's Committee, ACUA. Other national Catholic women's organizations existed at this time, but they were organized around a special interest, such as the Federation of Catholic Alumnae, or they were linked to fraternal societies, such as the Ladies of the Ancient Order of Hibernians.

12. The Committee on Women's Activities was under the auspices of the Committee of Special Activities of the War Council and under the direction of Father John Cooper who was trained as an anthropologist and had little administrative experience. Cooper was marginalized within the political structure of the War Council. The chairs of the other departments of that committee, including the Committee on Men's Activities, had representation on the Executive Committee, but Cooper was not on it. For an example of the frustration Cooper felt, see Fr. John Cooper to Fr. William Kerby, August 7, 1919, File 11–18, Box 36/39, Collection 10, NCWC Women's Committee, ACUA.

13. See "Report on Community Houses," File 19-2, Box 38, Collection 10, NCWC Women's Committee, ACUA.

thetic." "Without the hearty and spoken approval by our hierarchy," she wrote, "we are up against a stone wall." At the same time, Long declared that she found renewed energy for her work "when I hear Miss VanKleeck of the United States Industrial League speaking before three hundred women and quoting the Y.W. [the Young Women's Christian Association], the Jewish women and all other organizations, without thought or suggestion of our work."[14] Long especially chafed at the notion that only middle-class *Protestant* women were considered leaders in Americanization work, and vowed to make sure that Catholic women would no longer be ignored.[15]

In the fall of 1919, the bishops who led the War Council reorganized and created the National Catholic Welfare Council (NCWC) and introduced an ambitious post-war plan for Catholic-led social reform.[16] Working for women's rights was never part of the program for the NCWC, yet when it began to appear that women's suffrage would become a reality, many in the hierarchy felt they needed to act. A top priority of the priests and bishops who ran the NCWC was to create a national organization of Catholic laywomen, and the leadership framed this in terms of Catholics being competitive in national debates about women's issues. Father John Burke, the Executive Director of the NCWC, made this clear in a recruitment letter for the new women's organization: "the Protestant women of the country have the Young Women's Christian Association. The Jewish Women . . . have their Council of Jewish women. As yet, our Catholic women, with their great potential for good, have no similar cooperative board."[17] In his speech before the organizing convention in March 1920, Bishop Joseph Schrembs, the head

---

14. Margaret Long to Rev. John M. Cooper, March 13, 1919, File 19-4, Box 38, Collection 10, NCWC Women's Committee, National Catholic War Council Collection, ACUA.

15. The women who worked in the National Catholic Community Houses saw the YWCA as their particular competition, and the reports of the Field Secretaries were riddled with references to the "Y.W." and insinuations about how they would proselytize young Catholic women. For instance, in a report about South Amboy, New Jersey, Margaret Long warned that "the YW has made a special point of inviting both Catholic and Jewish girls to all their entertainments" and said that factory girls would "feel so much more at home if they could attend affairs given under Catholic auspices." Grace Ground, a field secretary in East St. Louis, proclaimed that the YWCA "fear us and are doing all they can do to knock our success which undoubtedly is generally known throughout the city." Report on Parlin, NJ by Margaret Long, November 19, 1918, File 41, Box 14, Collection 10 NCWC Executive Secretary Records, ACUA; Report of Grace M. Ground, Field Secretary, East St. Louis, IL, March 3–10, 1919, File 37, Box 14, Collection 10, NCWC Executive Secretary Records, ACUA.

16. Dolan, *The American Catholic Experience*, 344; See also Joseph M. McShane, SJ, *"Sufficiently Radical": Catholicism, Progressivism and the Bishop's Program of 1919* (Washington, DC: The Catholic University of America Press, 1986) and Elizabeth McKeown, "The National Bishop's Conference: An Analysis of Its Origins," *The Catholic Historical Review* 66 (October 1980): 565–583.

17. Form letter by John Burke, February 25, 1920, Box 98, NCWC/USCC General Secretary/Executive Department Files, ACUA.

Directors of the NCCW with Bishop Joseph Schrembs of Cleveland, Ohio, at their annual meeting in Washington, D.C., 1927. Left to right: Mrs. George Satory, Mrs. Anna Gamble; Mrs. Arthur Moller, Mrs. Wallace Benham, Mrs. John McMahon, and Mrs. Henry Keyser (Courtesy of editor, *U.S. Catholic Historian*).

of the NCWC Department of Lay Activities, defined the main purpose of the NCCW as "to ensure proper Catholic representation on, and the proper recognition of Catholic principles in, national committees and national movements affecting the religious, moral and material well-being of the country."[18]

Yet the women who attended the first convention received mixed messages. For instance, while Schrembs declared that he wanted the NCCW to be a "powerhouse of action," and claimed that the delegates would "be granted every liberty to express [themselves] honestly," he also cautioned the women that "we trust you to always prove yourselves obedient children to the Church, always receptive to its divine guidance."[19] In other words, Schrembs expected the women of the NCCW to understand that their freedom to operate as political actors had to be tempered by their submission to

---

18. Rt. Rev. Joseph Schrembs, "The National Catholic Welfare Council," "Proceedings of the 1920 Meeting of the National Council of Catholic Women," 3–19, Box 14, Collection 10, National Council of Catholic Women, ACUA.

19. Schrembs, "The National Catholic Welfare Council," 19.

Agnes Regan, first Executive Director of the National Council of Catholic Women (Courtesy of the American Catholic History Research Center and University Archives, Catholic University of America).

the Catholic hierarchy. Staking out a position that strayed from Church teachings, he warned, would not be possible.

As the convention began, it was not even clear that women would be put in charge of the new organization.[20] Burke, however, realized that to have any legitimacy in the political arena, the Women's Council would have to be run by women, and at the organizing convention, two unconventional Catholic women were appointed to leadership posts. Agnes Regan, a woman who never married and built an impressive career as a teacher, principal, and

---

20. When the convention began, Father John Cooper, who had run the War Council's Women's Committee, assumed that he would be in charge of the new organization. He had worked on setting up the Constitution of the NCCW and in the process had argued that the officers should be appointed rather than elected by the delegates because "I do not think our women are ready yet for direct elections." At the convention, Cooper had a run-in with the representative of Cardinal William O'Connell of Boston, and he ended up resigning from his position in the War Council and took up a post teaching anthropology at The Catholic University of America. See "Tentative Plan for Organizing of Nat. Cath. Women's Org," August 9, 1919, Folder 62, Box 9, Collection 10, National Catholic War Council, Muldoon and Burke Files, ACUA. For information on the founding of the NCCW, see Douglas J. Slawson, *The Foundation and First Decades of the National Catholic Welfare Council*, 76–80; Ruth Libbey O'Halloran, "Organized Catholic Laywomen: The National Council of Catholic Women, 1920–1995" (Ph.D. dissertation, The Catholic University of America, 1995), 17–23.

school board member in her native San Francisco, moved to Washington, D.C. at the age of fifty-one to take up the position of Executive Secretary of the NCCW.[21] Gertrude Gavin, who became the first President of the NCCW, was the daughter of James Hill, the railroad magnate. She had married into another wealthy New York family and became active in philanthropic causes, especially those dealing with the Catholic Church. Regan and Gavin ran a small executive committee based in Washington, D.C. while the bulk of the membership came from parish and diocesan women's groups who affiliated with the national body. In other words, the NCCW was set up to be a kind of umbrella organization that would coordinate the activities of local Catholic women's groups and at the same time present themselves as the representative of Catholic women in the United States. By the end of 1921, the NCCW claimed as affiliates over 800 organizations with approximately 12,000 members.[22]

After their organizing convention, Agnes Regan, Gertrude Gavin, and the other women of the NCCW set out on their challenging task—to be both outspoken women activists and good obedient Catholics. As it turns out, the political climate of the early 1920s provided them a chance to create a path between these seemingly contradictory goals.

The NCCW as Women's Activists

The passage of the Nineteenth Amendment in 1920 made this opportunity possible. Once women gained suffrage in the United States, Catholic laywomen found themselves in an unaccustomed position—they had some leverage over the hierarchy of their Church. Most leaders in the Catholic Church had worked against women's suffrage, albeit behind the scenes, both because they held traditional views of women's place in the family and because some in the movement resorted to anti-Catholic and anti-immigrant rhetoric.[23] Church leaders, however, could not ignore the fact that the suffrage movement, by uniting such diverse groups as Protestant temperance reformers,

---

21. For background on Regan, see her biographical file, Box 3, Collection 10, National Council of Catholic Women, ACUA.
22. "Catholic Womanhood in America," *NCWC Bulletin* (November 1921): 21. See also Mary J. Oates, *The Catholic Philanthropic Tradition* (Bloomington, IN: Indiana University Press, 1995), 95.
23. Some of the rhetoric of the women's suffrage movement emphasized that white Protestant women's votes would counteract the "Catholic contagion" of immigrant votes. James J. Kenneally, "Catholicism and Woman Suffrage in Massachusetts," *Catholic Historical Review* 53 (April 1967): 49. While some Catholics did support suffrage, overall the American hierarchy fought against the idea of the vote for women. See Paula M. Kane, *Separatism and Subculture: Boston Catholicism*, 241–244; John McGreevy, *Catholicism and American Freedom*, 95–96.

union members, settlement house workers, and radical feminists, gave women unprecedented political power.[24] Politicians began to propose what they believed to be "women's legislation," that is, legislation that broadened the rights of women or provided aid and protection to women and children.[25] The Church, Father Burke told the NCCW, needed Catholic women to claim their rights as citizens and assert themselves in these political debates in order for the Catholic view to be represented. If women's issues were to be addressed before Congress, Burke declared, "it does not do to send a priest over there." Instead, "it is the direct work of the woman who would stand up . . . and say that she represents the Catholic women of the country."[26]

At the same time, the aftermath of the suffrage movement provided new opportunities for Catholic women to forge alliances with other activist women. After women's suffrage became a reality, historians like Nancy Cott have shown, American feminist movements fractured between those who emphasized women's equality under the law and those who focused on expanding special protections for women.[27] This provided Catholic women with new opportunities to engage with certain feminist causes while adhering to the tenets of their faith. The women of the NCCW felt comfortable standing alongside women's groups who advocated protective legislation for women and children because they could frame these causes within Catholic teachings about the need for the community to take responsibility for the vulnerable members of society. At the same time, they could prove to male clergy that they were not radical feminists by standing with those same groups in opposition to the Equal Rights Amendment. Thus, the women of the NCCW used their political stands to prove to both women's groups and

---

24. For work that analyzes the broad coalition for women's suffrage, see Sarah Hunter Graham, *Woman Suffrage and the New Democracy* (New Haven: Yale University Press, 1996); Ellen Carol Dubois, *Harriot Stanton Balch and the Winning of Woman Suffrage* (New Haven: Yale University Press, 1997); Marilley, *Woman Suffrage and the Origins of Liberal Feminism in the United States, 1820–1920*; Beverly Beeton, *Women Vote in the West: The Woman Suffrage Movement, 1869–1896* (New York: Garland Publishing, 1986); Ellen Carol Dubois, *Feminism and Suffrage: The Emergence of an Independent Women's Movement in America, 1848–1869* (Ithaca, NY: Cornell University Press, 1978).

25. For examinations of women's political issues and activism in the 1920s, see Gwendolyn Mink, *The Wages of Motherhood: Inequality in the Welfare State, 1917–1942* (Ithaca, NY: Cornell University Press, 1995) and Robyn Muncy, *Creating a Female Dominion in American Reform, 1890–1935* (New York: Oxford University Press, 1991).

26. "Remarks of the Reverend John J. Burke, CSP to the meeting of the Board of Directors, National Council of Catholic Women, Washington DC, September 29, 1923," James H. Ryan Files, Collection 10, ACUA.

27. Nancy Cott, *The Grounding of Modern Feminism* (New Haven: Yale University Press), 1987. See also Sarah Alpern and Dale Baum, "Female Ballots: The Impact of the Nineteenth Amendment," *Journal of Interdisciplinary History* 16 (Summer 1985): 43–67; Susan D. Becker, *The Origins of the Equal Rights Amendment: American Feminism between the Wars* (Westport, CT: Greenwood, 1981).

the Catholic hierarchy that they deserved respect as equal citizens and as members of the Church.

Like other women's organizations that emphasized protection over equal rights, the women of the NCCW believed certain political issues and legislation to be the special purview of women. In the NCCW's first newsletter, an article titled "Our Real Work" proclaimed that Catholic women had a special duty to speak out on legislation "affecting the welfare of women and children."[28] In the early 1920s, the women of the NCCW did this by developing political alliances with activist women who championed causes such as protective labor legislation and the Sheppard-Towner Act, which allowed the Department of Labor's Children's Bureau to distribute mother's pensions.[29] For instance, May J. Williams, who worked in the Washington office of the NCCW, met with Florence Kelly, the head of the National Consumers League, and discussed mobilizing Catholic women, "particularly in states where the eight hour day, the minimum wage and other movements haven't been recognized."[30] Throughout the early 1920s, the newsletter of the NCCW promoted their association with secular women's groups such as the Women's Trade Union League and the National Consumers League and with political activists such as Kelly, Julia Lathrop, and Grace Abbott.[31] The women of the NCCW spoke out in support of welfare legislation, including a constitutional amendment outlawing child labor.[32]

Their fight against the Equal Rights Amendment (ERA) further allowed the women of the NCCW to work comfortably with women's activists who advocated protective legislation.[33] Feminist groups that emphasized

---

28. "National Council of Catholic Women Newssheet to Organizations," November 29, 1920, Box 62, Collection 10, ACUA.
29. For examinations of women's political issues and activism in the 1920s, see Gwendolyn Mink, *The Wages of Motherhood* and Robyn Muncy, *Creating a Female Dominion in American Reform*.
30. May J. Williams to Father Cooper, January 23, 1920, Box 36, File 4, Collection 10, Committee on Special War Activities, National Catholic War Council, ACUA.
31. See, for instance, "NCCW Newssheet to Organizations," May 1922; November/December 1922; Box 62, Collection 10, National Council of Catholic Women, ACUA. Grace Abbott also spoke at the Second convention of the NCCW in 1922. See "Proceedings: Second Annual Convention, National Council of Catholic Women, Washington D.C., November 21–25, 1922," Box 14, Collection 10, ACUA.
32. For their support of the Sheppard-Towner Act see, for example, "National Council of Catholic Women Newssheet to Organizations," August 1922, Box 62, Collection 10, ACUA. Their resolution in favor of a child labor amendment can be found in a letter from Mrs. Michael (Gertrude) Gavin to Mrs. Francis E. Slattery, October 20, 1924, File: Gavin, Mrs. Michael, President NCCW, 1921–1928, Box 44, James H. Ryan Files, Collection 10, ACUA.
33. The Church hierarchy and most Catholic women fought against the ERA. There were some exceptions however. See James J. Kenneally, "Women Divided: The Catholic Struggle for an Equal Rights Amendment," *Catholic Historical Review* 75, no. 2 (1989): 249–263.

women's equality, such as the National Women's Party, were promoting the ERA as the most efficient way to address the legal disadvantages of women.[34] The women of the NCCW made arguments against the ERA that were much like the ones secular women's organizations made—that the amendment would derail protective legislation that Progressive-Era women's organizations had worked so hard to pass. In 1922, for instance, they worked with members of the Women's Trade Union League to fight the ERA based on the effect it would have on minimum wage and eight-hour provisions for women workers.[35] In that same year, they argued that "the so-called Equal Rights Blanket will seriously jeopardize the remedial industrial legislation for women in industry now existing in many states and will postpone indefinitely passage of such legislation in states where such laws do not exist."[36]

At the same time, the women of the NCCW could also use their stance against the ERA to prove that they were upholding the Church's view on traditional gender roles. They framed their anti-ERA stand as one against the individualist culture of the United States that they insisted was eroding the integrity of the family and women's place within it. The 1922 resolution made it clear that the NCCW opposed the ERA because it would "affect seriously the whole attitude on the part of men and women to the obligations assumed as husband and wife" and that "through the amendment the unity of home and family life is seriously menaced." The same newsletter which included the resolution also reported that NCCW chairwoman Agnes Regan made these arguments at a meeting of the National Consumers League, declaring, that "the passage of such a law would be a direct blow at the home, which is the foundation on which society is built!"[37] Another NCCW statement from 1925 stated the case more fully, and put their critique of the ERA within a Catholic framework. It derided the ERA as "fundamentally unsound" because it operated under the assumption that equal rights must mean identical rights. The statement then pointed to natural law, the Catholic worldview that the divine order was set into nature, to argue that the "difference in function" between men and women, implied "essential differences in rights and duties." While conceding that there might be laws that discriminated against women, the statement concluded by saying that the purpose of laws should not be about giving women an unnatural equality

---

34. Lynn Duminel, *The Modern Temper: American Culture and Society in the 1920s* (New York: Hill and Wang, 1995), 104–105.
35. "National Council of Catholic Women Newssheet to Organizations," May 1922, Box 62, Collection 10, ACUA.
36. "National Council of Catholic Women Newssheet to Organizations," November/December 1922, Box 62, Collection 10, ACUA.
37. "National Council of Catholic Women Newssheet to Organizations," November/December 1922, Box 62, Collection 10, ACUA.

or the ability to satisfy their individual goals, but helping them to do "their full duty to themselves, their children and society."[38]

Even as they worked with non-Catholic women on legislative issues, then, the women of the NCCW stressed their Catholic identity to insist that women did not speak with a unified voice on political issues. As historian Dierdre Moloney argues, Catholic women's groups in the 1920s sought to "articulate their views on the role of women in America at a time when modern values began to resonate more widely in society as a whole."[39] So, for example, a 1921 newsletter warned that advocates were trying to get women's organizations to pass resolutions in support of birth control, and Catholic women had to be vigilant "to state the Catholic viewpoint on a question so vital to the stability of our country and which strikes at the very foundations on which society is built—the family unit."[40] They would also warn their members when divorce legislation was being considered, as in 1923, when they complained that the General Federation of Women's Clubs, an ally in their fight against the ERA, was advocating a uniform divorce bill.[41] Moreover, in their activism, the women of the NCCW continually emphasized that their main motivation was not enhancing their own political power as women, but "safeguarding those things which are near and dear to the hearts of the Catholics."[42] Those near and dear things were safeguarding the family and the ability of women to fulfill their natural role as wives and mothers, not granting women liberty from those obligations through birth control and divorce.

The motivation of protecting their faith became apparent when the women of the NCCW confronted measures that they believed would challenge Church power in the United States. For instance, they, along with the National Catholic Welfare Council, ardently opposed the Sterling-Reed Bill, which would have set up a system of providing federal funding to public schools and a federal Department of Education. They viewed it as a threat to Catholic schools, whose independence had been challenged in many states.[43]

---

38. "Bulletin of the National Council of Catholic Women," February 1925, Box 62, Collection 10, ACUA.
39. Dierdre M. Moloney, *American Catholic Lay Groups and Transatlantic Social Reform in the Progressive Era* (Chapel Hill, NC: University of North Carolina Press, 2002), 167.
40. "National Council of Catholic Women Newssheet to Organizations," May 1, 1921, Box 62, Collection 10, ACUA.
41. "National Council of Catholic Women Newssheet to Organizations," July/August 1923, Box 62, Collection 10, ACUA.
42. "National Council of Catholic Women Newssheet to Organizations," November 29, 1920, Box 62, Collection 10, ACUA.
43. For more on how the NCWC opposed a Department of Education (which was first proposed in the Smith-Towner Bill), see Slawson, *Foundation and First Decade of the NCWC*, 45–56.

In one newsletter, the leaders of the NCCW informed their members that groups they had fought with to oppose the ERA, like the Women's Trade Union League, were supporting the bill, and the fact "this bill bids fair to become known as a 'women's bill,' is a challenge to the NCCW and other Catholic women's organizations."[44] Thus, while they allied themselves with other causes that would lead to greater government involvement in the lives of women and children, they drew the line at any bill that seemed to attack Catholic institutions.

The NCCW and the Church

In 1921 Archbishop Messmer, who had declared that only men should fight the public battles, wrote a letter to the NCCW saying, "the interest of religion and morality in our times demand a strong and well-planned nation-wide organized body of Catholic women, just as much as a well-organized body of Catholic men." Debates over issues such as education, child welfare, divorce and birth control, he contended, "will depend, for better or for worse, upon the public and political action of the women in our land."[45] The somewhat grudging nature of this concession and the implication that women's activism might be for the worse instead of the better presaged problems the NCCW would face later in the 1920s. As the women of the NCCW sought to prove their equality to non-Catholic middle-class, activist women, they also had to constantly prove themselves to a hierarchy who were, at best, skeptical of the ability of Catholic women to be political actors and, at worst, saw organized women as a dangerous force. Even as the NCCW sought to defend Catholic values, the hierarchy would stymie their efforts for any control over their message or their alliances. This, in the end, limited the ability of the NCCW to influence public debate.

Part of the problem the women of the NCCW faced resulted from ethnic tensions between a largely Irish-Catholic hierarchy and recent southeastern European Catholic immigrants and priests.[46] In 1920, the NCCW took over the administration of the National Catholic Community Houses and they

---

44. "National Council of Catholic Women Newssheet to Organizations," July/August 1923 and April 1925, Box 62, Collection 10, ACUA.
45. "NCCW Newssheet to Organizations," December 1921, Box 62, Collection 10 NCWC/USCC General Secretary/Executive Department Files, ACUA.
46. For discussion of the attitudes of Polish immigrant Catholics, see Leslie Woodcock Tentler, "Who is the Church? Conflict in a Polish Immigrant Parish in Late Nineteenth-Century Detroit," *Comparative Studies in Society and History* 25 (April 1983): 241–276. For a discussion of the tensions between southeastern European immigrant Catholics and Irish-American Catholics, particularly those in the hierarchy, see Richard M. Linkh, *American Catholicism and European Immigrants* (New York: The Center for Migration Studies, 1975).

had to negotiate tensions between the mostly middle-class, second and third generation Irish-American secretaries who ran those houses and the priests in southeastern European immigrant parishes. The secretaries saw themselves as Americanizers and uplifters of immigrants, and yet as women and thus automatically outside the hierarchy of the Church, they had no authority to challenge the Polish or Italian priests who resisted their efforts. In Milwaukee, NCCW worker May J. Williams reported, "the Polish pastors were not supporting the work of the house," and that "no cooperation has been received from the Italian pastors who do not seem to realize the need for any community activities in the Italian district."[47] In East St. Louis, the secretaries faced especially strong resistance from Polish priests, and Julia Doyle, the head secretary of the house, let her superiors know that "the Poles are opposed to Americanization work," and that the pastor of the Polish parish "wants his people to be Polish first, last and always."[48] Doyle and May's frustration was palpable as they had to do the work the NCCW demanded of them within a power structure that undermined that work.

While NCCW workers faced hostility at the local level, Agnes Regan and Gertrude Gavin faced greater challenges from national Catholic leaders. Gavin, as an independent wealthy woman who had worked in many philanthropic organizations, seemed to chafe at these challenges the most. In a private letter to Regan, she wrote of the "strain" of organizing the first NCCW convention in 1921, and also pushed Regan to not put on the program Father John Ryan, the famous social-activist priest who ran the Department of Social Action for the NCWC. "He is so tactless," Gavin wrote, "and I have never heard him speaking in public that he doesn't make all kinds of trouble."[49] Ryan ended up writing the anti-birth control statement for the NCCW's 1921 convention, which he simply recycled from a previous publication.[50]

Gavin and Regan would face a bigger adversary when they ran up against Cardinal O'Connell of Boston.[51] He harbored hostility towards anything that suggested feminism and was critical of programs that provided social

---

47. "Report on Community Houses, Milwaukee, WI by May J. Williams, Representative of the NCCW," Folder 3, Box 98, Collection 10—NCWC/USCC General Secretary/Executive Department, ACUA.

48. Summary by Julia Doyle, August 5, 1920, File 31-4, Box 42, Collection 10, NCWC Women's Committee, ACUA.

49. Gertrude Gavin to Agnes Regan, September 26, 1921, Box 1, Collection 10—NCWC/USCC General Secretary/Executive Department, ACUA.

50. Tentler, *Catholics and Contraception*, 57.

51. O'Connell had been a critic of the Welfare Council and the NCCW right from the first, and he sought to influence the NCCW through the participation of his surrogate, Mrs. Francis Slatterry. See Slawson, *The Foundation and First Decade of the National Catholic Welfare Council*, 77-79.

welfare at the federal level.[52] In 1921, the NCCW made a public statement in support of the Sheppard-Towner Act, which empowered the Children's Bureau to provide mother's pensions.[53] Afterwards, a report of the NCCW stated that "it is understood that Cardinal O'Connell of Boston is greatly opposed to the bill and instructed the women's organization there to act accordingly," and "he expressed to Miss Regan great regret that the Women's Council had endorsed it."[54] The women of the NCCW continued to support the law, but in their newsletter, they were at pains to make it clear that it did not counteract Church teachings. In reporting that state boards were being set up to administer the Sheppard-Towner mother's pensions, a 1922 newsletter stated, "The Sheppard-Towner Bill must not be confused with propaganda on birth control and contraception. . . . On the contrary, by giving aid to prospective mothers and babies, it encourages and dignifies motherhood." The newsletter also insisted that Catholic women had to be leaders on this issue, and sit on state boards in order to "prevent any possible misuse of the Bill and will further the purposes for which it was intended."[55] O'Connell was not satisfied with this, or with the activism of the larger National Catholic Welfare Council, and in 1922, he urged Pope Pius XI to censure the Welfare Council.[56] The NCWC emerged from this fight still functioning but chastened, and in their new form, they sought to tighten the control of their subsidiary organizations, including the NCCW.

More and more after 1922, the leaders of the NCCW found themselves on the defensive for their political stands, particularly on issues dealing with the expansion of federal power. In 1923, for instance, Mary Workman, an

---

52. Kane, *Separatism and Subculture*, 153–154; 106.

53. "Council Favors Sheppard-Towner Maternity Bill: Catholic Women Urged to Combat Startling Mortality of Infants and Mothers," *National Catholic Welfare Council Bulletin* (January 1921): 15.

54. Report March 31-April 6, 1921, folder 3, Box 18, Collection 10, ACUA

55. "National Council of Catholic Women Newssheet to Organizations," April 1922, Box 62, Collection 10, ACUA.

56. In February of 1922, soon after Pius XI became pope, two American Cardinals, Dennis Dougherty of Philadelphia and William H. O'Connell of Boston, presented their case to the pope for the disbanding of the National Catholic Welfare Council. They argued that the organization had over-stepped its bounds and claimed to speak for all the American hierarchy. O'Connell, while sincere in his belief that the NCWC had overstepped its authority, also had other motives to discredit the organization. His nephew, a priest, had secretly married, and O'Connell worked to protect him. Certain members of the NCWC worked to discredit O'Connell in the eyes of the previous pope, Benedict XV. On March 22, 1922, the Pope Pius XI issued a decree of suppression against the Welfare Council. Douglas J. Slawson, "'The Boston Tragedy and Comedy': The Near Repudiation of Cardinal O'Connell," *Catholic Historical Review* 77 (October 1991): 616–643. They had to change their name to the National Catholic Welfare Conference, so as not to be confused with an official Church Council. For the complete story, see Slawson, *The Foundation and First Decade of the National Catholic Welfare Council*, 123–178.

NCCW director in Los Angeles, complained to Bishop John Cantwell about the Church's opposition to the Sterling-Towner Bill that would provide federal aid to education. She argued that she could not join in the attack and complained that "public school teachers, not unfriendly to Catholic interests" had been "antagonized" by the hostility of Catholics to this bill.[57] Cantwell wrote to NCCW Chair Agnes Regan, saying that he worried that "Miss Workman has been so long associated with Protestants, though she is a very devout Catholic, from time to time the Protestant element shows itself." He said that Regan should get Workman "into the habit of thinking with the Church."[58]

In 1924, Gertrude Gavin had a more direct confrontation with O'Connell. In that year, former Children's Bureau head Julia Lathrop spoke in Boston in favor of a child labor amendment, and mentioned that the NCCW passed a resolution at their 1923 convention supporting an amendment. In a letter to Bishop Schrembs, Gavin wrote that she was confronted by a priest from the Archdiocese of Boston who told her that Cardinal O'Connell was incensed by this—he felt that a child labor amendment would lead to too much power in the federal government and was of Bolshevik inspiration.[59] She complained that the priest insisted she should

> call a meeting of the Board of Directors at once, or telegraph them, stating that we wanted to take back the Resolution passed at the Convention of 1923, favoring a Child Labor Amendment. Then we were to communicate by telegram with every single delegate who had been at the convention, telling them that the amendment was a menace to the country, and they must work against it, and asking them to take back the Resolution.

Gavin stood her ground and told the priest that this plan of action was impossible, and that "our resolutions were only advisory, and that I knew very well that Cardinal O'Connell wouldn't like it if we were to send word up to his women to work for or against this or that because Archbishop Shaw [a more liberal bishop], for instance, wanted it."[60] O'Connell, meanwhile, successfully fought to defeat a child labor amendment in Massachusetts in 1924.[61]

---

57. Mary J. Workman to Bishop John J. Cantwell, February 11, 1923, Box 1, Collection 10, National Council of Catholic Women, ACUA.
58. Bishop John Cantwell, LA to Agnes Regan, February 15, 1923, Box 1, Collection 10, National Council of Catholic Women, ACUA.
59. For more on the way O'Connell clashed with the NCCW, see Slawson, *The Foundation and First Decade of the National Catholic Welfare Council*, 219–227.
60. Mrs. Michael (Gertrude) Gavin to Bishop Joseph Shrembs, October 22, 1924, Box 44, Collection 10, James H. Ryan Files, ACUA.
61. Kane, *Separatism and Subculture*, 217–218.

The NCCW in the Later 1920s

O'Connell's victory against the child labor amendment was a sign of other political changes in American society. By 1924, male political leaders realized that there was no longer any centrally organized "Woman's Movement" and that women were not going to vote as a block. The flurry of legislation dealing with the rights and protection of women and children tapered off, and by the late 1920s, Congress even began to reverse earlier provisions, such as defunding the Sheppard-Towner Act.[62] Activist women who had achieved so much during the Progressive Era, found their political power waning, as male politicians dismissed them and younger women eschewed political organizing and instead focused on expanding their options in the social realm of relationships, clothing styles, and public behaviors, such as smoking.[63] In light of these changes, the leadership of the NCWC began to see politically organized Catholic women as less of a priority, and the leaders of the NCCW had to struggle to prove their relevance.

Moreover, the women of the NCCW had to contend with the ways the National Catholic Welfare Conference changed as the 1920s progressed. After the NCWC was almost suppressed by Rome, it began take on a more defensive tone. The leadership of the Welfare Conference also began to recoil at the modern ideas of the 1920s, particularly those concerning sexuality, and they began to emphasize their critique of modern culture over social welfare goals. As historian Elizabeth McKeown writes, by the mid-1920s, the Welfare Council "spent its dollars and time defending Catholic interests, urging Catholics to keep a distance from culture, and concentrating on the management of its own internal organization."[64] These emphases eroded the ability of the NCCW to reach out to other non-Catholic women's organizations and work in common with them on issues like mother's pensions and workplace protections for women.

---

62. Gwendolyn Mink, *The Wages of Motherhood*, 66–72.
63. For scholarship on women's declining influence as political actors in the 1920s, see Amy Eilene Butler, *Two Views of Women's Equality: Alice Paul and Ethel Smith in the ERA Debate* (Albany, NY: SUNY Press, 2002); Wendy Sarvasy, "Beyond the Difference versus Equality Debate: Postsuffrage Feminism, Citizenship, and the Quest for a Feminist Welfare State," *Signs* 17 (Winter 1992): 329–362; Estelle Freedman, "Separatism as Strategy: Female Institution Building and American Feminism," *Feminist Studies* 5, no. 3 (1979): 512–529; Lynn Dumenil, *The Modern Temper*, 99–111. For more on changing perceptions of women during this time, see Cott, *The Grounding of Modern Feminism*, 143–174; Christina Simmons, "Modern Sexuality and the Myth of Victorian Repression," in *Passion and Power: Sexuality in History*, Kathy Peiss and Christina Simmons, eds. (Philadelphia: Temple University Press, 1989), 157–177.
64. Elizabeth K. McKeown, "The "National Idea" in the History of the American Episcopal Conference," in *Episcopal Conferences: Historical, Canonical & Theological Studies*, edited by Thomas J. Reese, SJ (Washington, DC: Georgetown University Press, 1989).

By 1925, the reports and newsletters of the NCCW rarely discussed working for welfare legislation and instead stressed that the NCCW was fighting against "the tendency toward the centralization of power" and "attempts to legislate concerning individual rights," such as the ERA.[65] The women of the NCCW also emphasized their role as arbiters of moral questions. For instance, one cause they took up was the restoration of "modest dress" for women in response to the new flapper look. A 1925 newsletter reprinted an article from the *Times Herald* of Newport News, Virginia, which praised the NCCW, saying that their campaign for modesty was "greater and nobler and more important work than all the political work, or welfare work or whatnot that the women are engaged in."[66] Even when they took political stands, they framed them much more explicitly in religious terms. For instance, in reporting that the National Women's Party was going to try again for an ERA, a 1927 newsletter declared that the NCCW was fighting for "not the attainment of a fictitious advantage for women, but for the restoration of the Reign of Christ."[67]

In the later 1920s, Regan continued her fight to prove that a Catholic women's political activism was essential. A top priority of the NCWC was fighting legislation that loosened restrictions on birth control, and Regan used this to her advantage. In a report to the bishops of the NCWC, Regan pointed out that legislatures saw this as a "woman's issue" and warned that "the Catholic voice will be virtually unheard . . . on these matters unless we have there capable women representatives who may truthfully say they represent the united Catholic women's organizations of the United States."[68] In another report, she used the argument that bishops and priests could not speak out on this issue because it would lead to "vulgar and harmful publicity," and Catholic sisters could not because "they do not know the situation." Therefore, the report said, it was "the definite responsibility of the Catholic lay woman to put the message across, not only for the sake of the Catholic Church, but also for the benefit of America."[69] These arguments, however, had little impact in gaining more support for the NCCW. NCWC leaders like Father John Ryan and Father John Burke did not believe women

---

65. "Report of the Executive Secretary NCCW, 1926," File 3, Executive Secretary Reports, Box 1, Collection 10, ACUA.
66. "National Council of Catholic Women Newssheet to Organizations," December 1925, Box 62, Collection 10, National Council of Catholic Women, ACUA.
67. "National Council of Catholic Women Newssheet to Organizations," August 1927, Box 62, Collection 10, National Council of Catholic Women, ACUA.
68. "Report of Membership of NCCW, September 1925," File 2, General Organization and Development, Box 1, Collection 10, ACUA. See also the reports of Agnes Regan for 1926, 1927, and 1928 in File 3, Executive Secretary Reports, Box 1, Collection 10, ACUA.
69. "Report of Membership of NCCW, June 1925," File 1, General Organization and Development, Box 1, Collection 10, ACUA.

could effectively speak out on the birth control issue and still maintain their modesty.[70]

By 1926, the NCCW was forced to cut back on staff and programs. In her report for 1927, Regan stated frankly that they were not getting enough membership dues and it had become necessary to "plan retrenchments."[71] In that year, an NCCW field worker, Dr. Anne Nicholson, reported in a letter to a friend that Regan was "at the lowest ebb" about the NCCW's situation and complained that if archbishops and bishops in the NCWC "should say 'we wish every organization of Catholic women to belong to the NCCW, all would be well.'"[72] Few bishops, however, offered any sort of support, and the NCCW limped along through the rest of the 1920s. By 1930, after ten years of existence, the new NCCW president Mary G. Hawks wrote privately to Father Burke and asked "why . . . must we spend so much time convincing the bishops that the NCCW is 'useful and necessary'"? Burke agreed it was a problem that a number of bishops had little use for the NCCW, but offered no real solution.[73]

Conclusion

During their first years as an organization, the leaders and members of the NCCW seized the opportunity to define their civic identities on their own terms. A piece in their newsletter, titled "Legislation for Women," argued that Catholic women had to be public participants in legislative debates in order to both uphold "principles and customs which we have always held to be sacred," and prevent measures that "would slowly undermine the democratic principles on which our nation was founded."[74] The women of the NCCW defined their role as speaking out, with their authority as Catholics and as women, to fight against ideas and laws that would erode their religion and their nation. In the end, however, the political and cultural changes of the later 1920s stymied the efforts of the women of the NCCW to sustain their political maneuverings between non-Catholic women activists and the male Catholic hierarchy. While they continued to be an organization that allowed women's diocesan councils and individual Catholic women to have a voice in national debates, the NCCW never achieved their original goal to be as politically powerful as a group like the Young Women's Christian Association.

---

70. Tentler, *Catholics and Contraception*, 57.
71. "Report of the Executive Secretary, 1927," File 3, Box 1, Collection 10, ACUA.
72. Dr. Anne Nicholson to Miss Mary Carmichael, January 23, 1927, Dr. Anne Nicholson Correspondence File, Box 1, Collection 10, ACUA.
73. Mary G. Hawks to Fr. John Burke, June 29, 1930, Folder 2, Box 98, Collection 10, National Council of Catholic Women, ACUA.
74. "National Council of Catholic Women Newssheet to Organizations," July/August 1923, Box 62, Collection 10, National Council of Catholic Women, ACUA.

Yet the formation of the NCCW gave Catholic women an opportunity they never had before. They claimed their right to civic inclusion and used it to speak in the public arena as equals of other women. They found common cause with some women's groups on questions dealing with the protection of women and children, but they also insisted that their stand had special meaning since it derived from the teachings of the Catholic Church. Moreover, long before the phrase "family values" entered the political lexicon, the women of the NCCW articulated a political identity for themselves as defenders of fixed gender roles in the family and traditional views of sexuality and opponents of any legislation or movements that fought for women's autonomy. By operating on a national stage and fighting for or against legislation, the women of the NCCW took part in forging Catholic positions on women's issues that stressed communalism over individualism and women's responsibilities over women's rights. In the process, they charted an unconventional political path that straddled the left-right political divides in the United States. These women laid a foundation for distinctive Catholic responses to twentieth-century gender issues that affects American politics to this day.

Mother Katharine Drexel's Benevolent Empire: The Bureau of Catholic Indian Missions and the Education of Native Americans, 1885–1935

*Amanda Bresie**

Between 1885 and her retirement from ministry due to ill health in 1935, Mother Katharine Drexel had a significant impact on the effort to educate and evangelize Native Americans. While historians have acknowledged her monetary donations, the full scope of her partnership with the Bureau of Catholic Indian Missions (BCIM) has remained unexplored, in part because Drexel preferred to keep much of her work secret. Drawing heavily from BCIM correspondence, this article chronicles Drexel's financial contributions, highlighting her guidance of the bureau's work. Drexel provided the BCIM with millions of dollars to finance construction projects, insure churches and schools, publish reports and fundraising magazines, spread Catholic material culture, pay missionaries' salaries, and establish a Catholic presence at government Indian schools. Promotion of strict accounting practices and attentiveness to her investments enabled Drexel to closely monitor her vast benevolent empire. These policies created tensions in a church not accustomed to such behavior from a female religious. This work examines the intersection of money and mission in the late nineteenth and early twentieth century Church in the United States.

In 1904, Father William Ketcham, the Bureau of Catholic Indian Missions' director, warned U.S. Catholics: "Had it not been for one devoted woman, raised up by Almighty God for the edification of the American people and for the succor of poor abandoned races, the whole system of Catholic Indian schools would have collapsed and the Indian children been given over to schools decidedly anti-Catholic."[1] That "devoted

---

*This essay originally appeared in *U.S. Catholic Historian* 32, no. 3 (Summer 2014): 1–24.
1. William Ketcham, *Report of the Director of the Bureau of Catholic Indian Missions for 1903–1904* (Washington, DC: Bureau of Catholic Indian Missions, 1904), 2–3. Ketcham was

woman," Katharine Drexel, founded the Sisters of the Blessed Sacrament for Indians and Colored People (SBS) and donated more than $100,000 each year for religious and educational outreach to Native Americans. Drexel, daughter of banking magnate Francis Drexel and heir to a sizeable fortune, founded the SBS in 1891. Her aim was to extend Catholic educational and social outreach to these two groups which she believed the Church had underserved. Using the interest from her father's $15 million estate, she financed the Church's expansion into the home missions.[2] By her death in 1955 the SBS ran dozens of schools and social settlements, including Xavier University in Louisiana. In addition to their own schools, the SBS supported the African American and Indian missions of many other religious congregations.[3] From her initial donations following her father's death in 1885 to her retirement from ministry in 1935, no one had a larger impact on the Catholic mission to educate and evangelize Native Americans. Because she preferred to donate anonymously or through other agencies, tracing her monetary contributions is difficult, but she spent an estimated $15 to $20 million on mission projects. Generous contributions, however, tell only part of her story. Through shrewd business practices, indefatigable research, political acumen, and steely resolve, Drexel shaped Catholic Indian policy for nearly five decades.

Her considerable financial investments in Catholic missions meant clergy had to adapt to her philanthropic business model—one that held clerics accountable for her treasure and attempted to aid as many as possible. Following this model she built mission schools, churches, and convents for the Bureau of Catholic Indian Missions. Her reach extended to government-run

---

the director of the BCIM from 1901 until his death in 1921. He was born in Sumner, Iowa, in 1868 to non-Catholic parents. He entered Mount St. Mary's Seminary in Cincinnati, and then went to Oklahoma to be ordained for the Vicariate of the Indian Territory in 1892. Before assuming the directorship of the BCIM in 1901 he had extensive missionary experience with the Choctaw of Oklahoma. "Monsignor Ketcham," *The Indian Sentinel* 2, no. 9 (January 1922): 402–410, Bureau of Catholic Indian Mission Collections, Marquette University Archives, Milwaukee, Wisconsin (hereafter MUA).

2. Her father died with an estate valued at roughly $15.5 million. In the initial settling of the estate, $1.5 million was disbursed to charities. The remainder was put in a trust benefiting Francis Drexel's three daughters: Elizabeth, Katharine, and Louise. Each sister received a third of the trust's income. After Elizabeth died in childbirth in 1890, the amount was split between Katharine and Louise (who died in 1943).

3. For more on Drexel and the SBS, see Consuela Marie Duffy, SBS, *Katharine Drexel: A Biography* (Bensalem, PA: Mother Katharine Drexel Guild, 1966); Patricia Lynch, SBS, *Sharing the Bread in Service: Sisters of the Blessed Sacrament, 1891–1999* (Bensalem, PA: Sisters of the Blessed Sacrament, 1998); Lou Baldwin, *Saint Katharine Drexel: Apostle to the Oppressed* (Philadelphia: The Catholic Standard and Times, 2000). A scholarly account of her work in the West can be found in Anne M. Butler, *Across God's Frontiers: Catholic Sisters in the American West, 1850–1920* (Chapel Hill, NC: University of North Carolina Press, 2012), 191–230.

schools through her contacts on reservations. She developed an interest in Indian rights and wielded considerable lobbying power in Washington, D.C. In an age when few women, particularly Catholic women, exercised authority, Drexel carefully controlled millions of dollars and prompted the Church hierarchy to solicit her opinions. Though Church officials did not always agree with the wealthy nun, without her fiscal and policy contributions to Catholic Indian missions, the Church's outreach program could never have been implemented. While historians have acknowledged some of Drexel's financial gifts, their magnitude and her influence on policy has not yet been fully recognized.

Her canonization in 2000 has further contributed to this lacuna. The Church's investigation into her sanctity looked for proof of heroic virtue rather than investigating her worldly activities. Those interviewed regarding Drexel's career focused on the abdication of her high station in life and her financial generosity. During her lifetime, many in the male hierarchy were uncomfortable with Mother Katharine's outsized influence on policy, and they frequently chose to downplay her ability to shape the Church's mission work. The glossing over of Drexel's contributions is symptomatic of a larger absence of women religious in the missionary narrative. Sisters primarily staffed the schools and mission centers Mother Katharine funded, but the sisters are remembered most often for their connection to missionary priests. For instance, the famed Franciscans Anselm Weber and Berard Haile rightly deserve praise for their linguistic and ethnographic work at St. Michael's Mission on the Navajo Reservation, but Mother Katharine bought their land, paid their salaries, and financed the publication of their books. Throughout the missions sisters labored in the school, cooked, cleaned, and did the priests' laundry. They worked on the Church's front lines with little recognition—then and today.[4] Ketcham, however, had a clearer understanding of Drexel's significance: "The fate of our Indian missions hangs in the balance; it depends, apparently on the life of one true Catholic woman—Mother M. Katharine Drexel."[5]

---

4. Recent scholarship has begun to correct this gap. Anne Butler's *Across God's Frontiers* covers a wide range of women religious' activities in the American West including Indian missions. See Butler, *Across God's Frontiers*, 233–246. Other important works on religious sisters and Catholic Indian missions include James T. Carroll, *Seeds of Faith: Catholic Indian Boarding Schools* (New York: Garland Publishing, 2000); Irene Mahoney, OSU, *Lady Blackrobes: Missionaries in the Heart of Indian Country* (Golden, CO: Fulcrum Publishing, 2006); and Susan Peterson, "A Widening Horizon: Catholic Sisterhoods on the Northern Plains, 1874–1910," *Great Plains Quarterly* 5, no. 3 (Spring 1985): 125–132.

5. Wm. H. Ketcham, *Our Catholic Indian Missions: A Paper Read Before the Catholic Missionary Congress, Chicago, November 16, 1908* (Washington, DC: Byron S. Adams, 1908), 15.

Business woman and saint, Mother Katharine Drexel maintained detailed records of her mission work with the Bureau of Catholic Indian Missions (Courtesy of the Archives of the Sisters of the Blessed Sacrament, Bensalem, Pennsylvania).

Forming a Philanthropic Partnership

As early as 1876 Katharine Drexel had begun corresponding with her spiritual director, Bishop James O'Connor of Omaha, Nebraska, about her interest in Catholic Indian missions. Her interest heightened when the Drexel family took several extended tours of western missions and outposts in the 1880s. Having met personally with Indians such as the Oglala Lakota Chief Red Cloud, Drexel became determined to aid the missions. She reported that the Indians she met on her western tours asked for Catholic schools. As historian Anne M. Butler has asserted, Drexel believed the Indians were crying out for the Catholic faith. More likely, however, they were searching for "any advantage a receptive listener might provide."[6] The Northern Plains chiefs whom Drexel met had ulterior motives for requesting Catholic schools. Many of them recognized missionary Pierre-Jean DeSmet, SJ, as a trustworthy man of peace, who could serve as a peace-broker with the United States government. In addition Red Cloud had a French Canadian son-in-law who advocated for the Jesuit missionaries. Consequently, a number of chiefs became Catholic converts and demanded "Black Robe" (Catholic) schools for their reservations in order to facilitate what they

---

6. Butler, *Across God's Frontiers*, 199.

believed would be a lasting peace with the government.[7] In any case, these meetings as well as the opportunity to witness the poverty of the reservations piqued Drexel's missionary interests.

In addition, Drexel's involvement stemmed from her acquaintance with Father Martin Marty, OSB, the Bishop of Sioux Falls, a diocese then covering all of North and South Dakota, and Father Joseph A. Stephan, the first head of the Bureau of Catholic Indian Missions.[8] In 1885, shortly after the death of Francis Drexel, the clerics arrived unannounced at the Drexel home's doorstep in Philadelphia wishing to obtain funds from the philanthropic sisters. They could not have anticipated that their begging mission would garner such an avid partner in their affairs. Between her 1885 meeting with the two priests and 1895, Katharine Drexel donated nearly $1 million to the Bureau of Catholic Indian Missions, established a $50,000 fund for BCIM operations, and constructed dozens of schools.[9]

The BCIM, established in 1874 to lobby the government on behalf of Catholic mission interests, desperately needed Drexel's financial assistance to expand its presence in the West at the end of the nineteenth century. While the BCIM received some funding from the federal government and from the Church-sponsored Lenten Collection for Indian and African American Missions instituted after the Third Council of Baltimore (1884), the Drexel family financed the bulk of the Catholic Indian missions in the late nineteenth century. Mother Katharine was at least partly responsible for erecting

---

7. Karl Markus Kreis, ed., *Lakotas, Black Robes, and Holy Women: German Reports from the Indian Missions in South Dakota, 1886–1900*, trans. Corinna Dally-Starna (Lincoln, NE: University of Nebraska Press, 2007), 22–27; Peter J. Rahill, *The Catholic Indian Missions and Grant's Peace Policy, 1870–1884* (Washington, DC: Catholic University of America Press, 1953), 24–25. See also Ross Enochs, *The Jesuit Mission to the Lakota Sioux: A Study of Pastoral Ministry, 1886–1945* (Kansas City, MO: Sheed and Ward, 1996), 18–28.

8. Martin Marty, OSB (1836–1896) was born in Switzerland where he joined the Benedictine order in 1855.He came to the United States to head the Abbey at St. Meinrad, Indiana, in 1859. In the 1870s he became an important advocate for Indian missions and began the mission at Fort Yates, North Dakota. He later became Vicar Apostolic of the Dakota Territory and in 1889 was named the Bishop of Sioux Falls. He also worked with the government as an Indian commissioner from 1889 to his death in 1896. Joseph A. Stephan (1822–1901) began his theological training in his native Germany before immigrating to the United States in 1847. He was ordained a priest for the Diocese of Cincinnati. Stephan served in various positions along the American frontier and grew increasingly interested in Indian missions. He served as an Indian agent for Standing Rock starting in 1878. He became head of the Bureau of Catholic Indian Missions in 1884. For more complete biographical information see, "Bishop Martin Marty, OSB, Apostle of the Sioux," *The Indian Sentinel* 1, no. 1 (January 1920): 7–10, and Kevin Abing, "Directors of the Bureau of Catholic Indian Missions, 2; "Joseph A. Stephan, 1884–1901," Explanatory Note, Bureau of Catholic Indian Mission Papers, MUA.

9. *The Bureau of Catholic Indian Missions, 1874–1895* (Washington, DC: The Church News Publishing Company, 1895), 19, BCIM Records, Series 4/2 and 3: Reports and Publications, reel 1, MUA.

over thirty schools prior to her entrance into religious life. Her philanthropy was essential because collections never raised enough money to grow or even sustain Indian mission work. The first Lenten collection in 1887 reaped $81,898 from which the mission aid organization, the Society for the Propagation of the Faith, took a portion before it was divided between Indian and African American missions. Though the first collection was small, successive collections were even more meager.[10] The collection grew in the twentieth century, though it never amounted to more than a few pennies per Catholic each year. Other sources of money such as the Society for the Preservation of the Faith among Indian Children, the Association of the Holy Childhood, and the Marquette League also failed to collect sufficient funds.[11] Drexel's money, thus, proved essential for Catholic Indian missionary work.

The onset of Drexel's career as a philanthropist coincided with her discernment of a religious vocation. For several years Drexel struggled with the decision and told no one except her spiritual director, Bishop James O'Connor. Deeply interested in Indian missions and desperate for her money, O'Connor at first tried to persuade Drexel to remain in the world. Finally sensing she would not relent, he determined that she should found a religious community and maintain control of her fortune.[12] To prepare for her role as foundress of a religious congregation, she completed her novitiate with the Sisters of Mercy in Pittsburgh. When she entered the convent in 1889, she had the daunting task of learning poverty and humility while performing her role as chief executive of a multi-million dollar charitable empire. During her novitiate, the nuns allowed her several hours each day to manage the voluminous correspondence necessary to continue her work with the BCIM while her brother-in-law Edward Morrell handled her finances.[13] By the time she professed vows in her religious community, the Sisters of the Blessed Sacrament, in 1891, Drexel had become integral to the survival of the U.S. Catholic Indian missions.

The Drexel fortune provided the funds for the building of dozens of schools in the West, though the exact number constructed with Drexel's

---

10. *The Bureau of Catholic Indian Missions, 1874–1895* (Washington, DC: The Church News Publishing Company, 1895), 20.

11. For example in 1906, the Preservation Society raised $14,957, the Marquette League $2,200, and the Association of the Holy Childhood, $4,000. Mother Katharine supplied over $100,000 in the same year. *Report of the Director of the Bureau of Catholic Indian Missions for 1905–1906* (Washington, DC: BCIM, 1906), and *Report of the Director of the Bureau of Catholic Indian Missions for 1906* (Washington, DC: BCIM, 1906), 29, 78.

12. Anne M. Butler, "Mother Katharine Drexel: Spiritual Visionary for the West" in *By Grit and Grace: Eleven Women Who Shaped the American West*, ed. Glenda Riley and Richard W. Etulain (Golden, CO: Fulcrum Publishing), 200–205.

13. Duffy, *Katharine Drexel*, 145.

Drexel Hall at Holy Rosary School, now Red Cloud Indian School, on the Pine Ridge Reservation in South Dakota, was named after Mother Katharine, the mission's primary benefactor; photograph ca. 1890-1900 (Courtesy of Marquette University Special Collections, Holy Rosary Mission-Red Cloud Indian School Records).

support is unknown. Drexel's earlier gifts, before she took vows as a sister, were more substantial. For example, one of her first behests (1890) was St. Boniface School in Banning, California. She bought 258 acres in the San Bernardino Mountains, supplied the construction costs, purchased the animals for industrial education, and contributed annual operating funds.[14] Later, when her fortune supported her own congregation's schools, she contributed more modestly to the works of other religious communities. When a priest approached her about building a school for the Zuni in Arizona in 1923, for example, she offered a loan rather than a gift.[15] Her largesse became such a trope that in 1914 the history of Sacred Heart Institute, Vinita, Oklahoma, simply stated, "[T]his school shares the history of most other Catholic Indian schools, namely that it was made possible chiefly by the generosity of Mother Katharine Drexel."[16]

In addition to purchasing land and constructing buildings, Mother Katharine often covered the insurance premiums for mission schools. Having

---

14. Tanya Rathbun, "Hail Mary: The Catholic Experience at St. Boniface," in *Boarding School Blues: Revisiting American Indian Educational Experiences,* ed. Clifford Traafzer, Jean A. Keller, and Loene Sisquoc (Lincoln, NE: University of Nebraska Press, 2006), 156.
15. Mother Katharine Drexel to Charles Lusk, January 19, 1923, BCIM Correspondence, Series 1-1, Reel 114, MUA.
16. "Sacred Heart Institute in Vinita, Oklahoma," *The Indian Sentinel* (1914): 15.

seen fire destroy several schools she had built, Drexel understood the importance of property insurance. She also supplied statues, crucifixes, medals, and holy cards to missionaries, believing these material objects attracted nonbelievers to the Catholic faith. The SBS never travelled without sacramentals to give away. Upon first arriving at the Yankton Mission in Marty, South Dakota, in 1922, for example, the sisters visited Indian homes handing out "miraculous medals," showing an image of the Virgin Mary. These gifts helped to mark the Indians' homes with the stamp of Catholic culture.[17] Drexel described the power of material culture: stained-glass windows, statues, and crucifixes "all make mute appeal to the hearts of the Indians."[18]

Mother Katharine and the Church School Wars

Drexel's work building and supporting mission schools through gifts large and small brought her and the BCIM into conflict with the U.S. government. As the government gradually withdrew funds from Catholic schools, with which the government had "contracted" to provide educational services, missionaries increasingly depended upon Drexel. In the 1890s, Protestant missionary groups joined the chorus calling for government-run schools for Native Americans, gradually relinquishing its schools and missions for Indians. The Protestant exodus meant Catholics began receiving a greater proportion of the government contracts for Indian education. In 1874 the Church received only $8,000 for Indian school contracts, but by 1890, $500,000.[19] As Catholics obtained a greater portion of the federal school money, sectarian tensions increased. The appointments of Thomas Jefferson Morgan as Commissioner of Indian Affairs and Daniel Dorchester as Superintendent of Indian Schools further heightened tensions as Catholics claimed both were anti-Catholic. BCIM director Father Stephan's vitriolic protests against the two men caused Morgan to sever ties between the Bureau of Indian Affairs and the Bureau of Catholic Indian Missions in 1891.[20] While the bureaus restored relations, the relationship remained acrimonious.

Facing Protestants who began to champion "non-sectarian" government-run education which would deliver a basic Protestant message without delving into the doctrinal differences separating the various branches of

---

17. A Sister of the Blessed Sacrament, "Yankton Mission, South Dakota," *The Indian Sentinel* 2, no. 11 (July 1922): 503–504.
18. Mother Katharine Drexel, "Mother Katharine Drexel at Yankton," *The Indian Sentinel* 4, no. 1 (January 1924): 21.
19. Mark Clatterbuck, *Demons, Saints, and Patriots: Catholic Visions of Native America through the* Indian Sentinel, *1902–1962* (Milwaukee, WI: Marquette University Press, 2009), 39.
20. Francis Paul Prucha, *The Churches and the Indian Schools, 1888–1912* (Lincoln, NE: University of Nebraska Press, 1979), 10–24; also see Carroll, *Seeds of Faith*, 86–88.

Christianity, the BCIM vowed to fight for the government/Church partnership that they had cultivated for thirty years. The ensuing struggle which played out largely in the press, created an anti-Catholic backlash.[21] Between the 1890s and the start of World War I, Protestants and Catholics engaged in a battle for funding and cultural hegemony. In this struggle, Drexel became the Catholic Church's most valuable asset.

In the 1890s agitation from anti-Catholic groups such as the American Protective Association caused the U.S. Congress to rapidly withdraw support from Catholic schools. The government, not the Church, supporters believed, should take responsibility for the assimilation and Americanization of Indians. President Grover Cleveland's appointment of Daniel M. Browning as Indian Commissioner in 1892 further turned the tide against Catholic Indian missions. In 1896, Browning not only convinced Congress to slash contracts to religious schools by twenty percent, but asserted that Indian children must attend a government school if one were close to their homes. Catholics resented the interference. The "Browning Ruling" forbade Indian parents from designating which school their children would attend.[22] By the turn of the century, sectarian schools received only fifteen percent of the federal money allocated for Indian education in 1895. Congress for a time eliminated food rations for Indian students attending sectarian schools. In short, Catholic Indian missions could no longer rely on the U.S. government for support and survival.[23]

In 1898, to keep mission schools solvent after Congress slashed funding, Drexel developed a complicated subsidy system that paid schools the difference between their original government contracts and the reduced subsidies, provided that they maintained a quota of students.[24] In 1899, the difference amounted to $92,046, not including the churches she built, nor the costs of running her religious congregations' schools.[25] She allocated, on average, $80,000 annually for Indian schools, though the amount lessened by the 1930s as some schools closed and others became more self-sufficient. Between 1895 and 1928, Drexel estimated that she supplied almost

---

21. Prucha, *The Churches and Indian Schools*, 26–41. For anti-Catholicism during the time period, see Justin Nordstrom, *Danger on the Doorstep: Anti-Catholicism and American Print Culture in the Progressive Era* (Notre Dame, IN: University of Notre Dame Press, 2006), 1–18.
22. Ironically, as James Carroll has pointed out, the Browning Ruling actually strengthened Catholic schools as Indian parents subverted the rule. Carroll, *Seeds of Faith*, 100.
23. Prucha, *The Churches and the Indian Schools*, 40.
24. Mother Katharine Drexel to J. A. Stephan, August 1, 1898, BCIM Records, Series 1-1, Box 36, Folder 31, MUA.
25. J. A. Stephan to Mother Katharine Drexel, June 10, 1899, BCIM Records, Series 1-1, Box 38, Folder 1, MUA.

TABLE 1. Aid to Native American Schools
Lenten Collections and Drexel's Subsidies, 1898–1924

Year	Lenten Collection	Drexel Subsidies
1898	$64,242.75	
1899	$60,880.47	
1900	$79,853.42	$231,096.87 (between 1898 and 1901)
1901	$82,798.20	$82,333.65
1902	$119,687.00	$83,827.48
1903	$121,206.61	$86,003.25
1904	$87,175.18	$84,548.49
1905	$148,672.31	$73,839.51
1906	$171,816.76	$79,980.96
1907	$103,415.62	$89,255.94
1908	$89,162.72	$70,604.87
1909	$97,358.38	$57,564.78
1910	$92,520.23	$73,316.82
1911	$113,309.86	$73,260.27
1912	$109,549.35	$41,031.39
1913	$117,446.96	$70,024.31
1914	$112,668.53	$51,166.29
1915	$109,354.04	$48,746.62
1916	$144,705.13	$46,722.13
1917	$135,013.61	$44,873.72
1918	$147,617.81	$39,481.71
1919	$155,971.40	$41,263.70
1920	$210,717.64	$42,292.02
1921	$196,242.22	$39,784.43
1922	$215,190.35	$38,938.75
1923	$231.047.05	$39,518.25
1924	$273,241.00	$39,862.35

*Some Catholic schools received additional support from Indian tribal funds beginning in 1905. As both tribal funding and the Lenten collection rose, Drexel's subsidies fell. These numbers do not represent the sum of Drexel's donations to the missions during the year. She frequently made anonymous gifts under the pseudonym "A Friend of the Indian Missions." Table compiled from *Reports on Mission Work among the Negroes and the Indians: What is Being Accomplished by Means of the Annual Collection Taken up for Our Missions, 1887–1925*, BCIM Records, Series 7–2, reel 1, MUA.

$6,000,000 to the Indian missions for buildings, maintenance, and subsidies, not counting funds for the SBS schools.[26] Though Drexel supported more than fifty schools, her involvement remained an "open secret." Schools received a stipend each quarter with the designation: "From a Friend of the Indian Missions," but most everyone understood the money came from the heiress nun's coffers.

In addition to crucial support subsidizing students in mission schools, Drexel facilitated the missions in myriad ways. She provided an estimated $1,300,000 to construct churches, schools, convents, and rectories between 1895 and 1928, in addition to financing the BCIM's daily activities. She purchased the BCIM headquarters in Washington, D.C., in 1888, gave the BCIM a quarterly stipend, and covered the director's travel expenses until 1933.[27] In 1920, the SBS purchased a second residence near the BCIM headquarters and sent three sisters to handle BCIM business. The sisters assigned to the Washington, D.C. residence (called Tekakwitha House), answered correspondence for the Society for the Preservation of the Faith among Indian Children, the bureau's fundraising arm, performed administrative tasks such as typing, accounting, and payroll, and edited *The Indian Sentinel*, the society's official organ. For many years the bureau owed its existence to the talents and treasure of the SBS. While attaching her sisters to the BCIM undoubtedly helped the bureau, it also gave Drexel unfettered access to the center of power. Through her sisters she gained key information about missionaries' work, the legitimacy of monetary requests, and any potential sources of conflict. SBS editing of *The Sentinel* helped her shape the public debate about Indian missions. Consequently, Mother Katharine was able to assert control over the bureau all while professing to be its most humble servant.

Inroads into Government Schools

While Drexel, like most Catholics, believed Catholic-affiliated mission schools were the key to the education and assimilation of Native Americans—the "Indian Problem"—she did not ignore the reality that most Native Americans attended government-run schools. In 1916, the BCIM noted that more than 5,000 Catholic Indians attended government schools.[28] Drexel and her cohorts at the bureau feared Protestant influence

---

26. Mother Katharine Drexel to J. B. Tennelly, July 24, 1928, BCIM Records, Series 1-1, Roll 151, MUA. During the same time period, she also donated an estimated $5.8 million to churches and missions for African American pupils.
27. Mother Katharine Drexel to Rev. William Hughes, January 5, 1933, BCIM Records, Series 1-1, reel 186, MUA.
28. "Catholic Instruction in Government Boarding Schools," *The Indian Sentinel* 1, no. 3 (Winter 1916): 20.

of the government schools which she claimed robbed Indian students of their religion.[29] To combat this perceived loss of faith, Drexel offered financial support for Catholic education and instruction at government schools.

Not limiting their work to their own Catholic schools, the SBS made assisting in religious education at government schools a significant part of their undertaking. Drexel's sisters coordinated the religious education of students at government boarding schools in Carlisle, Pennsylvania; Santa Fe, New Mexico; Fort Defiance, Arizona; and Chin Lee (Chinle), Arizona. They traveled to the schools on Sundays to assist the priests at Mass, coordinated catechism classes, and prepared students to receive the sacraments. In addition, the sisters sometimes brought government students to nearby missions for religious services and retreats.[30] Since the religious congregation did not have enough sisters to visit every government school, Drexel built chapels near the schools and recruited priests to attend to the students. By the 1920s, she allocated $7,000 annually for Mass stipends for priests providing ministry to Indians in government schools.[31]

Federal policy dictated that for students to receive religious education, the parents had to sign a paper stating their religious preference. This stipulation launched frenzied missionaries deep into reservation territory hunting for signatures. She recruited and financed the efforts of priests to gather signatures of Indian parents which ensured that their children would receive Catholic education while attending government schools.[32] As Drexel told the American Board for Catholic Missions, "One never knows how many miles are implied in the lift of an Indian's chin."[33] Drexel's gifts worked on the presumption that money was best spent when it could affect the greatest number of people, whether in Catholic or government schools.[34]

---

29. Mother Katharine Drexel, "MMK Talks to Tekakwitha Club, February 28, 1933," H10A Box 30, Folder 16, Archives of the Sisters of the Blessed Sacrament, Bensalem, Pennsylvania (hereafter ASBS).
30. Father Egbert Fischer, "The Fort Defiance School," *The Indian Sentinel* (1914): 42–46.
31. "Quarter Ending December 29, 1929," BCIM Records, Series 1–1, reel 151, MUA.
32. Rev. William Hughes to Rev. Marcellus Troester, OFM, March 8, 1923; Rev. Marcellus Troester to Mother Catherine (sic), March 3, 1923; Fr. Brendan Haile, OFM to Mother Katharine Drexel, April 9, 1923, BCIM Records, Series 1–1, reel 110, MUA.
33. Mother Katharine Drexel, "Report 1935 to American Board for Catholic Missions," MMK Talks, Box 30, folder 16, ASBS.
34. H.A. Leduc to William Ketcham, October 26, 1920, BCIM Records, Series 1–1, reel 97, MUA; William Ketcham to H.A. Leduc, November 2, 1920, BCIM Records, Series 1–1, reel 97, MUA.

Drexel and Political Reform

In addition to her direct support of education, Drexel encouraged practical reform, using her influence in Washington, D.C. to lobby for Native Americans.[35] She donated funds to defray the cost of legal fees for Indians fighting to retain their land. In 1897, for example, she donated $6,000 to finance the legal team representing the Cupeño and Digueño tribes who had been removed from their land in California.[36] The California Supreme Court ruled against the tribes in 1899; the United States Supreme Court followed suit in 1901, rejecting their claim.[37] Drexel's interest in the group's plight did not fade, however, and in 1906 she paid the travel expenses for three Indians to come to Washington, D.C. to lobby for protective legislation.[38]

Drexel pressured the BCIM to intercede for Indians with government officials. For example in June 1899, she prodded Father Stephan to inform the Department of the Interior of the conditions of the Indians at San Ildefonso Pueblo, resulting in some additional funding.[39] The following year, she spurred the bureau to investigate a water dispute between the Pueblo Indians and the Canal Company.[40] When the bureau did not move quickly enough on the issue, Drexel wrote more forcefully: "I think some energetic means should be taken otherwise there will be a famine amongst these poor Indians next summer. If the Bureau cannot do anything I am thinking seriously of interesting the Indian Rights Association in the matter. Something should be done and promptly."[41] This assertion is all the more dramatic considering the BCIM's long and contentious relationship with the Indian Rights Association, which the Church viewed as thoroughly anti-Catholic. She stunned Father Ketcham with her support of a bill proposed in 1904

---

35. Mother Katharine's brother-in-law Edward Morrow served in Congress between 1902 and 1907. Her other brother-in-law Walter George Smith was president of the American Bar Association and sat on the Board of Indian Commissioners. In addition to these immediate ties to the government, the Drexel name and the financial houses it represented commanded much respect.

36. Mother Katharine Drexel to Msgr. J.A. Stephan, June 23, 1897, BCIM Records, Series 1-1, Box 35, Folder 26, MUA.

37. Stephen M. Karr, "The Warner's Ranch Indian Removal: Cultural Adaptation, Accommodation, and Continuity," *California History* 86, no. 4 (2009): 26-29.

38. Charles Lusk to Mother Katharine Drexel, December 28, 1906, BCIM Records, Series 1-1, Box 52, Folder 6, MUA.

39. Mother Katharine Drexel to J.A. Stephan, June 6, 1899, BCIM Records, Series 1-1, Box 38, Folder 1, MUA; J.A. Stephan to Mother Katharine Drexel, June 10, 1899, BCIM Records, Series 1-1, Box 38, Folder 1, MUA.

40. Mother Katharine Drexel to Charles Lusk, March 15, 1900, BCIM Records, Series 1-1, Box 39, Folder 19, MUA; Mother Katharine Drexel to J.A. Stephan, August 3, 1900, BCIM Records, Series 1-1, Box 39, Folder 19, MUA.

41. Mother Katharine Drexel to Charles Lusk, undated (ca. 1902), BCIM Records, Series 1-1, Box 40, Folder 1, MUA.

which would have evicted all white people from Indian land. He demurred, suggesting, "Right or wrong, you could as easily remove the Atlantic from our eastern coast as you could remove the hundreds of thousands of white people from the Indian Territory."[42] Her commitment to justice, in this case, meant a willingness to work beyond accepted channels, and she saw politics as a means to accomplish spiritual ends.

Terms and Conditions

Despite her generous benefactions, the money issued from Drexel came with strings attached. Mother Katharine kept detailed records and demanded financial accountability. Anyone who accepted her funding agreed that it would be used exclusively to benefit Native Americans. If a school closed or ceased to serve Indians, she asked for the return of her original investment. Those who did not agree to her stipulations were politely, but firmly, informed no funds would be provided. An uncooperative priest who wanted assistance in building a chapel for the Crows but refused to sign her standard contract was informed, "I do not wish to force you into anything you do not approve of, only without such a contract I cannot conscientiously help you." Drexel warned, "Other Indians in the United States require help as urgently as the poor Crows. I shall look about me for an Order who will bind itself to such a perpetual contract & help these other Indians whose souls are as precious in God's sight as are the Crows."[43]

Drexel never wavered in demanding contractual stipulations, despite the pleas of clerics to forgo the requirement. When she purchased a home for a priest in Antlers, Oklahoma, for instance, it was contingent on the bishop agreeing to forfeit the house if the mission no longer served Native Americans. Though Father Ketcham had expressly asked that the bishop not be forced to sign the agreement, Drexel forwarded it to the bishop, breezily informing Ketcham, "As he has signed papers of this kind before, I do not think he will hesitate about this. As soon as he returns the papers duly signed I hope if I live to be able to send you the money as promised."[44] When she reported that the bishop had indeed completed the necessary paperwork, Ketcham retorted, "Since your experiment turned out so nicely, I am only too happy you took

---

42. Rev. William Ketcham to Mother Katharine Drexel, December 28, 1904, BCIM Records, Series 1-1, Box 46, Folder 11, MUA.
43. Mother Katharine Drexel, "Writings 3161," ASBS.
44. Mother Katharine Drexel to Father William Ketcham, November 20, 1917, BCIM Records, Series 1-1, reel 84, MUA. She wrote "if I live" on all her promises of money because her father's will stipulated that if his daughters died without heirs, his money would be distributed to several charities upon their deaths. Her ability to support BCIM projects would die with her.

Mother Katharine Drexel is greeted on a visitation of St. Michael's Mission on the Navajo Reservation (ca. 1925, likely at Chinle or Lukachukai, Arizona) by Navajo leader Charlie Mitchell and Father Clementin Wottle, OFM (Courtesy of the Archives of the Sisters of the Blessed Sacrament, Bensalem, Pennsylvania).

the initiative."[45] She had a similar confrontation in 1923 with then-BCIM director Father William Hughes when she insisted over his objections that a donor sign a note for a loan because it was "a little more businesslike."[46] She only funded projects which she felt had a great likelihood of success. Indeed, missionaries came to understand that their ability to gain funding from the hierarchy depended on Mother Katharine's stamp of approval.[47] Drexel meticulously counted every penny and demanded it all be used, as she often put it, *ad maiorem Dei gloriam*, for the greater glory of God.

The daughter of an accomplished businessman, Katharine Drexel took the cautions to control her own finances. She demanded painstaking record

---

45. Rev. William Ketcham to Mother Katharine Drexel, December 1, 1917, BCIM Records, Series 1–1, reel 84, MUA.
46. Father William Hughes to Norine Prudom, January 7, 1923, BCIM Records, Series 1–1, reel 111, MUA.
47. For example, before appealing for money from the Negro and Indian Mission Board, Father Sylvester Eisenman and Father William Hughes made sure the committee led by Cardinal Dougherty saw Mother Katharine's letters of approval for the mission in Marty, South Dakota. Rev. William Hughes to Father Sylvester Eisenman, September 18, 1923, BCIM Records, Series 1–1, Reel 111, MUA; Father Sylvester Eisenman to Rev. William Hughes, October 9, 1923, BCIM Records, Series 1–1, Reel 111, MUA.

keeping practices in a church setting that was not always comfortable with a woman dictating the terms of business. As Carol K. Coburn and Martha Smith have pointed out in their history of American sisters, "Women religious who challenged male authority often found themselves ostracized and labeled 'unladylike' and their very sanity questioned."[48] That the loss of Drexel's support would have brought the entire Catholic Indian mission system to a halt meant that priests and bishops, unused to consulting with women and hesitant to treat them as equals, swallowed their pride in order to insure Drexel's continued assistance.

Accustomed to having great authority over religious sisters, priests and bishops addressed Mother Katharine's concerns and satisfied her conditions in order to access her money. Some had difficulty acknowledging her ability to shape the Church's work. In 1928, when Drexel sent an additional agenda item for the meeting of the Negro and Indian Mission Board, the secretary Father J. B. Tennelly first sent word to Cardinal Dennis Dougherty of Philadelphia stating,

> Mother Katharine says nothing in the letter which accompanies these documents (regarding SBS contributions to home missions) which would lead me to infer that she had consulted Your Eminence in regard to laying her request before the Board. For this reason I thought that it would be only proper for me first to ask if I have Your Eminence's authorization to include the matter. . . .[49]

While Dougherty instructed Tennelly to comply with Drexel's wishes, Tennelly's letter demonstrates the hesitancy to acknowledge Drexel's authority.[50] Despite her difficulty getting an item placed on the meeting agenda, the board acquiesced with her request that the SBS be granted $25,000 from the Lenten fund to be continued in perpetuity. This grant continued in full, even during the Depression when the mission board cut all other payments by twenty-five percent.[51] The bishops felt they could not say no to Mother Katharine. Though she regularly signed letters to bishops and cardinals with fawning statements such as "Kneeling to kiss the sacred Purple and to beg the blessing of Your Eminence," Mother Katharine often held the upper

---

48. Carol K. Coburn and Martha Smith, *Spirited Lives: How Nuns Shaped Catholic Culture and American Life, 1836–1920* (Chapel Hill, NC: University of North Carolina Press, 1999), 94.
49. Rev. J.B. Tennelly to His Eminence Dennis Cardinal Dougherty, November 1, 1928, BCIM Records, Series 1-1, reel 151, MUA.
50. Cardinal Dougherty to Rev. J.B. Tennelly, November 2, 1928, BCIM Records, Series 1-1, reel 151, MUA.
51. J. Tennelly to His Eminence Dennis Cardinal Dougherty, January 18, 1933, BCIM Records, Series 1-1, reel 186, MUA.

hand in negotiations.[52] Perhaps for this reason, the Church hierarchy readily praised her generosity and her holiness, but never her business skills nor her political acuity.

The combination of disrupted gender conventions and Drexel's exacting business methodology sometimes proved contentious. She insisted on control, liked to handle details personally, and wished to be included in all phases of a project. When reporting on a visit from Drexel, Father Sylvester Eisenman, a priest in Marty, South Dakota, ministering to the Yankton Sioux, joked about her fastidiousness, "Of course she admires everything. She even admired St. Paul's Mission from the cellar all the way to the garret."[53] While her attention to detail amused Eisenman, it could sometimes create hardship for the missions. Before signing checks, Mother Katharine personally pored over reports and receipts. When she was away from the convent on her lengthy visitation tours, schools waited for payments. The delays created hardship for schools needing to purchase food and supplies. In 1922, for example, her long absence caused BCIM Secretary Charles Lusk to send letters to the schools explaining that he hoped to send their checks in the near future—but the timing depended entirely on Drexel.[54]

While her own travels occasionally delayed payments, she held missionaries strictly accountable to the terms in her contracts. In 1899, she angrily informed Father Stephan that several of the schools she had agreed to subsidize had not supported the agreed-upon number of students, and she pointed out many discrepancies in their reports. Drexel threatened to cut off support to any school or mission that did not promptly file its paperwork.[55] In fact, in 1904, tired of chronically late or incomplete reports from two schools, she delayed payments in order to make a point. She explained to Ketcham that the reports to the two schools came after she had already written a check covering the others, noting, "It seems to me that Mother Francis said last year when these reports were delinquent without <u>any good reason</u> they would have to wait until the next quarter, and as she was in retreat when these came, and had previously sent the cheque for those which were received <u>on time</u> I simply made no response on the matter."[56] Ultimately she

---

52. Mother Katharine Drexel to His Eminence Dennis Cardinal Dougherty, November 4, 1932, BCIM Records, Series 1–1, reel 180, MUA.
53. Father Sylvester Eisenman to Father William Hughes, November 3, 1922, BCIM Records, Series 1–1, reel 105, MUA.
54. Charles Lusk to Rt. Rev. Frederick Eis, August 14, 1922, BCIM Records, Series 1–1, Reel 105, MUA.
55. Mother Katharine Drexel to J.A. Stephan, September 1, 1899, BCIM Records, Series 1–1, Box 38, Folder 1, MUA.
56. Mother Katharine Drexel to William Ketcham, August 18, 1904, BCIM Records, Series 1–1, Box 46, Folder 10, MUA.

delivered the money, but she wanted her displeasure for shoddy business practices noted.

Tensions and Turmoil

Not all priests and missionary sisters appreciated her guidelines, nor did her system always work smoothly. In 1917, Father Thomas Grant, a priest who served at St. Labre in Montana, complained to Father Ketcham, "You require us to carry 55 children in order to get the full pay for the 17 provided for by the Bureau and the 28 provided for by Mother Catherine (sic). But you make no provision in your contract for any in excess of this number while you expressly cut down the payment when the number falls below 55." He continued his polemic, adding, "Moreover, you only consider the Bureau bound to the contract on the condition that it can get the funds. A contract to be square should work both ways, namely, when the number goes below and pay is reduced on that account, it should be increased when the number goes above the number called for."[57] While the BCIM director agreed with the frazzled priest and responded that a more equitable system would indeed pay per student, he firmly added

> The system we have is an arrangement between the Bureau and Mother Katharine, whose contribution is a matter of absolute necessity and which I understand she promised on condition that this system should be carried out. So it appears to be a choice between forfeiting her contribution or retaining the system.[58]

While her provisos were designed to maximize the recruitment and retention of students, her byzantine subsidy system undoubtedly caused headaches for priests and sisters in the missions.

No matter how generously Drexel spread her largesse, missionaries in the field demanded more, and the heiress nun increasingly lost her ability to favorably answer supplicants. By the early twentieth century, many letters to the BCIM complained of deteriorating physical plants and poor conditions. Poverty was endemic. In one particularly pitiful letter, a priest lamented that he did not even have the money to buy his unfortunate constipated assistant a laxative.[59] Others spoke of forgoing running water and furniture while

---

57. Father Thomas Grant to William Ketcham, March 8, 1917, BCIM Records, Series 1-1, reel 84, MUA.
58. Father William Ketcham to Father Thomas Grant, March 19, 1917, BCIM Records, Series 1-1, reel 84, MUA.
59. Father Francis Redman to Father William Hughes, September 12, 1923, BCIM Records, Series 1-1, reel 110, MUA.

living from the small stipends from the BCIM and Mother Katharine.[60] As Drexel had constructed many of the schools, priests and sisters often believed it fell to her and the bureau to complete repairs, despite making it clear on all her contracts that her support could only be guaranteed "while I live" and providing no promises of continued aid. When she began her donations in the 1880s, Drexel believed the schools would eventually support themselves through their industrial work. As Ketcham noted in 1912, however, "Experience shows that no Indian school ever became self-supporting and I have given up the idea that any ever will."[61] As such, Drexel found herself continually besieged with requests for building improvements for schools which she had constructed decades earlier as a onetime benefaction.

Strains on the Philanthropic Model

In the twentieth century, Drexel's philanthropic model and missionaries' continual demand for additional funds strained even Drexel's vast resources. As per the instructions of her father's will, she received half of the interest on a trust of about $15 million—roughly $220,000 per year by the 1920s.[62] Though a large sum of money, it was never enough to meet the missions' demands, especially as she increased the scope of the work. As the number of SBS-run schools proliferated in the twentieth century, money for outside missions dwindled. As SBS superior, she put the needs of her own congregation first, and consequently she had less to spend on other schools and churches. Despite a constriction in funds, she consistently dismissed critics who urged against opening more missions. In 1904 when Ketcham wrote her a letter hotly contesting her desire to add another school when she might not be able to support it forever, she responded, "You must pardon me, Father, when I tell you that the vision of no less than your venerable self, waxing warm on the prospect of new schools . . . was too much for my gravity, and although I was very busy, I actually had to take the time to laugh." She added, "Never mind, Father, all these things will come to an end," and she urged him to trust in divine providence.[63]

Providence, however, could not protect them from the federal income tax's implementation in 1913. The tax, combined with overextension in the mission field, created considerable financial strain for the SBS who depended

---

60. Hubert A. Van Rechem to Joseph H. Fargis, January 18, 1906, BCIM Records, Series 1–1, Box 53, Folder 6, MUA.
61. Father William Ketcham to Hubert Post, September 13, 1912, BCIM Records, Series 1–1, reel 62, MUA.
62. Butler, *Across God's Frontiers,* 216.
63. Mother Katharine Drexel to Father William Ketcham, December 12, 1904, BCIM Records, Series 1–1, Box 46, Folder 11, MUA.

on the income from Drexel's inheritance. By 1920, with post-World War I inflation, the situation was dire. Indeed, the BCIM had to lend Drexel money to help her cover expenses at SBS schools.[64] When an Ursuline sister wrote Ketcham asking for a raise in her school's stipend, he had to report, "She cannot do anything because the high prices have crippled her institutions likewise and the income tax has eaten into her funds so that it will be impossible to expect any further help from her—that is more than she is giving." He further mused, "In fact, I wonder that she has been able to keep up as well as she has. I know that she has stinted herself and her own institutions."[65] In 1923, when the BCIM requested money, Drexel provided a loan rather than a donation, complaining that she did not have even six dollars to give. She blamed the income tax: "It requires some degree of resignation to render cheerfully 'to Caesar the things that are Caesar's.'"[66] The situation brightened in 1924 when Pennsylvania Senator George Wharton Pepper moved a tax exemption for people who donated more than ninety percent of their income for the previous ten years to charity. This exemption, which at the time applied only to Drexel, saved her roughly $100,000 annually.[67]

The reprieve occasioned a rapid expansion of SBS missionary activity, especially in the South, in the 1920s, but the Depression deeply damaged Mother Katharine's ability to bankroll the BCIM. In 1933, she ruefully reported to BCIM director Father William Hughes, "We have been accustomed in the past to give all the financial help we could possibly afford to missionary works outside of our Congregation, but we have finally reached the limits of our resources."[68] While Drexel continued to financially back the BCIM through the 1930s (over $100,000 each year), she could no longer singlehandedly finance operations.

Conflicting Responses to Indian Education Reform

Her decreasing ability to dispense financial aid and tensions with the BCIM director Father William Hughes (who had succeeded Ketcham in 1922) resulted in a decreasing role for Drexel in the bureau in the 1930s.

---

64. Father Ketcham to Rt. Rev. Mathias C. Lenihan, Bishop of Great Falls, Montana, April 28, 1920, BCIM Records, Series 1–1, Reel 97, MUA.
65. Father Ketcham to Sr. M. Loyola, May 20, 1920, BCIM Records, Series 1–1, Reel 98, MUA.
66. Mother Katharine Drexel to Father William Hughes, October 19, 1923, BCIM Records, Series 1–1, Reel 114, MUA.
67. "Income Tax Exemption for Mother Katharine Drexel," *The Indian Sentinel* 4, no. 3 (July 1924): 102.
68. Mother Katharine Drexel to Rev. William Hughes, December 11, 1933, BCIM Records, Series 1–1, Reel 186, MUA.

Hughes consulted Drexel on fewer projects, though he continued to ask for money and utilized SBS talent in his office.[69] One source of disagreement between Drexel and Hughes arose when increasing numbers of Indian students began attending federally-funded public day schools.[70] During the 1930s, the government, pressured by John Collier, Franklin Roosevelt's Commissioner of Indian Affairs, built between forty and fifty day schools, and in 1934, Congress passed the Johnson-O'Malley Act, easing more Indian children into public schools.[71] Hughes embraced the new government policy, while Drexel saw it threatening the Catholic educational empire she had devoted her life to building.

When the government announced plans to build additional day schools in the Pueblos to meet student needs up to the eighth grade, Drexel warned Hughes, "I consider that if acted upon this would be detrimental to the Catholicity of the Pueblo Indians." She anticipated that Hughes would instruct the SBS to close St. Catherine's and teach in the Pueblos instead, but she wondered, "Who would build the day schools in the Pueblos? Who would provide the mid-day meal for the pupils and the bus where necessary to bring them to the school? Who would build the Convents in each Pueblo—and there are about ten of them?" Having reached the end of her financial resources, an irate Drexel questioned his dedication to Catholic boarding schools and begged for reassurance.[72] Not willing to accept Hughes' approval of the government plan, Drexel went behind his back and contacted U.S. Indian Commissioner John Sullivan and asked him to lobby Congress against the plan.[73] Hughes rebuked her, expressing his doubt that the Church could possibly stop the government plan; in fact, he insisted that

---

69. Drexel pulled SBS administrative support at the end of 1932, claiming that the sisters were needed elsewhere. She also informed Cardinal Dennis Dougherty that she needed the Washington residence as a house of studies for the many sisters enrolled at Catholic University of America. Though both of these were compelling, it is likely that personal tensions precluded continued work. Mother Katharine Drexel to His Eminence, D. Cardinal Dougherty, D.D., November 4, 1932, Correspondence Files, BCIM, Series 1-1, Reel 180, MUA.

70. This move was in large part a reaction to the 1928 publication of the Meriam Report which harshly condemned boarding schools as overly institutional, unsafe, and cruel – places that did not suit Indians' educational needs. The report specifically criticized missionaries for destroying Indian religion and rightly pointed out that too many schools were in poor physical condition. The report pushed for more day schools and more Indian autonomy. Lewis Meriam, *The Problem of Indian Administration* (Baltimore: Johns Hopkins Press, 1928), see especially 815–847.

71. Margaret Connell Szaz, *Education and the American Indian: The Road to Self-Determination since 1928* (Albuquerque: University of New Mexico Press, 1974), 63–91.

72. Mother Katharine Drexel to Rev. William Hughes, January 17, 1931, BCIM Records, Series 1-1, Reel 173, MUA.

73. Mother Katharine Drexel to William Hughes, February 28, 1931, BCIM Records, Series 1-1, Reel 173, MUA.

the government and the Church were working for the same objective: "the bringing of the Indians, where possible, into her ordinary (which is to say parochial) organization." Despite her sharp words to Hughes, Drexel supported Catholic day schools, stating, "It is the ideal of Catholic education to have day schools for the children whence they may return at night to the family circle, and, what is particularly desirable in the case of a pagan people, the children may carry into the home the lessons of faith and morality learned in the classroom."[74] Her actions stemmed not from ideological differences over the efficacy of day schools, but rather from the fear of having to shutter the institutions she and the SBS had labored to nurture. Hughes' refusal to leap to the defense of Catholic boarding schools and his support for Collier's policies surely rankled the woman who had devoted her life to the idea of saving souls, at least in part, through Catholic education.[75]

The more Hughes stressed Church-government cooperation and the transition to day schools, the more Drexel insisted upon her approach. For instance, while Hughes wanted to sell the long-vacant St. Mary's School in Miami, Oklahoma, and allocate the money elsewhere, Drexel remained hesitant for fear of losing souls. She explained that she still hoped to attract missionaries to reopen the school. Drexel told Hughes of a boy who had been educated first at St. Mary's and then boarded at St. Catherine's while attending St. Michael's College in Santa Fe—"proof that the Faith implanted in the heart of the child at school will assert itself later on in life, and make the boy or girl realize what a gift it is and it will lead them right."[76] Instead of retreating, she proposed paying a missionary priest to visit local Indians or conducting a summer school there to interest young people in the faith. Though a gifted business woman who surely understood the cost of refusing a property sale, Drexel's religious principles required her to reach as many as possible, sometimes leading to decisions others found unpalatable. Her fortune, her connections to power, and her iron will, however, put the hierarchy in the uncomfortable position of accepting her gifts on her terms or losing much-needed revenue.

---

74. William Hughes to Mother Katharine Drexel, March 31, 1931, BCIM Records, Series 1-1, Reel 173, MUA; Mother Katharine Drexel, "MMK Talks to Tekakwitha Club 28 February 1933," H 10A Box 30, Folder 16, ASBS.

75. Mother Katharine Drexel to William Hughes, March 1932, BCIM Records, Series 1-1, Reel 180, MUA. For more on Hughes' support of Collier, see William Hughes, "What of the New Indian Bill?" *The Indian Sentinel* 14, no. 2 (Spring 1934): 30–36; William Hughes, "Collier Indian Bill Passes," *The Indian Sentinel* 14, no. 3 (Summer 1934): 54–55, 65; and William Hughes, *Indians on a New Trail*, pamphlet (July 1934), BCIM Records, Series 4/2 and 3, Reel 2, MUA.

76. Mother Katharine Drexel to William Hughes, January 27, 1934, BCIM Records, Series 1-1, Reel 192, MUA.

Two Sisters of the Blessed Sacrament accept a buckskin dress on behalf of Mother Katharine at the 1924 St. Francis Catholic Congress, Rosebud Indian Reservation, South Dakota. The dress was a gift from the Sioux to Mother Katharine as a token of appreciation for her many donations to Sioux missions (Courtesy of Marquette University Special Collections, Bureau of Catholic Indian Missions Records, image no. 01386).

By the time a massive heart attack forced her into retirement in 1935, Drexel's influence at the BCIM had waned considerably. Ultimately, Mother Katharine's goal of providing Catholic education to as many Indian students as possible floundered. The SBS managed to continue their schools, some into the twenty-first century, but far more congregations shuttered schools' doors. From a peak of over 7,500 Indian students in Catholic schools in 1931, by the late 1930s the BCIM supported only 4,582 pupils, a number which continued to decrease as more students attended public schools. Some Indians applauded the decline, calling the schools sites of "cultural genocide." To many Indians, the schools serve as painful reminders of a colonial past, and some former students remember the mission sites Mother Katharine funded as places of abuse and neglect rather than as centers of redeeming love.[77] In other places, however, Indian communities have

---

77. For example, activist Mary Crow Dog who attended St. Francis Mission School called the school a "curse for our family for generations." Mary Crow Dog and Richard Erodes,

worked with religious congregations to create schools that are models of cooperation and cultural enrichment. The transformation of Holy Rosary Mission on the Pine Ridge Reservation into Red Cloud Indian School epitomizes this interest in cultural accommodation.[78]

Often overlooked in this complicated and frequently painful debate are Mother Katharine's methods and motives. Exploring her contributions—both financial and philosophical—however, enriches historical understanding of the administration of Catholic Indian missions and the male/female power dynamics in the Church in the late-nineteenth and early-twentieth centuries. In the years after the codification of canon law in 1917, a period which scholars have lamented as "religious communities of women religious calcified under the weight of ecclesiastical hegemony," Mother Katharine and the Sisters of the Blessed Sacrament grew increasingly interested in economics and politics and more willing to contest the hierarchy's policies.[79] As the SBS superior, Drexel never hesitated to offer clergy her opinions about the best way to meet minority communities' needs. When the Church failed to act, she forged ahead. A shrewd business woman and powerful force for change in an era when the Church welcomed neither, Mother Katharine Drexel carved out a unique and unprecedented role as the chief operating officer of a benevolent empire balancing dollars and souls.

Lakota Woman (New York: Harper Perennial, 1991), 31. Growing scholarly literature confirms that both Catholic and government-run Indian schools failed to live up to their lofty promises. In the 1990s, studies such as Robert A. Trennert Jr.'s exploration of the Phoenix Indian School (Arizona) and K. Tsiannia Lomawaima's study of the Chilocco Indian School (Oklahoma) have characterized the schools as harsh institutions where students were bullied and stripped of their identities. Native scholars such as Debra K. S. Barker have called on personal experience to inform their academic research and have labeled the boarding schools "an instrument that emotionally scarred generations of Indian children, leaving them and their children, as well, victims of institutionalized cultural genocide." See Sally McBeth, *Ethnic Identity and the Boarding School Experience of West Central Oklahoma American Indians* (Washington, DC: University Press of America, 1983); Robert A. Trennert, *The Phoenix Indian School: Forced Assimilation in Arizona, 1891–1935* (Norman, OK: University of Oklahoma Press, 1988); K. Tsiannia Lomawaima, *They Called it Prairie Light: The Story of Chilocco Indian School* (Norman, OK: University of Oklahoma Press, 1993); Debra K. Barker, "Kill the Indian, Save the Child: Cultural Genocide and the Boarding School," 47–78, in *American Indian Studies: An Interdisciplinary Approach to Contemporary Issues*, ed. Dane Morrison (New York: Peter Lang, 1997); David Wallace Adams, *Education for Extinction* (Norman, OK: University of Oklahoma Press, 1995); and Brenda Child, *Boarding School Seasons: American Indian Families, 1900–1940* (Lincoln, NE: University of Nebraska Press, 1998).

78. Christopher Vecsey, *Where the Two Roads Meet* (Notre Dame, IN: University of Notre Dame Press, 1999), 10, 21–22, 69–78.

79. Coburn and Smith, *Spirited Lives*, 225.

The Daughters of Charity as Cultural Intermediaries: Women, Religion, and Race in Early Twentieth-Century Los Angeles

Kristine Ashton Gunnell*

In early twentieth-century Los Angeles, California, the Daughters of Charity employed their religious identity as sisters to cross cultural boundaries, acting as intermediaries between the church, the city's charitable establishment, and the Japanese and Mexican immigrant communities. As the Catholic Church's support for Americanization programs grew in the 1910s and 1920s, the sisters shaped their charitable efforts to fit within this framework, providing personnel to teach English in a Japanese school, expanding their settlement work by providing disaster relief to flood victims in 1914, and by encouraging the efforts of middle and upper-class Mexican immigrants who wished to aid their less fortunate countrywomen by forming Las Señoritas de la Caridad *("Spanish Ladies of Charity"). This article questions the sisters' role in Americanization and suggests that they used these programs primarily as a vehicle to further their long-standing commitment to aid those in poverty irrespective of race or ethnicity.*

As Catholic nuns and sisters ventured into the American West during the nineteenth-century, they became important links between cultures and classes in the diverse communities they served. As Anne M. Butler argues, Catholic sisters made religion a significant part of the western experience by actively participating in cultural exchanges. These French, German, Irish, Spanish, and American sisters ate new foods, learned new languages, and lived in conditions that many would have previously thought unfathomable. They established hospitals and schools where Native Americans, Mexicans, Asians, and European immigrants received valuable social

---

**This essay originally appeared in U.S. Catholic Historian 31, no. 2 (Spring 2013): 51–74.

and educational services.[1] Importantly, Catholic sisters constructed their institutions as *community* services, thereby mitigating some of the religious tensions that characterized eastern cities at the time and fostering cooperation between Catholics, Protestants, and Jews. Religious women acted as lynchpins in complex social structures, connecting the middle-class and the elite with the poor from many racial backgrounds. And although religious tensions increased as western cities grew, one community of religious women, the Daughters of Charity, maintained their position as cultural intermediaries in Los Angeles well into the twentieth century.

The social landscape in which the sisters operated changed dramatically in the early twentieth century. Los Angeles had shed its reputation as "Queen of the Cow Counties," and the city's population increased from 100,000 to 577,000 between 1900 and 1920. Ten years later, its population reached 1.24 million.[2] Although white Protestants remained in control of most of the city's economic and political institutions, the influx of Mexican, Japanese, and African American migrants created some uneasiness among the white middle class. The economic chaos produced by the Mexican Revolution caused the city's Mexican population to increase fivefold between 1910 and 1920. Its size and immigrants' assumed connections to political radicals like the Flores Magón brothers made Mexicans targets both for racial restrictions and altruistic reform.[3]

---

1. Anne M. Butler, *Across God's Frontiers: Catholic Sisters in the American West, 1850–1920* (Chapel Hill, NC: University of North Carolina Press, 2012). For more on Catholic sisters' experience in the American West, see Carol Coburn and Martha Smith, *Spirited Lives: How Nuns Shaped Catholic Culture and American Life, 1836–1920* (Chapel Hill, NC: University of North Carolina Press, 1999); Michael E. Engh, SJ, *Frontier Faiths: Church, Temple, and Synagogue in Los Angeles, 1846–1888* (Albuquerque, NM: University of New Mexico Press, 1992); Barbra Mann Wall, *Unlikely Entrepreneurs: Catholic Sisters and the Hospital Marketplace, 1865–1925* (Columbus: Ohio State University Press, 2005); Sioban Nelson, *Say Little, Do Much: Nurses, Nuns, and Hospitals in the Nineteenth Century* (Philadelphia: University of Pennsylvania Press, 2001); M. Ursula Stepsis, CSA and Dolores Ann Liptak, RSM, eds., *Pioneer Healers: The History of Women Religious in American Health Care* (New York: Crossroad, 1989); Susan Carol Peterson, *Women with Vision: The Presentation Sisters of South Dakota, 1880–1985* (Urbana, IL: University of Illinois Press, 1988).
2. Robert M. Fogelson, *The Fragmented Metropolis: Los Angeles, 1850–1930* (Berkeley, CA: University of California Press, 1993), 78–83; Michael E. Engh, SJ, "Practically Every Religion Being Represented," in *Metropolis in the Making: Los Angeles in the 1920s*, ed. Tom Sitton and William Francis Deverell (Berkeley, CA: University of California Press, 2001), 202–203. By 1930, 14.2 percent of Angelenos were considered nonwhite, giving Los Angeles the distinction of having the second largest proportion of nonwhites of any major city in the U.S. (second only to Baltimore). Fogelson, *The Fragmented Metropolis*, 83.
3. Mark Wild, *Street Meeting: Multiethnic Neighborhoods in Early Twentieth-Century Los Angeles* (Berkeley, CA: University of California Press, 2005), 30; Douglas Monroy, *Rebirth: Mexican Los Angeles from the Great Migration to the Great Depression* (Berkeley, CA: University of California Press, 1999), 217–221.

World War I further heightened fears of national disunity and sparked Americanization movements throughout the United States. As Judith Raftery and Gayle Gullett have shown, California clubwomen spearheaded the state's Americanization movement under the auspices of the Home Teacher Act of 1915. Organizers sponsored courses to instruct Mexican women in the English language, citizenship, and Anglo-American values. Stephanie Lewthwaite notes that instructors encouraged the production of Mexican handicrafts, ostensibly celebrating immigrant culture while essentializing and racializing the programs' participants.[4] While riddled with contradictions and questionable results, Americanization programs did gain some political currency in the late 1910s and early 1920s. U.S. bishops took note and incorporated Americanization into diocesan charitable efforts.

Conscious of Protestant overtones associated with the movement, Bishop John J. Cantwell embraced Americanization as a "Catholic responsibility" during World War I. In doing so, he adopted the approach of the National Catholic War Council (later renamed the National Catholic Welfare Conference), which emphasized patriotism and assimilation to counter charges of Catholic disloyalty. Cantwell encouraged clergy, religious women, and lay charity workers to establish Americanization programs in Los Angeles. He endorsed a training course in Americanization techniques sponsored by the University of California Extension Division in 1919, including English instruction and citizenship. The diocese invested considerable resources in the Mexican community by sponsoring religious education classes, providing charitable relief, and endorsing social service programs for immigrants at the Brownson House and *El Hogar Feliz* settlements. The diocese also recruited Spanish-speaking sisters for the parochial school at the Plaza Church, appointed Spanish-speaking priests to establish "Mexican missions" in some parishes, and sought to build a church dedicated to Our Lady of Guadalupe.[5]

---

4. Gayle Ann Gullett, "Women Progressives and the Politics of Americanization in California, 1915–1920," *Pacific Historical Review* 64, no. 1 (February 1995): 71–94; Stephanie Lewthwaite, *Race, Place, and Reform in Mexican Los Angeles: A Transnational Perspective, 1890–1940* (Tucson, AZ: University of Arizona Press, 2009), 95–119; Judith Rosenberg Raftery, *Land of Fair Promise: Politics and Reform in Los Angeles Schools, 1885–1941* (Stanford, CA: Stanford University Press, 1992), 68–86. See also Frank Van Nuys, *Americanizing the West: Race, Immigrants, and Citizenship, 1890–1930* (Lawrence, KS: University Press of Kansas, 2002).

5. Michael E. Engh, SJ, "Female, Catholic, and Progressive: The Women of the Brownson Settlement House of Los Angeles, 1901–1920," *Records of the American Catholic Historical Society of Philadelphia* 109, no. 1 (1999): 113–126; "For Extending Work of Americanization," *Los Angeles Times*, December 14, 1919; "Many Attend Course on Americanization," *Los Angeles Times*, November 24, 1919; Jeffrey M. Burns, "The Mexican Catholic Community in California," in *Mexican Americans and the Catholic Church, 1900–1965*, ed. Jay P. Dolan and Gilberto Miguel Hinojosa (Notre Dame, IN: University of Notre Dame Press, 1994), 155–175; Robert E. Wright, OMI, "Mexican-Descent Catholics and the U.S. Church, 1880–

For their part, the Daughters of Charity continued their efforts to offer unconditional charity to the city's newcomers, particularly to the Mexican immigrants living in the shantytowns near their orphanage in Boyle Heights.

This article examines the ways that the Daughters of Charity employed their religious identity as Catholic *sisters* to cross cultural boundaries, acting as intermediaries between the city's charitable establishment and immigrant communities. The Daughters participated in Catholic Americanization programs but shaped them according to the spirit of their vocation. The religious community's founders, Vincent de Paul and Louise de Marillac, emphasized respect for the individual and human dignity. Applying these values counteracted some of the most pernicious aspects of Americanization, which often denigrated immigrant cultural traditions and minimized their potential contributions to American society.

The Daughters of Charity and the Mexican Community in Boyle Heights

Industrial expansion in the southwestern United States combined with the economic disruptions of the Mexican Revolution to produce one of the most dramatic migrations in U.S. history. An estimated one million people—approximately ten percent of Mexico's population—migrated to the United States between 1910 and 1930. By then, George J. Sánchez notes that the Los Angeles barrio had become the "largest Mexican community in the world outside of Mexico City."[6] Many recent Mexican immigrants gathered in shantytowns, or "Boxcarvilles" along the banks of the Los Angeles River, while others lived in the flood-prone areas of Fickett Hollow and Bernal Gully, near Boyle Heights.[7] Russians, Jews, Italians, Japanese, Greeks, and African Americans also claimed the neighborhoods of Boyle Heights as their home. The Daughters of Charity's Los Angeles Orphan Asylum sat on the bluffs overlooking the river, in the heart of one of the most diverse neighborhoods in the city.

There the Daughters of Charity actively worked with Californio-Mexican children and their families throughout the late nineteenth and early twentieth centuries. Between one-third and one-half of children living in the Los

---

1910: Moving Beyond Chicano Assumptions," *U.S. Catholic Historian* 28, no. 4 (Fall 2010): 87–88; Jay P. Dolan, *In Search of an American Catholicism: A History of Religion and Culture in Tension* (Oxford; New York: Oxford University Press, 2002), 141–146.

6. George J. Sanchez, "'Go After the Women': Americanization and the Mexican Immigrant Woman, 1915–1929," in *Unequal Sisters: A Multicultural Reader in U.S. Women's History*, ed. Vicki L. Ruiz and Ellen Carol DuBois, vol. 2 (New York: Routledge, 1994), 284–297.

7. Wild, *Street Meeting*, 27, 31.

Los Angeles Orphan Asylum, 1896 (Courtesy of Vincentian Archives, Rue de Desvres, Paris).

Angeles Orphan Asylum had some Mexican or Native Californian heritage in 1880, and the diocesan newspaper, *The Tidings*, reported that one-third of the children were Mexican in 1919.[8] Because of the "revolving door" system that characterized Catholic orphanages, children often had brief stays at the institution. Most children lived there one or two years before returning to parents or relatives, and some may have had several short visits. Many children continued to interact with parents or relatives, thereby giving the sisters the opportunity to assist these families. Even when a child was placed out, the sisters often required adoptive or foster parents to report on his or her welfare.[9] The sisters' social services provided an avenue for greater involvement in the Mexican community. Immigrants regarded the sisters as a source of support, whether they needed food, clothing, or medical assistance. When

---

8. "Our Diocesan Charities: The Los Angeles Orphan Asylum," *The Tidings*, October 17, 1919; *U.S. Census, Los Angeles, 1880*.

9. For example, when a young girl was placed with a family in Los Angeles after what Linda Gordon has called the "Great Arizona Orphan Abduction," the Sisters of Charity of New York required the adoptive family to report to them every six months. This was a common practice. Thomas J. Conaty, D.D., to Dr. W.J. Davis, May 18, 1905, Conaty Papers, 535, D-1905, Archives of the Archdiocese of Los Angeles; Teresa Vincent, D.C., to Thomas J. Conaty, D.D., April 24, 1905, Conaty Papers, 777, V-1905, Archives of the Archdiocese of Los Angeles.

Sister Cecilia Craine died in 1940, one mourner remembered, "She did not know how to say 'No' and would always find a way to help the situation, were it the petty worries of a child or those of a jobless man or a hungry family, and that without question."[10]

The Daughters of Charity often worked informally with the Mexican community in Los Angeles, but the 1914 flood inaugurated a new phase in the sisters' activities. Beginning on February 18, a fierce rainstorm inundated the city. The deluge lasted four days and flooded gullies and boxcarvilles on the banks of the Los Angeles River. Wind and water scattered the contents of homes into the yard, soaking clothing and bedding. Everything was covered in mud. During a break in the storm, Craine and another sister "ventured out, carrying bread, potatoes, and soup to the sufferers."[11] With the gully flooded and bridge washed out, the sisters carefully crossed a narrow wooden plank separating them from the residents, carefully protecting their pots from the rushing current below.

Other groups also offered assistance to the flood victims, but racial antagonism fostered suspicion between Mexican immigrants and Anglo relief organizations. Between 1913 and 1918, nativists reacted to the surge of Mexican migrants by scapegoating them as the cause of the city's economic problems and by heightening public suspicions about immigrants' political radicalism. Particularly after Pancho Villa's raid in New Mexico in 1916, nativists convinced city officials to increase the police presence in Mexican neighborhoods and to place an embargo on sales of guns and liquor to Mexican residents.[12] In addition, the Salvation Army, the Presbyterian Church, and other Protestant missionary groups actively proselytized the Mexican community. These organizations offered charitable assistance and social services for the needy, but the aid came with strings attached. Accepting Protestant charity often meant attending religious services and opening one's home to "friendly visitors," who may not have fully appreciated immigrants' culture or traditions. Charity workers often equated "Americanization" with "Protestantization," and some immigrants saw their actions as unwarranted intrusions into their families.[13]

---

10. "An Account of Sister Cecilia Craine's Illness and Death," c. 1940, Maryvale Historical Collection, Box 2, Folder 12, Maryvale, Rosemead, California (hereafter MHC).

11. "California," *Annals of the Congregation of the Mission: Letters from the Missionaries and the Daughters of Charity* 22, no. 1 (1915): 51–57.

12. Ricardo Romo, *East Los Angeles: History of a Barrio*, vol. 1 (Austin, TX: University of Texas Press, 1983), 89–111, especially 101–102.

13. Derek Chang, "'Brought Together Upon Our Own Continent': Race, Religion and Evangelical Nationalism in American Baptist Home Missions, 1865–1900," in *Immigrant Faiths: Transforming Religious Life in America*, ed. Alex Stepick, et al. (Walnut Creek, CA: Alta Mira Press [Rowman and Littlefield], 2005), 36.

In contrast, the Daughters of Charity sought to support Mexican immigrants' religious traditions. Readily identifiable in their blue habits and cornettes, the sisters acted as symbols of Catholic identity and community. Commitment to serving those living in poverty regardless of race or creed made the Daughters of Charity less judgmental than their Protestant counterparts. When approached by Salvation Army representatives in 1914, the Mexicans in Boyle Heights declined their help, saying "the Sisters were taking care of them." Flood victims also rejected the Municipal Charities Commission's efforts to provide temporary shelter, and they even turned away white Catholic women offering food and dry clothing, confusing them for "Salvation Lassies."[14] The sisters had to intervene before the residents would accept the women's help. Apparently, these residents equated whiteness with Protestantism, and an organization that did not necessarily serve their best interests. Admittedly, Mexican immigrants' responses are filtered through the sisters' voices. So far, Mexican accounts of their interactions with the Daughters of Charity have not surfaced. However, the sisters' records demonstrate their conscious use of religious identity to act as intermediaries among racial groups.

Building on the work of multiracial feminists, Henry Goldschmidt argues that race, nation, and religious identities are co-constituted, meaning "they are constructed in and through each other, and through other categories of difference."[15] Although Mexican flood victims appear to have conflated whiteness with a Protestant religious identity (i.e. the "Salvation Lassies"), race did not necessarily determine residents' decisions to reject aid from charity organizations. Nearly all Daughters of Charity serving at the Los Angeles Orphan Asylum in the 1910s were also white.[16] Though it is unclear how many sisters spoke Spanish in 1914, they visited families and provided food and other necessities for their struggling neighbors even before the flood, thereby bridging cultural differences through acts of serv-

---

14. "California," 52–55.
15. Henry Goldschmidt and Elizabeth A. McAlister, *Race, Nation, and Religion in the Americas* (New York: Oxford University Press, 2004), 7.
16. In 1910, fourteen out of twenty sisters either emigrated from Ireland themselves or their parents had. By 1920, that number rose to eighteen. According to the census data, two sisters appear to have Hispanic backgrounds in 1910; Sister De Sales's parents were born in Spain, while Sister Carmelito and her parents were all born in California. Two other sisters were born in Germany, while the remaining two were German-American. *U.S. Census, Los Angeles, 1910*; *U.S. Census, Los Angeles, 1920*. A majority of entrants to the community during the first century of its history (known as the Sisters of Charity of St. Joseph's from 1809–1849 and the Daughters of Charity, Province of the United States, after 1850) were born in the United States (55%). Twenty-four percent of entrants were born in Ireland, but many of the American sisters may have had Irish heritage. Betty Ann McNeil, DC, "Demographics of Entrants: Sisters of Charity of St. Joseph's, 1809–1849 and Daughters of Charity, Province of the United States, 1850–1909," *Vincentian Heritage Journal* 31, no. 1 (April 2012): 85.

ice. Sister Leonide Bowling, a German-American woman from Pennsylvania, took special notice of Mexican families living along the river. She brought food and medicine to the sick and elderly, providing comfort and sustenance to their families. At age thirty-eight, Bowling died of a sudden illness, and the Mexican community mourned her passing. Sister Mary Cain remembered Bowling's funeral as an outpouring of love:

> It was not the *rich* who filled the Chapel at Boyle Heights, but one half of it was *filled* by the *poor lowly Mexicans,* and as the casket was carried down the aisle, their sobs, cries, and aspirations, would touch your very heart. She loved her poor Mexicans, and her kind acts were many and frequent and now she is reaping the reward of her charity to-day (sic) at hands of the God of Charity for devotion to His own poor in general. Her death was a shock to all.[17]

Such instances suggest that the Daughters built cooperative relationships by extending humanitarian service, rather than letting racial or national prejudices dominate their interactions with others.

Disaster relief comprised one aspect of what a sister described as their "settlement work."[18] While the Catholic settlement movement has received attention for expanding laywomen's opportunities outside the home, the Daughters of Charity engaged in similar types of activities. In Chicago, the Daughters operated two settlements: the Catholic Social Center opened in 1914, and the sisters took over operations at the De Paul Settlement and Day Nursery in 1916. These settlements primarily provided daycare services and kindergarten classes, but the De Paul Settlement also had an information bureau for those seeking to provide or secure employment. In 1911, Sister Brendan O'Bierne started an outreach program that included home visits and emergency aid to some Mexican residents in Dallas, and Sister Cecilia Craine worked at the Guardian Angel Settlement in St. Louis before taking the reins of the Los Angeles Orphan Asylum in October 1913. Under Craine's leadership, the sisters in Boyle Heights developed a comparable program offering religious education and material assistance as needed.[19] Even

---

17. Mary Cain, DC to Eugenia Fealy, DC, Los Angeles, May 26, 1919, MHC. Copy consulted in Maryvale Collection at St. Vincent Medical Center Historical Conservancy (hereafter SVMCHC); "Sister Leonide," c. 1919, MHC. Copy consulted in Maryvale Collection at SVMCHC. Emphasis in the original.

18. "California," 51.

19. Daniel Hannefin, DC, and Vincentian Studies Institute (U.S.), *Daughters of the Church: A Popular History of the Daughters of Charity in the United States, 1809–1987* (Brooklyn, NY: New City Press, 1989), 197–199; Deborah A. Skok, *More Than Neighbors: Catholic Settlements and Day Nurseries in Chicago, 1893–1930* (DeKalb, IL: Northern Illinois University Press, 2007), 126–163, 190; "Death Takes Sister Cecilia, Head of Orphanage 26 Years," *Los Angeles Times,* July 12, 1940; "Minutes, October 9, 1913," Maryvale Historical Collec-

before the February flood, the sisters opened a "supply-station" in the quarantine cottage at the orphanage, which provided food, clothes, and other donated supplies for the struggling Mexicans, Italians, and others residing in the surrounding neighborhoods.

While the Daughters of Charity extended helping hands to impoverished immigrants with different cultural traditions, they also acted as intermediaries among people of varying class backgrounds. Since their arrival in 1856, the sisters chose to cross cultural borders in order to build cooperative relationships with the city's elite Spanish-Mexican, Irish, German, and French families. These benefactors donated funds to purchase land for an orphanage and school, and also supported the orphans' fairs and other fundraising projects. The Daughters maintained their relationships with many Spanish-Mexican families for at least two generations.[20] These relationships signified *californios'* ongoing importance within the Church when, as a group, their economic and political influence diminished in the aftermath of the American conquest.[21]

---

tion, Book 32, Los Angeles Orphan Asylum Minute Book, June 21, 1869-July 13, 1940, MHC. See also Deirdre M. Moloney, *American Catholic Lay Groups and Transatlantic Social Reform in the Progressive Era* (Chapel Hill, NC: University of North Carolina Press, 2002). The literature on the activities of Catholic laywomen is growing, which Skok reviewed in 2008. See Deborah A. Skok, "The Historiography of Catholic Laywomen and Progressive Reform," *U.S. Catholic Historian* 26, no. 1 (Winter 2008): 1–22. Other examples include Michael E. Engh, SJ, "From the City of Angels to the Parishes of San Antonio: Catholic Organization, Women Activists, and Racial Intersections, 1900–50," in *Catholicism in the American West: A Rosary of Hidden Voices*, ed. Roberto R. Treviño and Richard V. Francaviglia (Arlington, TX: University of Texas at Arlington, 2007), 42–71; Kathleen Sprows Cummings, *New Women of the Old Faith: Gender and American Catholicism in the Progressive Era* (Chapel Hill, NC: University of North Carolina Press, 2009).

20. The family of Ygnacio and Ysabel del Valle provides a good example. The del Valles hosted the Daughters of Charity when they first arrived in Los Angeles in 1856. Ysabel donated almond trees to the orphanage in 1870. Ysabel and her daughter, Josefa del Valle Forster, donated time and funds to the orphanage fundraisers in the 1870s and 1880s. Forster and her sister Ysabel del Valle Cram also donated to the new St. Vincent's Hospital in 1927. Mary Scholastica Logsdon, DC, to Ysabel del Valle, January 26, 1870, Del Valle Collection (1002), Document 814, Box 6, Seaver Center, Los Angeles; Kristine Ashton Gunnell, "Women's Work: The Daughters of Charity Orphans' Fairs and the Formation of the Los Angeles Community, 1858–1880," *Southern California Quarterly* (January 2012): 373–406; "St. Vincent's Hospital Donor Plaque," 1927, SVMCHC, Los Angeles.

21. *Californio* and *californiana* are regional terms for those born and raised in the territory during the first half of the nineteenth century. After Mexican independence in 1821, *californios* tended to identify more with the land of their birth than with a far-off government in Mexico City. Those who belonged to the elite *ranchero* class owned large tracts of land and wielded considerable economic, political, and social power. After the American conquest in 1848, many of these families sought to preserve their social status by retaining their identity as *californios,* thereby distinguishing themselves (and their descendants) from Mexican immigrants who arrived in the state after 1880. Rose Marie Beebe and Robert M. Senkewicz, eds. *Lands of Promise and Despair: Chronicles of Early California, 1535–1846* (Berkeley, CA:

The Daughters of Charity continued to reach out to benefactors from several different ethnic groups in the early twentieth century, notably the middle- and upper-class immigrants who fled the war-ravaged regions of Mexico. After the 1914 flood, four young women from St. Vincent's Parish visited the orphanage, offering their services and support for flood victims. As one sister described, Emilia Taylor, María Armendáriz, Ana McManus, and María de Jesús Espinosa "were anxious to form a society of the Ladies of Charity to work among the Mexicans." Sister Cecilia Craine gave each young woman a rosary and a Miraculous Medal, and the sister-author hoped that "God might grant them the grace of vocation."[22] The young women founded a sewing circle, offering poor Mexican women an opportunity to sew clothing for their families at the orphanage, while also encouraging them to practice their religion.[23]

The society grew slowly until Armendáriz met several granddaughters of General Luis Terrazas who happened to be staying at the same hotel in 1919. Revolutionaries had expelled the long-time governor of Chihuahua and patriarch of the family's economic empire from Mexico in 1912. Of Terrazas' fourteen children and seventy-one grandchildren, many fled to Los Angeles to avoid capture and violence.[24] The Terrazas family had extensive experience in charity work in Chihuahua, and their interest reinvigorated the Ladies of Charity. Daniel Riofrio, C.M., arranged a tour of the orphanage for the Mexican young women who belonged to St. Vincent's Parish, and afterwards, they reorganized the association as *Las Señoritas de la Caridad,* or Young Ladies of Charity. They elected María Armendáriz as president, and Riofrio became their spiritual advisor. Ninety-five young women

---

Heyday Books, 2001), 485; Douglas Monroy, "The Creation and Re-creation of Californio Society," in *Contested Eden: California Before the Gold Rush*, eds. Ramón A. Gutiérrez, Richard J. Orsi (Berkeley, CA: Published in association with the California Historical Society by University of California Press, 1998), 173–195; Eileen V. Wallis, "Keeping the Old Tradition Alive: Spanish-Mexican Club Women in Southern California, 1880–1940," *Southern California Quarterly* 91, no. 2 (2009): 133–154. For more on the economic consequences of American conquest on Spanish-Mexican families, see Leonard Pitt, *The Decline of the Californios: A Social History of the Spanish-speaking Californians, 1846–1890* (Berkeley, CA: University of California Press, 1970); Richard Griswold del Castillo, *The Los Angeles Barrio, 1850–1890: A Social History* (Berkeley, CA: University of California Press, 1979).

22. "California," 56.
23. Ibid.; "Las Señoritas de La Caridad," *Tidings*, December 12, 1919.
24. Luis Terrazas was governor of the Mexican state of Chihuahua from 1860–1873, 1879–1884, and 1903–1907. Terrazas used his political connections to amass an economic empire that included 3.5 million acres of land, a large cattle-raising operation, textile manufacturing and food processing plants, banking, and other enterprises. He was related either by blood or marriage to the state's wealthiest families and his sons and sons-in-law managed his vast empire. Mark Wasserman, *Capitalists, Caciques, and Revolution: The Native Elite and Foreign Enterprise in Chihuahua, Mexico, 1854–1911* (Chapel Hill, NC: University of North Carolina Press, 1984), 27–32, 43–70, 165.

enrolled between August and December 1919, including fifteen of the Terrazas granddaughters, of whom one, Ester Urueta, served as secretary. Like the Terrazas family, the other young women of *Las Señoritas* were born in Mexico, and all those identifiable in the census had immigrated to the United States since 1913. All but one young woman were between the ages of sixteen and thirty-one. Many lived with widowed mothers, a few had household servants, and all could read and write.[25] As Sister Cecilia Craine noted, these middle- and upper-class young women "have time and money at their disposal, which they are happy to employ for the benefit of their countrywomen."[26]

Las Señoritas functioned as a charity organization and a social group. Each member paid twenty-five cents per month, which, along with other donations, bought fabric for the Mexican women who wished to come to the orphanage on Wednesday afternoons and sew clothing for themselves or their children. In October 1919, about fifty women from the neighborhood participated in the project, and *Las Señoritas* taught catechism to seventy-five children at the same time. Craine noted that the young women taught the children their prayers *in English,* suggesting that some, if not most, members of the society were fluent in the language.[27] Besides the sewing circle, the association also sponsored a choir, and they may have participated at the Mass celebrating the feast of Our Lady of Guadalupe at St. Vincent's Church.[28] *Las Señoritas* gave recent immigrants an opportunity to demonstrate their respectability, display their talents, and practice their faith. As Timothy Matovina demonstrates, pious societies like *Las Señoritas* also provided culturally acceptable venues for socializing and space for women to develop leadership skills and a degree of autonomy.[29] The Daughters of

---

25. Estela Yberri, the oldest member at age thirty-one, lived with her widowed mother, two sisters, and her sisters' children. Yberri came to the United States in 1918. Margarita Gaxiola, the youngest at age ten, was likely admitted because her two older sisters, Beatrix (age eighteen) and Graciela (age seventeen) were also members. The Gaxiolas also came to the United States in 1918. "Mexican Young Ladies Heed the Voice of Charity," *Tidings*, August 29, 1919; "Las Señoritas de La Caridad," *Tidings*, December 12, 1919; *U.S. Census, Los Angeles, 1920*; *U.S. Census, Los Angeles, 1930*; Wasserman, *Capitalists, Caciques, and Revolution*, 167–170.

26. "Letter of the Sister Servant of the Orphan Asylum at Los Angeles California to Our Most Honored Mother, October 30, 1919," *Annals of the Congregation of the Mission: Letters from the Missionaries and the Daughters of Charity* 27, no. 2 (1920): 280.

27. "The Spanish Ladies of Charity," *Tidings*, October 31, 1919; "Letter of the Sister Servant of the Orphan Asylum at Los Angeles California to Our Most Honored Mother, October 30, 1919," 280.

28. "The Spanish Ladies of Charity," *Tidings*, October 31, 1919; "Festival of Our Lady of Guadalupe Celebrated," *Tidings*, December 19, 1919.

29. Timothy M. Matovina, *Guadalupe and Her Faithful: Latino Catholics in San Antonio, from Colonial Origins to the Present* (Baltimore: Johns Hopkins University Press, 2005),

Charity encouraged *Las Señoritas* to provide direct service to the poor, interacting with the women and children who attended sewing circles and catechism classes, rather than just donating money. In this way, the Daughters acted as intermediaries between individuals who shared a common religious and cultural heritage, but different class backgrounds.

Ethnic rivalries remained prevalent within the U.S. Catholic Church during the late nineteenth and early twentieth centuries. Although adherents shared a commitment to Catholicism, other loyalties competed for attention and members had to negotiate the varying claims of ethnicity, language, nationality, and class as they practiced their faith. Historically, U.S. bishops organized ethnic or "national" parishes to accommodate the needs of immigrants who sought to preserve their language and culture. Some congregations of religious women also founded hospitals, orphanages, and schools to serve particular ethnic communities.[30] Susan S. Walton and Deborah A. Skok also illustrate the complicated interplay of religion and class in Catholic charitable endeavors. In Boston, Walton claims that class biases crept into the work of the St. Vincent de Paul Society, as "they preached not just Christian love, but middle-class respectability."[31] Leaders sought to promote Catholic unity and strengthen Catholic identity through their charitable network, but they also looked outward, wanting to demonstrate that Catholics had a distinct, yet equal, place in society. These dual goals often had contradictory results and could lead to an ambivalent attitude towards the poor.[32] In contrast, Skok asserts that settlement work in Chicago demonstrates that cross-class cooperation boosted the fortunes of the Catholic community as a whole. Settlement leaders relied on the labor of upper-, middle-, and working-class women for institutional survival, and leaders often parlayed their experiences into professional opportunities in government welfare agencies

---

112, 114. See also Roberto R. Treviño, *The Church in the Barrio: Mexican American Ethno-Catholicism in Houston* (Chapel Hill, NC: University of North Carolina Press, 2006), 70–71, 127–153, 168–171.

30. George C. Stewart, *Marvels of Charity: A History of American Sisters and Nuns* (Huntington, IN: Our Sunday Visitor, 1994), 270–308; Stephen Joseph Shaw, "The Cities and the Plains, a Home for God's People: A History of the Catholic Parish in the Midwest," in *The American Catholic Parish: A History from 1850 to the Present*, ed. Jay P. Dolan (New York: Paulist Press, 1987), 306–317, 333–345; Maureen Fitzgerald, *Habits of Compassion: Irish Catholic Nuns and the Origins of New York's Welfare System, 1830–1920* (Urbana, IL: University of Illinois Press, 2006), 156–162; Dolan, *In Search of American Catholicism*, 90–99, 136–146. See also Stephen Joseph Shaw, *The Catholic Parish as a Way-station of Ethnicity and Americanization: Chicago's Germans and Italians, 1903–1939* (Brooklyn, NY: Carlson Pub., 1991); Dolores Ann Liptak, RSM, *Immigrants and Their Church* (New York; London: Macmillan; Collier Macmillan Publishers, 1989).

31. Susan S. Walton, *To Preserve the Faith: Catholic Charities in Boston, 1870–1930* (New York: Garland Publishing, 1993), 100.

32. Ibid., 1–7, 106–108, 127, 145–152, 162–168.

to continue aiding Catholics in need.³³ As these scholars suggest, relationships between nation, religion, and class are intricately linked, but an individual's response to these differences could vary based on their relative importance in a given set of historical circumstances.

Furthermore, a woman's identity as a consecrated member of a religious community could also shape her perspective on social differences. In her study of the *Petites Franciscaines de Marie* (PFM), Florence Mae Waldron argues that these women selectively used their individual national identities as Americans, Canadians, or French Canadians as needed to serve their community in the late nineteenth and early twentieth centuries. Unlike Father Joseph Brouillet, who fiercely defended what he saw as French Canadian Catholic interests in Worcester, Massachusetts, Waldron argues that for the PFM "such national allegiances in and of themselves were not a direct route to power, influence, or the ability to make a difference in either Quebec or New England at the time."³⁴ Their identity as Catholic nuns retained the utmost importance; other allegiances were subsumed underneath this umbrella. National identities served as tools employed as needed to accomplish their mission.³⁵ While not applicable for all sisters, Waldron's assessment provides a lens from which to view the "co-constitution" of identities for communities of religious women founded in the United States. Race, cultural heritage, and citizenship matter, but not as much as one's commitment to Christ and service to and through the religious community.

In evaluating the actions of the Daughters of Charity in Los Angeles from the foregoing perspective, mission comes first. These women committed to assist those in temporal or spiritual distress, whether sheltering flood victims or teaching children the fundamentals of their faith. The sisters fostered the charitable impulses of the *Las Señoritas* and encouraged others to put personal differences aside in order to better serve poor persons. However, these conclusions must be qualified. The sisters' accounts cited here were intended for *public* consumption, at least among Daughters of Charity serving in the United States. An unnamed sister, most likely Sister Cecilia Craine, reported these activities to James J. Sullivan, C.M., the director of the Daughters of Charity Western Province of the United States (1910–1927). An edited version of the letter was reprinted in *Annals of the Congregation of the Mission: Letters from the Missionaries and Daughters of Charity*, a quarterly publication printed at St. Joseph's House in Emmitsburg, Mary-

---

33. Skok, *More Than Neighbors*, 4–9.
34. Florence Mae Waldron, "Re-Evaluating the Role of 'National' Identities in the American Catholic Church at the Turn of the Twentieth Century: The Case of Les Petites Franciscaines De Marie (PFM)," *The Catholic Historical Review* 95, no. 3 (July 2009): 535.
35. Ibid., 535, 539–541.

land. Distributed throughout the United States, the publication aimed to edify and strengthen other members of the religious community. Editors selected narratives that reflected ideal attributes of a Daughter of Charity, particularly a commitment to aid those in poverty, regardless of race or creed. Accounts of individual sisters struggling to live up to these standards seldom appear. Nevertheless, the sisters' published reports demonstrate that they chose to cross cultural and racial boundaries, emphasizing their responsibility as *sisters* to serve all who were in need.

Interestingly, the unpublished letter suggests that the dualities Walton identified in Boston also existed in Los Angeles in the 1910s. Certainly, Daughters of Charity looked inward by caring for Mexican Catholics, providing relief for their physical and spiritual needs. But they also looked outward, considering Catholics' overall place within the city's charity circles. The letter suggests that the sisters felt a degree of satisfaction—perhaps, even triumph—when flood victims preferred their ministrations to those of their Protestant counterparts. The author also expressed surprise when Dr. Milbank Johnson, director of the Municipal Charities Commission, asked the Daughters to house flood victims and offered to reimburse their expenses, since he led the "honorable board that has been giving us so much trouble and annoyance the past few months inspecting us and everything around here."[36] Someone excised this comment before the letter was printed in the *Annals,* but it indicates that some friction existed between city charity leaders and the Daughters, and that at last, Johnson recognized the valuable contribution that sisters made to the city.

Americanization and the Japanese Community

Consistent with their philosophy to serve poor persons regardless of race or creed, the Daughters of Charity did not limit their work to Mexican immigrants. Between 1915 and 1920, the sisters also became involved with Los Angeles' Japanese community. After the Chinese Exclusion Act of 1882, Japanese immigrants started to fill California's insatiable demand for labor. As Ronald Takaki notes, the Japanese population in the United States grew from

---

36. Unnamed Sister to J.J. Sullivan, CM, February 22, 1914, 3, Maryvale Historical Collection, Box 2, Folder 13, MHC. In October 1913, Johnson started to develop a plan to consolidate the funding for charity organizations in Los Angeles, and he intended to investigate all charitable institutions and learn about their operations. "Public Session Today: Municipal Charities Commission to meet at City Hall to Discuss Betterment Plans," *Los Angeles Times,* October 14, 1913. Earlier in the year, County Health Officer E.O. Sawyer called for inspections of all orphan asylums in Los Angeles County located outside the city limits (of which the Los Angeles Orphan Asylum was the most notable), charging that "Conditions are bad," and that they improperly handled the adoption of babies. See "To Regulate Orphanages," *Los Angeles Times,* February 4, 1913.

72,257 to 138,834 between 1900 and 1920, and most lived on the Pacific Coast. According to Brian Hayashi, the Japanese community in Los Angeles also grew dramatically, from less than 200 in 1900 to more than 11,000 two decades later. He notes that Los Angeles County had the largest Japanese community in the contiguous forty-eight states by 1930.[37] *Issei* (first-generation immigrants) and *Nisei* (second-generation) found economic niches in agriculture and established small businesses, including hotels, restaurants, laundries, poolrooms, and grocery stores. Because the Alien Land Laws (1913 and 1920) limited the ability of those deemed "ineligible for citizenship" to lease or own property, *Issei* farmers tended to specialize in short-term crops like berries or vegetables, which they trucked from El Monte and other outlying regions to sell in the city's markets.[38] Although these farmers formed an important part of California's agricultural economy, Japanese residents often struggled against social and legal discrimination. Japanese were regularly called names, spat on in the streets, and refused services. Like Mexicans and the Chinese, public health officials regarded the Japanese as potential sources of disease. According to officials, this new "yellow peril" could be more dangerous than the Chinese because Japanese farmers were intimately linked to the city's food supply.[39] Along with other non-whites, Japanese immigrants struggled to create a place for themselves in an Anglo-dominated society.

Even so, missionaries, settlement workers, and other "Americanizers" sought to include Japanese immigrants and their children in their pluralist vision. Although tacitly understood that non-whites would remain in a subordinate position, Mark Wild argues that missionaries and settlement workers "all hoped to incorporate immigrants . . . into a larger 'American society' anchored in Anglo-American traditions, language, living standards, patriotism, and, sometimes, Christian beliefs."[40] However, all immigrants were not equal, and California Commission on Immigration and Housing officials often employed hierarchies of race. European immigrants had the most potential to assimilate, although Wild notes that as business owners, Japanese immigrants' reputation for industriousness placed them higher on the ladder than Mexicans, Chinese, and African Americans.[41]

---

37. Brian Masaru Hayashi, *For the Sake of our Japanese Brethren: Assimilation, Nationalism, and Protestantism among the Japanese of Los Angeles, 1895–1942* (Stanford, CA: Stanford University Press, 1995), 3–4; Ronald T. Takaki, *Strangers from a Different Shore: A History of Asian Americans*, updated and revised ed. (Boston: Little, Brown, 1998), 180–181.
38. Takaki, *Strangers from a Different Shore*, 186, 189–194, 203–212.
39. Natalia Molina, *Fit to be Citizens?: Public Health and Race in Los Angeles, 1879–1939* (Berkeley, CA: University of California Press, 2006), 55–60; Takaki, *Strangers from a Different Shore*, 181–182.
40. Wild, *Street Meeting*, 72.
41. Wild, *Street Meeting*, 50.

The Catholic Church became more attentive Japanese immigrants' needs in the 1910s. Father Albert Breton ministered to the small Japanese Catholic community through St. Xavier Francis Mission.[42] The Daughters of Charity first became involved in the work in 1915, when Breton invited four women from *Aikukai*, a lay religious organization in Kagoshima, Japan, to teach catechism to Japanese-American children in Los Angeles.[43] Known as the Order of Visitation or *Homonkai*, four additional women joined the original sisters over the next three or four years. Led by Margaret Matsumoto, the Japanese sisters established a kindergarten and primary school in Little Tokyo.[44] Although not yet officially recognized as a religious community, these women patterned their religious life after the Daughters of Charity. Upon their arrival, Breton took the Japanese sisters to visit the Daughters of Charity. The sisters made habits for the Japanese women, a blue dress and a "black veil with a white border."[45] Although the blue dress was likely made of the same material as the habits of the Daughters of Charity, the Japanese sisters did not take the cornette headdress or have any official ties with the religious community. Breton hoped to establish an official community for Japanese sisters, one "adapted to their nationality."[46]

Besides offering material aid to the *Homonkai*, the Daughters of Charity also became involved in their educational outreach programs. In 1919, Breton asked the Daughters to assign two sisters to teach classes at the *Homonkai* school. Breton hoped to attract students by teaching English, while also exposing them to a Catholic environment. Since the *Homonkai* sisters spoke little or

---

42. See Michael E. Engh, SJ, "From the City of Angels," 46–47. Yuki Yamazaki, "St. Francis Xavier School: Acculturation and Enculturation of Japanese Americans in Los Angeles, 1921–1945," *U.S. Catholic Historian* 18, no. 1 (2000): 56–57.

43. Because of Japanese immigration patterns, few *Issei* immigrated to the United States as children. Between 1890 and 1908 most Japanese immigrants to the United States were men. Under the Gentlemen's Agreement, the Japanese government stopped issuing passports to laborers, but it continued to allow wives, children, and parents to emigrate until 1924. In 1920, twenty-nine percent of the 71,000 people of Japanese descent living in California were born in the United States. Many of them were children, so it is likely that most, if not all, of the students attending St. Xavier Francis School were Japanese American. David Yoo, *Growing up Nisei: Race, Generation, and Culture Among Japanese Americans of California, 1924–49* (Urbana, IL: University of Illinois Press, 2000), 3–5.

44. Harry K. Honda, "The Maryknoll Story in Little Tokyo, Little Tokyo Historical Society Meeting, March 24, 2007, at the Japanese American Cultural and Community Center, Los Angeles," 1–2, Japanese American National Museum, Los Angeles. Transcript available at www.discovernikkei.org. Michael Engh lists the names of the original four sisters as Sue Matsumoto, Toi Oe, Eki Fujisawa, and Tsui Yamano. See Engh, "From the City of Angels," 47.

45. "Letter of the Sister Servant of the Orphan Asylum at Los Angeles California to our Most Honored Mother, October 30, 1919," 278. See also Hannefin, *Daughters of the Church*, 205–206.

46. "Letter of the Sister Servant of the Orphan Asylum at Los Angeles California to our Most Honored Mother, October 30, 1919," 278.

St. Francis Xavier School, Los Angeles, from *The Field Afar*, October 1920 (Courtesy of the Maryknoll Mission Archives, Maryknoll, New York).

no English, Breton charged them with teaching catechism to students in Japanese after Mass. But he needed English-speaking teachers to make the overall program work. The Daughters agreed to supply two sisters on a temporary basis. Visitatrix Eugenia Fealy, superior of all Daughters of Charity in the western United States, assigned Sisters Zoe Reid and Stephanie Lynch, both experienced teachers, to the Japanese school. At age forty-nine, Sister Zoe Reid had served in a school or orphan asylum for twenty-five years, and Sister Stephanie Lynch had seven years of teaching experience.[47]

---

47. Albert Breton to Eugenia Fealy, DC, Los Angeles, August 5, 1919, MHC. Copy consulted in Maryvale Collection, SVMCHC. "Letter of the Sister Servant of the Orphan Asylum at Los Angeles California to our Most Honored Mother, October 30, 1919," 279. Born in Toronto, Canada, on March 25, 1870, Sister Zoe (Mary) Reid entered the community of the Daughters of Charity in 1894. She served at St. Columba's School in Chicago, St. Rose's Asylum in Milwaukee, and St. Stephen's School in New Orleans before coming to Los Angeles. Sister Stephanie (Leonora) Lynch, born in New Orleans on July 24, 1892, entered the Daughters of Charity in 1911, and started teaching at the Holy Cross School in Santa Cruz, California in 1912. "Zoe Reid, DC," entry in Daughters of Charity Database, Archives

To assist in their duties, Reid and Lynch enrolled in an Americanization course offered by the University of California Extension Division in November 1919. Along with one hundred other Catholic volunteers, Reid and Lynch learned strategies for teaching English as a second language and techniques used in the Home Teacher program, focusing on teaching American cooking, health, and hygiene practices to immigrant mothers and their children. Lecturers also addressed topics such as housing problems, sanitation, citizenship, and industrial management.[48] During the previous year, Bishop Cantwell secured a $50,000 grant from the National Catholic War Council (NCWC) to conduct Americanization work within the diocese, and the university course acted as part of this program. The diocese also established a branch office under the direction of the local Bureau of Catholic Charities with the stated purpose of organizing Americanization efforts.[49] The bishop's endorsement of the university's Americanization course and the sisters' participation therein shows some willingness to adapt secular methods to Catholic needs.

Reid and Lynch managed the school, consisting of a day nursery, kindergarten, and classes for the first, second, and third grades. The *Homonkai* sisters supervised the day nursery and instructed the children in Japanese, while Reid and Lynch taught English to the Japanese sisters and their students. Sister Cecelia Craine reported that the Japanese sisters "learn[ed] with astonishing facility," but Reid became frustrated with the children's limited progress at the beginning of the school year, noting, "Our Japanese are very slow and it will take a long time to make them like our own children."[50] From her letters, she appeared a little overwhelmed with sixty kindergarteners, but Reid immediately connected with some older children, describing seven-year-old Marjorie Yamamoto as "a little saint."[51] Over the course of the year, Reid and Lynch developed a love for the children, but their letters elicit some of the paternalism typical of the day by referring to the children as "our little Japs" and "poor little pagans."[52]

---

of the Daughters of Charity Province of St. Louise, St. Louis Campus, St. Louis, Missouri. "Stephanie Lynch, DC," entry in Daughters of Charity Database, Archives of the Daughters of Charity Province of St. Louise, St. Louis Campus, St. Louis, Missouri.

48. "Training Course for Americanization Workers," *Tidings*, October 24, 1919.

49. Engh, "Female, Catholic, and Progressive," 120; "For Extending Work of Americanization," *Los Angeles Times*, December 14, 1919; "Many Attend Course on Americanization," *Los Angeles Times*, November 24, 1919; Craine to Williams, July 13, 1920, SVMCHC.

50. "Letter of the Sister Servant of the Orphan Asylum at Los Angeles California to our Most Honored Mother, October 30, 1919," 279; Zoe Reid, DC, to Eugenia Fealy, DC, Los Angeles, September 9, 1919, MHC. Copy consulted in Maryvale Collection at SVMCHC.

51. Zoe Reid, DC, to Eugenia Fealy, DC, September 9, 1919, MHC. Copy consulted at SVMCHC.

52. Zoe Reid, DC, to Eugenia Fealy, DC, July 22, 1920, MHC. Copy consulted at SVMCHC; Stephanie Lynch, DC, to Eugenia Fealy, DC, March 10, 1920, MHC. Copy consulted at SVMCHC.

As a missionary endeavor, St. Francis Xavier School did not limit its services to Japanese Catholics. Breton purposely reached out to non-Catholics and non-Christians through the school, and about twenty of the 125 students were baptized by the end of the academic year.[53] The school drew students from throughout the county, and Breton hired a driver to transport the children to and from Little Tokyo. According to Reid, the route encompassed seventy-five miles, and some students did not return home until five o'clock in the evening.[54] The school provided valuable educational services, but Breton believed the "aim of [the work was] exclusively the conversion of pagan souls."[55] Actions of the Daughters of Charity mirrored Breton's spiritual focus, as they interacted with students' families whenever given an opportunity. Lynch even surreptitiously baptized an infant who was near death during a visit to one of her student's homes, an exceptional occurrence. Breton baptized other children during the course of the year, but he may not have been available at this particular time.[56]

Besides providing school teachers, the Daughters of Charity assisted the *Homonkai* in their fundraising activities. In 1919, Father Breton and some of the "charitable ladies" organized a festival to raise funds for the purchase of a new house for the Japanese sisters. Breton asked Craine to donate some of the refreshments. Despite their own financial struggles at the orphanage, she agreed to donate four hundred rolls made by the older students in the orphanage's bakery. While the other sisters "considered this too generous a gift," Craine believed that God would reward their generosity: "Do not worry," I said to them, "what we do for love of God for these Japanese, much poorer than we are, will not remain unrewarded."[57] The very same day, a Los Angeles baker sent 800 loaves of bread to the asylum, enough for the orphans and the Japanese sisters. The Japanese sisters purchased a home for $8,000, and Craine believed her efforts had done some good. She commented, "This is not the only occasion in which our Lord has given us sen-

---

53. Reid to Fealy, July 22, 1920, SVMCHC.
54. Reid to Fealy, September 9, 1919, SVMCHC; Craine to Williams, July 13, 1920, SVMCHC.
55. Breton to Fealy, August 5, 1919, SVMCHC.
56. Reid explained, "I asked Sister Stephanie, to go with the Japanese sister, to see the child and baptize him if the doctor said that there was no hope. The father would not bother the mother just then but promised to have him baptized when he got better. Poor sister did not know what to do, the mother would not let the child out of her arms, so Sister filled her handkerchief with water and baptized him while his mother thought she was cooling his head, that was about one o'clock, he was in heaven at four." Reid to Fealy, July 22, 1920, SVMCHC. Lynch reported that Breton baptized one of her second-graders when he was ill, and the child recovered and returned to school. Lynch to Fealy, March 10, 1920, SVMCHC.
57. "Letter of the Sister Servant of the Orphan Asylum at Los Angeles California to our Most Honored Mother, October 30, 1919," 279.

Father Albert Breton occasionally drove the St. Francis Xavier School Bus on its 75-mile route, from *The Field Afar*, June 1920 (Courtesy of the Maryknoll Mission Archives, Maryknoll, New York).

sible proofs of the value He attaches to the little service we are enabled to render to these dear Sisters."[58]

Despite its initial success, the collaboration between the Daughters and the *Homonkai* only lasted one year. After five years in Los Angeles, Father Breton wished to return to his work in Japan and he sought a more permanent arrangement for the St. Francis Xavier Mission. In 1919, he petitioned the Maryknoll Fathers to staff the Japanese mission in Los Angeles. Maryknoll, officially known as the Catholic Foreign Missionary Society of America, acted as a missionary arm of the Catholic Church in the United States. Besides sending missionaries to China, Maryknoll took responsibility for ministry to Japanese Catholics on the Pacific Coast. Assuming that this ministry would be a stepping stone to further missionary work in Japan, the religious community agreed to maintain Breton's mission in Los Angeles and they assigned two sisters to teach there in 1921.[59] Since the Japanese sisters

---

58. "Letter of the Sister Servant of the Orphan Asylum at Los Angeles California to our Most Honored Mother, October 30, 1919," 279–280.

59. Although Maryknoll originally included only men, Pope Benedict XV approved the formation of the Maryknoll Sisters by early 1920. Officially named the Foreign Mission Sisters of Saint Dominic, the Maryknoll sisters established a house of formation in Ossining, New York, headquarters for the Catholic Foreign Mission Society of America. Although Maryknoll was designed as a foreign mission society, the sisters' work was initially confined to the United States. Father Breton decided that the Japanese sisters' work in Los Angeles best fit the Maryknoll charism. "Papal Authorization for the Maryknoll Sisters," *Annals of the Congregation of the Mission: Letters from the Missionaries and the Daughters of Charity* 27, no. 1 (1920): 147–148.

were now formally associated with another religious community, the Daughters withdrew Reid and Lynch from the Japanese school, although they trained the Maryknoll sisters, neither of whom had teaching experience.[60]

The work of the Daughters of Charity with the *Homonkai* and the students at St. Francis Xavier School illustrate the sisters' willingness to cross racial and cultural boundaries to further their mission, whether by providing bread to the impoverished sisters for their fundraiser, educating students, or providing spiritual sustenance for children and their families. Sisters Zoe Reid and Stephanie Lynch used Americanization training as one tool in their established kit of teaching experience. Their efforts must have met with some success as the school grew from ninety-four to one hundred twenty-five students over the course of the year. Four students were Christian when they started the year; twenty had become Catholic by the end. Ten students regularly went to confession and three made their first communions.[61] Yet, Americanization at the mission school did not operate as a one-way street. The Daughters of Charity provided English instruction, but the *Homonkai* continued to support the students' language and culture. Parents likely sent their children to the school because students could learn English without completely relinquishing their cultural traditions. Yet, extant records do not reveal whether the Daughters' relationships with the Japanese sisters and students' parents were entirely harmonious. Lynch notes that one Japanese sister "felt rather suspicious of our methods of Americanization" after a frightened child made a disrespectful comment during a visit from an archbishop from Japan.[62] However, she does not elaborate on her relationship with the Japanese sisters, or comment on when or if, the issues were ever resolved. What her letters reveal, however, is a genuine desire to serve and affection for her students.

Conclusion

Religious identity played a pivotal role in the sisters' abilities to act as cultural intermediaries in the Mexican and Japanese communities during the early twentieth century. Recognized in their habits, the sisters were welcomed when Mexican residents turned away civic officials and Protestant missionaries. The sisters also harnessed the enthusiasm of young Mexican women to assist impoverished migrants by sewing clothing and teaching

---

60. Stephanie Lynch, DC, to Eugenia Fealy, DC, Los Angeles, July 22, 1920, MHC. Copy consulted in Maryvale Collection, SVMCHC.
61. Reid to Fealy, September 9, 1919, SVMCHC; Reid to Fealy, July 22, 1920, SVMCHC.
62. Lynch to Fealy, March 10, 1920.

Catholicism and English simultaneously. Laywomen did not just collect funds; sisters encouraged *Las Señoritas de la Caridad* to become actively involved in works of charity. At St. Francis Xavier School, sisters provided English instruction to Japanese American children and offered spiritual support within a Catholic environment. In both cases, the Daughters of Charity extended their service to those in poverty beyond the orphanage doors, continuing a tradition of working among the people of their assigned communities. In the process, the sisters built and maintained relationships with different segments of the community, reaching across cultural borders by emphasizing their religious identity.

But the question remains, did the Daughters of Charity see themselves as active agents of Americanization? Or, did they view their efforts as part of a long-standing tradition to offer charity without regard to race or creed? In their reports, the sisters framed their activities in terms of Americanization, thus conforming to the vision of the National Catholic War Council and the priorities of other Church leaders. In July 1920, Sister Cecilia Craine reported that "we have been engaged in Americanization work among the Mexicans for the past six years."[63] Two sisters taught catechism on Sunday afternoons and another supervised the *Las Señoritas*' sewing circle. She also noted, "On Fridays a Sister accompanied by a committee of ladies visits these poor people in their homes to teach them how to care for their children and manage their households as Americans do."[64] Though it is unclear if the "committee of ladies" included members of *Las Señoritas* or other Americanization workers trained by the Catholic Bureau of Charities, these efforts reflect popular trends in Americanization work at the time, while remaining firmly rooted in the teachings of Vincent de Paul and Louise de Marillac. Since the 1850s, the Daughters had acted as intermediaries between cultures, races, and classes in Los Angeles. De Paul and de Marillac founded the religious community so that sisters could provide assistance to the sick poor in their homes, so while discussions of household management and child-rearing may have been new, home visits were consistent with the sisters' religious traditions. They blended Americanization with long-established charity practices. The Daughters of Charity had also provided disaster relief by nursing Mexican and Native American smallpox victims in Los Angeles from the 1860s through the 1880s. Extending relief to flood victims in 1914 continued this tradition. By 1920, the Daughters of Charity had been actively involved in charitable efforts in the Californio-Mexican community in Los

---

63. Cecilia Craine, DC, to Michael Williams, July 13, 1920, Enclosure in Cecilia Craine, DC, to Eugenia Fealy, DC, July 13, 1920 in MHC. Copy consulted at SVMCHC.

64. Ibid. See also "Letter of the Sister Servant of the Orphan Asylum at Los Angeles California to Our Most Honored Mother, October 30, 1919."

Angeles for over sixty years. Whatever needs the Church had, the Daughters of Charity continued focusing on their core spiritual mission: service to those living in poverty.

Likewise, the Daughters of Charity taught *Las Señoritas* to give personal service to those in need. Middle- and upper-class Mexican women sewed with Mexican women from the poorer classes, as they sought to help their children understand their religious heritage and nurture their faith. Learning the language of prayer in English could foster their assimilation into the U.S. Catholic community and provide a foundation for economic advancement. *Las Señoritas* learned the sisters' lessons so well that they expanded beyond St. Vincent's Parish, taking up good works in other parts of the city, most notably teaching catechism at the new Catholic Social Center completed on the site of *El Hogar Feliz* in February 1920.[65] The Daughters sought to facilitate communication and foster relationships among those with differing class or ethnic backgrounds. Americanization served as a useful tool in their charitable service, not an end unto itself.

Furthermore, what did participation in Americanization work mean for *Las Señoritas*? Few, if any, of these young women were U.S. citizens, so why would they engage in activities to help immigrants assimilate into American society? I would suggest that these young women did not define their service in terms of Americanization. They sought to "devote their energies of youth, piety and education to serve their countrymen of the poor class" and to foil "religious seducers" trying to draw the immigrants away from the Catholic faith.[66] These young women taught catechism, not civics. If included in the sisters' home visits, they may have acted as translators rather than proffering advice on childrearing. While the bishop and the sisters placed *Las Señoritas'* service under the umbrella of Americanization, the young women saw it simply as an act of charity.

Interestingly, the young women's participation in these programs facilitated their assimilation into the Church in the U.S. Their membership provided a sense of purpose and a degree of social status within the parish. At its founding, the association's leaders met with Bishop Cantwell and received his approval to begin their work. He introduced them to Father William E. Corr, Bureau of Catholic Charities director. Since one of Corr's major projects was developing a network of Catholic social centers like the one at *El*

---

65. "Las Señoritas de La Caridad," *Tidings*, December 12, 1919; "Work at the Centers," *Tidings*, March 5, 1920.
66. "*Comunicaronse sus deseas de consagrar sus energías de juventud, de piedad y de educación al servicio de sus conterraneos de la clase pobre tan numerosa en Los Angeles y tan apetecida por los seductores religiosos;*" "Las Señoritas de La Caridad," *Tidings*, December 12, 1919.

Hogar Feliz, he likely invited *Las Señoritas* to teach catechism at the center. Cantwell and Corr attended the Mass to celebrate the feast of Our Lady of Guadalupe, where Cantwell blessed a picture of the virgin donated by members of St. Vincent's Parish. *Las Señoritas* garnered attention from church leadership, and their activities were reported in the diocesan newspaper.[67] Membership in the association provided recent immigrants with an entry point into Catholic society in Los Angeles. The sisters' supervision of the society facilitated this transition, and the Daughters of Charity continued their work as cultural intermediaries, not only for the poor, but for middle- and upper-class immigrants as well. Emphasizing their religious identity as *sisters* helped to mediate cultural differences between these women and other Catholics and allowed the Daughters of Charity to strengthen their relationship with at least two immigrant communities in Los Angeles. Although we do not always know how their actions were received, the sisters sought to construct a space where they could enact their vision of a compassionate and just society.

---

67. "Mexican Young Ladies Heed the Voice of Charity"; "Work at the Centers"; "Festival of Our Lady of Guadalupe Celebrated"; "The Spanish Ladies of Charity." Interestingly, when *Las Señoritas* sought to expand their work, they submitted an article to the *Tidings,* one of two articles printed in Spanish in the last half of 1919. The organization was seen as important enough to be included, though the newspaper primarily published in English. "Las Señoritas de La Caridad," *Tidings,* December 12, 1919.

Dorothy Day and César Chávez: American Catholic Lives in Nonviolence

Anne Klejment*

While Dorothy Day and César Chávez belonged to different generations and different ethnicities, they shared a profound commitment to religiously inspired nonviolent direct action. A comparative analysis of the lives of Day and Chávez finds that they shared the experience of poverty during childhood, activism as a young adult, the influence of a mentor at a crucial stage in their spiritual development, and an openness to cross denominational boundaries. These pioneer lay activists drew inspiration from the Bible, particularly the example of Jesus, papal encyclicals, the catechism, and the lives of saints. Additionally, the influence of Mohandas Gandhi and Protestant proponents of nonviolence shaped their spirituality and activism. Day and Chávez were dedicated to labor and economic justice, racial justice, and a world without war. During the tumultuous 1960s, Day's Catholic Worker movement and Chávez's United Farm Workers union found support from committed members and a larger group of lay, clerical, and religious supporters.

During the 1960s, a socially awakened U.S. Catholic laity would come to understand nonviolence as a powerful spiritual response to injustice. Many of them would regard its practice as legitimate, moral, and consistent with—even essential to—their faith. What factors contributed to this outpouring of Catholic activism? Papal social encyclicals and an ecclesiology that emphasized the universal nature of the Church continued to shape the social vision of Catholics in the 1960s. The rich teachings

---

*A version of this essay originally appeared in *U.S. Catholic Historian* 29, no. 3 (Summer 2011): 67–90. The author gratefully acknowledges the assistance of M. Christine Athans, BVM, Catherine Cory, Richard Gribble, CSC, Christine Igielski, Andrew Jacobs, Ann Kenne, Andrew J. Leet, Joanne Lucid, BVM, Timothy Matovina, James S. Rogers, Charles Schuman, Scott K. Wright and audience comments at the January 2011 American Historical Association and American Catholic Historical Association meeting.

of John XXIII, Paul VI, and Vatican II encouraged greater engagement with the modern world. The leadership of Dorothy Day and César Chávez was a vital catalyst which invited further lay involvement and a new appreciation of the Beatitudes and the Works of Mercy.

During the postwar era, American Catholics witnessed the efficacy of nonviolence in a newly nuclear world, first in Gandhi's campaign for an independent India, and later, with Martin Luther King, Jr. Together, they addressed racism, war, and imperialism. Better educated than previous generations of Catholics, better informed by the mass media, and beneficiaries of a growing economy, they were challenged to participate in this deeply spiritual quest for social justice. A Catholic president's call for sacrifice inspired their participation in projects of social reform and economic development at home and abroad.

At the moment when Catholics were showing unparalleled receptivity to the message of social activism, two of their co-religionists provided a living example of what nonviolent direct action might accomplish. Dorothy Day of the Catholic Worker movement, whose nonviolent "revolution of the heart" dated back to the 1930s, was creating a spiritual foundation for American Catholics to engage in nonviolent direct action in pursuit of justice in labor relations, international peace, and the dignity of the most marginalized human beings.[1] Her work enlarged Catholic conscientious objection and draft resistance during the Vietnam War, drawing the young to her movement, while César Chávez's grape and lettuce boycotts focused attention on the situation of farm workers.

By the early 1950s César Chávez had begun a campaign for the improvement of Mexican-American dignity through community organizing to address needs through political empowerment, such as voter registration initiatives. Prevented from engaging in union organizing by the sponsor of his community efforts, the Community Service Organization (CSO), Chávez abandoned secure employment in 1962 to found a union for farm workers, the majority of them Americans of color and many of them immigrants. At first Chávez's efforts were little known outside of California. During the Delano strike that began in 1965, his nonviolent campaign garnered considerable attention from the religious press and mass media. By 1968 Robert F.

---

1. Day's experience as a journalist enabled her to widely disseminate her spirituality of nonviolence and her critique of modern society. Not only had she edited and published the *Catholic Worker* paper, but she also wrote several books. Her autobiographical *The Long Loneliness* (1952) was widely available in inexpensive paperback editions as well as her account of Catholic Worker activities in *Loaves and Fishes* (1962). The peripatetic Day addressed large audiences, including college students. On certain campuses, attendance at her talk was mandatory (St. Mary's, Winona, Minnesota). Conversation with Thomas McCarver, January 2011.

Kennedy's presidential campaign and his support for Chávez's movement provided still greater visibility. Catholic school students could learn about the nonviolent activism of Day and Chávez in their courses. Activist students and professors supported the United Farm Workers (UFW) boycotts of non-union lettuce and Gallo wines.[2] As the head of the union, eventually known as the United Farm Workers, Chávez raised social awareness about agricultural laborers throughout North America and Europe, while demonstrating the effectiveness of nonviolence deeply rooted in his Mexican-American Catholic spirituality.[3] By the end of the 1960s, Chávez's nonviolent movement mobilized farm workers and multitudes of comfortable people, many of them young, eager to work for the movement or at least to uphold the grape boycott in solidarity with the *campesinos*.

As devout lay Catholics, Day and Chávez were formed by their faith in dialogue with their social environment. Having absorbed the message that human dignity originated in God's creation and that humanity was created "in the image and likeness of God," their words and deeds embodied the message of the ubiquitous Baltimore catechism and Jesus's teaching to love God and neighbor.[4] Their witness helped to empower American Catholics and others to move beyond an insular "Jesus and me" spirituality and a materialistic culture to meet their faith requirement to worship and live in socially responsible ways while working to enhance human dignity by challenging social and economic injustice. Two ordinary lay Catholics, representing different generations, ethnicities and classes, became activists and introduced Catholics to nonviolent direct action as an authentic Catholic way to engage in social change.

During this tumultuous era, lay Catholics increasingly challenged the political, social, and economic status quo as they protested injustices such as racial inequality, farm workers' conditions, and the Vietnam War. Lay Catholic activism had begun to take deep root during the Great Depression,[5] with Vat-

---

2. The author, a high school senior in 1968, was taught by the Sisters of St. Joseph (SSJ), some of whom championed progressive causes. The UFW fast was understood to be a "Catholic" event, as was the boycott. As a graduate student at the State University of New York at Binghamton, 1972–1976, the author remembers a rigidly enforced Gallo boycott and a contentious situation in dining halls, where labeled bowls of union and non-union lettuce appeared at the salad bar. Boycotting Gallo wine and non-union lettuce shaped the behavior of many students, professors, and ordinary Americans.

3. For an analysis of the mixed publicity of Catholic and Protestant magazines, see Andrew Jacobs, "Friends and Foes: Religious Publications and the Delano Grape Strike and Boycott (1965–1970)," *American Catholic Studies* 124 (Spring 2013): 23–42.

4. *A Catechism of Christian Doctrine No. 2 (Revised Edition of the Baltimore Catechism No. 2)* (Paterson, NJ: St. Anthony Guild Press, 1961), 9.

5. Day and Chávez practiced public activism that addressed political issues unlike earlier Catholic lay persons who created or worked within an exclusively Catholic domain. For late nineteenth and early twentieth century Catholic activism, see Deirdre M. Maloney, *American*

ican approved Catholic Action initiatives. During the 1930s Catholic initiatives addressed poverty, racism, and the exploitation of industrial workers, usually through prayer and modest explicitly and exclusively Catholic reform efforts. Thanks to the efforts of lay Catholic activists of the 1960s, such issues as war, racism, exploitation of agricultural workers, and sexism, for instance, penetrated American Catholic culture. Nonviolent lay Catholic activists boldly challenged the system: American government, capitalism, and white middle-class values. The Second Vatican Council itself helped to create a refreshing environment, open to renewal, ecumenism, and engagement with the world and infused greater numbers of the Catholic laity with a sense that nonviolent direct action, when grounded in Catholic practice, constituted an essential expression of faith.

The Early Life of Dorothy Day

Born in Brooklyn in 1897, Dorothy Day belonged to an earlier and possibly more rebellious generation than César Chávez. Hers was an up-and-coming White Anglo Saxon Protestant family, privileged by white skin, British Isles lineage, nominal Protestant identity, and middle-class status. Her forebears had fought proudly in the American Revolution and on both sides of the Civil War.[6]

John I. Day and Grace Satterlee Day, nonobservant mainline Protestants, privatized their religious belief. Years later, Day recalled that since childhood, the Bible had "meant much to me." She had discovered it on her own, "not by example of others" or from her parents. In the Day household, she mused, "To speak of religion, to bear [sic] one's soul was as bad as to bare one's body."[7] Progressive-era social gospel Christianity failed to appeal to the other members of her family.[8]

While the Days enjoyed class, ethnic, and race privileges over the Chávez family, the upwardly mobile Days did experience bouts of economic instabil-

---

Catholic Lay Groups and Transatlantic Social Reform in the Progressive Era (Chapel Hill: University of North Carolina Press, 2002) and Kathleen Sprows Cummings, *New Women of the Old Faith: Gender and American Catholicism in the Progressive Era* (Chapel Hill: University of North Carolina Press, 2009). David O'Brien's *American Catholics and Social Reform: The New Deal Years* (New York: Oxford University Press, 1968) represented a major scholarly step in interpreting the history of social Catholicism.

6. For a more detailed narrative relating to Day's early life, see Jim Forest, *All Is Grace: A Biography of Dorothy Day* (Maryknoll, NY: Orbis Books, 2011), 4–104.

7. Robert Ellsberg, ed., *The Duty of Delight: The Diaries of Dorothy Day* (Milwaukee: Marquette University Press, 2008), 514.

8. Essential sources on Day's early years include her fictionalized *Eleventh Virgin* (1924), *From Union Square to Rome* (1938), and, of course, *The Long Loneliness* (1952). Each follows a similar chronology but there are differences in interpretation since they were written over the course of thirty years.

ity. John Day worked his way up to positions as editor and sportswriter for large daily newspapers and to partner at Hialeah Race Track.[9] Although a white collar worker, he periodically faced unemployment. During these interludes, the Days lived in poorer neighborhoods and endured reduced circumstances. Relocating to better or worse neighborhoods in the same city, or other times crisscrossing the continent, the family's moves increased Dorothy's awareness of the fragility of the economy and of family prosperity. The move to Chicago's South Side from a tasteful Oakland bungalow meant that the family shared "a dingy, six-room flat," furnished with "curtains over fishing rods" and "stools out of nail kegs." People of humble means, their new neighbors, became more visible and human to Dorothy and her siblings, if not to her parents.[10]

Years after the devastating 1906 San Francisco earthquake, Dorothy Day recalled both the horror of the event and a positive outcome. The loss that had fractured economic activity and security had briefly led to the creation of a community of mutual concern. Neighbors in need helped each other during the disaster and temporarily broke through the barriers of the nuclear family. Day privileged this development as a vision of genuine Christian community otherwise lacking in white middle class society.[11] Despite her parents' lack of interest in social advocacy, several of her siblings supported social revolution as young adults. Dorothy Day alone developed a social conscience that responded to a gospel message that haunted her: Christ's command to love your neighbor.[12]

By the standards of the era, she was well educated, since she had attended the University of Illinois in Urbana-Champaign for two years. In lieu of college coursework, she substituted voracious and insightful reading of a broad range of literature of her choice, which she developed into a lifelong habit.[13] Already having absorbed the progressive ethos that experience can be a source of education, Day never completed college, preferring to live fully and to write authentically from experience whenever possible, or at least from close observation.

---

9. The 1900 U.S. Federal Census listed him as a "shipping clerk." By 1910 he had become an "editor." Accessed at Ancestry.com. Later in life, he covered horse racing, served on a state racing commission, and was a partner at a race track. See also William D. Miller, *Dorothy Day: A Biography* (San Francisco: Harper & Row, 1982), 2.
10. Day, *Long Loneliness*, 22–24, 26.
11. Ibid., 20–21.
12. For a deeper analysis of Day's adolescent spirituality, see Anne Klejment, "The Spirituality of Dorothy Day's Pacifism," *U.S. Catholic Historian* 27, no. 2 (Spring 2009): 2–4.
13. Day's journals and published writings mention a staggering selection of her readings about many subjects. Her letters document her less than enthusiastic appraisal of a college education.

An exposure to progressive and radical ideas and activism sparked Dorothy Day's desire to record, to advocate, and to participate in social change as an "advocacy journalist." Before she had turned twenty, she publicly opposed militarism, imperialism, and U.S. entry into the First World War. Comfortable with left wing socialists and anarchists, the so-called "Lyrical Left," she identified with rebels who discarded Victorian propriety in favor of social and sexual experimentation, cultural modernism, and socialism.[14] Impulsive to the core, the young radical approved of the limited use of force in class warfare and on occasion managed to defy bourgeois convention by defending her interests with her fists.[15] She rejected socialist politics that aimed to elect decent men like Eugene Debs to office. Instead, she preferred those anarchists, socialists, communists, and Wobblies (Industrial Workers of the World—IWW) who engaged in direct action, sometimes nonviolently, in order to demonstrate the democracy of action over the compromise of elective politics.[16] Wartime repression and romantic relationships temporarily shifted Day's priorities.

After the war's end, Day focused less on activism and more on finding domestic bliss. Long attracted to Catholicism, Day had her child baptized and, a year later, entered the Church herself in 1927. Conversion, Day feared, ended any possibility of working in the radical movement. While she struggled with her domestic partner—hoping for a marriage proposal—she searched for ways to support herself and her daughter and to find a way of living Christ's commandment to love while working for systemic change. The Church, as she knew, disapproved of communism and all of the other radical "isms" to which she had been attracted. Her young faith was challenged by the "scandal of business like priests." Quoting Romano Guardini on how "the Church is the Cross on which Christ was crucified," Day found to her dismay that the Church provided bountiful charity "but too little [support for] justice."[17] For five years she searched for a way to live her faith while remaining true to a radical sensibility that informed her faith and urged her to attack the roots of poverty, injustice, and inequality.

In the late 1920s, after having left the communist affiliate, All America Anti Imperialist League, Day found office work with the interdenominational

---

14. For an overview of the Lyrical Left, see John Diggins, *The Rise and Fall of the American Left* (New York: W.W. Norton, 1992), 93–143.
15. On Day's use of force, see Anne Klejment, "The Radical Origins of Catholic Pacifism: Dorothy Day and the Lyrical Left during World War I," in Anne Klejment and Nancy L. Roberts, eds., *American Catholic Pacifism* (Westport, CT: Praeger, 1996), especially 19–21.
16. Day's early connection to radicalism is explored in Klejment, "Spirituality of Pacifism," 4–11.
17. Day, *The Long Loneliness*, 150.

Fellowship of Reconciliation (FOR), which advocated opposition to war and promoted economic justice.[18] These were causes dear to Day's heart. Although its leaders were Protestants—and Catholics were trained to avoid their wiles—at least she was finally in touch with socially engaged Christians, including radicals who favored revolution. She shared their struggle to discern how to live the Christian law of love. Day wrote little about her work with the FOR, but there she discovered possibilities for an alternative radical Christian life dedicated to nonviolent social revolution on behalf of Christ's poor.

Before Mohandas Gandhi became widely known to Americans during his March to the Sea in 1930, a protest against salt tax and British imperialism in India, the Fellowship was helping to create America's "Gandhian moment." John Haynes Holmes had already figured in arranging for the first U.S. edition of Gandhi's autobiography.[19] Whether Day discovered Gandhi through her employment at the FOR is unclear. However, when it became available, she read Richard Gregg's work on Gandhian nonviolence, another effort by a FOR leader to popularize *satyagraha* (soul force), the approach of the century's most influential global advocate of direct action without force and discussed Gandhi's approach in *The Catholic Worker*.[20]

But how did these disparate influences relate to Catholic social teaching and spirituality? As an adult convert, Day had learned about Catholic attitudes toward charity, less about social justice. "I knew no work I could do within the framework of the Church," she lamented.[21] To find an answer, she needed a mentor.

Peter Maurin became her unlikely teacher. Literally the answer to a prayer whispered in the crypt of the unfinished National Shrine of the Immaculate Conception in Washington, D.C., Maurin had appeared at her door. A loquacious French immigrant, he was born in 1877 to a large peasant family in southern France. Once a Christian Brother and homesteader in the Canadian West, Maurin was subsisting on odd jobs. His life could not have been more different from Day's.[22]

---

18. Although Day mentioned FOR in her writings, her employment there was apparently so insignificant that an examination of the FOR records in the Swarthmore College Peace Collection did not document her presence. For a lucid discussion of the issues confronting the Fellowship of Reconciliation during the twenties and thirties, see Joseph Kip Kosek, *Acts of Conscience: Christian Nonviolence and Modern American Democracy* (New York: Columbia University Press, 2009), especially 49–145.
19. Kosek, *Acts of Conscience*, 85–87.
20. Ellsberg, ed., *The Duty of Delight: The Diaries of Dorothy Day*, 36. She found the newly published volume absorbing. "Up until one thirty last night," she confessed.
21. Quoted in Dorothy Day with Francis J. Sicius, *Peter Maurin: Apostle to the World* (Maryknoll, NY: Orbis Books, 2004), 38.
22. Day, *The Long Loneliness*, 171.

Having abandoned a life of respectability in Chicago as a teacher of French, Maurin began to proclaim the "Green Revolution," a nonviolent alternative society. He favored Catholic rural community and simple living over the bourgeois culture, alienated individualism, and finance capitalism of modern urban industrial society. Indifferent toward comfort, Maurin extolled communal Catholic society, rooted in a romantic understanding of medieval monasticism. A Union Square soapbox orator, Maurin sought out Day as a promising socially conscious Catholic journalist who could publicize the Green Revolution, after, of course, he had thoroughly indoctrinated her. Two papal encyclicals blessed Catholic efforts to establish social justice in modern society, Leo XIII's *Rerum Novarum* (1891) and Pius XI's *Quadragesimo Anno* (1931). Familiar with the statements of Catholic bishops, Maurin agreed with the nuanced positions that several pronounced on communism. By noting that they accepted communist criticism of rugged individualism, he assisted Dorothy Day's developing Catholic radicalism, which led to the founding of the Catholic Worker movement in 1933.[23]

In the first test of her vocation as a radical Catholic activist committed to nonviolence, Day acknowledged her earlier connection to secular radicalism and refused to demonize her former comrades. Well aware of popular anti-radical sentiment, government actions against radicals, and Catholic condemnation of communism, she scrupulously documented her earlier connections to American radicalism.[24] After launching the Catholic Worker movement, her positions on the economy, worker rights and civil rights, imperialism and war alarmed the most rabid anticommunists, since her positions resembled those taken by socialists and communists. Widespread Red-baiting did not weaken her resolve to engage in radical social criticism and activism inspired by the teachings of Christ.

The Spirituality of Nonviolence: Dorothy Day

Day found emerging movements within the Church that reinforced the teachings of Jesus and the catechism. Both the liturgical movement and Catholic Action, each rooted in Mystical Body theology, emphasized community, complete with mutual rights and obligations.[25] Informed and active

---

23. Peter Maurin, *Easy Essays* (1936) (London: Sheed and Ward, 1938), 56.
24. The FBI started compiling an extensive file on Day in September 1940 after she publicly opposed the military draft and shortly thereafter linked her to the Left as early as 1917. "Dorothy Day, Catholic Worker," FBI-FOIA, File Number 62–61208, volume 1, especially 100-7885, 2.
25. Mark and Louise Zwick, *The Catholic Worker Movement: Intellectual and Spiritual Origins* (New York: Paulist Press, 2005), 58–74, and Brigid O'Shea Merriman, OSF, *Searching for Christ: The Spirituality of Dorothy Day* (Notre Dame, IN: University of Notre Dame Press, 1994), 75–82.

participation at daily Mass provided a constant reminder that the Eucharist was a call to the baptized to sacrifice themselves for others. Catholic Action advocated by Pope Pius XI addressed how the laity might sacrifice for others by participating in Catholic programs that addressed pressing human needs. Living one's faith, she understood, continued after prayers were recited. Faith required action—here and now. Prayer and spiritual discipline were also essential.

Day's unshakeable belief in the unlimited power of grace supported her view that "weapons of the spirit," such as prayer and fasting, bested the weapons of force in ways often incomprehensible to human logic.[26] Prayer, she believed, was an underappreciated weapon of the spirit. "We can do nothing without prayer," she had discovered, and advocated private and communal prayer as essential elements in her nonviolent revolution.[27] By itself, without action, prayer insufficiently fulfilled one's Christian duty. Pray and work and leave the rest to God, since "'God can change things in the twinkling of an eye,'" Day believed.[28]

Day's spirituality, which revered "the little way" of St. Thérèse of Lisieux, the "Little Flower," advocated consistent daily practice of small acts of nonviolence as needed rather than the occasional heroic gesture. "Today," she wrote, "we are not content with little achievements, with small beginnings. We should look to . . . the Little Flower, to walk her little way, her way of love."[29] "Little way" spirituality minimized discouragement when activist efforts fell short of reaching a goal. Equally important, it challenged "American Way" ideology. At midcentury, this secular mindset, which seduced many American Catholics who had survived depression and war, measured success by such indicators as greatness and size. Numbers of followers, quantities of meals served—these meant little to Dorothy Day, since such calculations dehumanized Catholic Worker volunteers and guests. "Ours is not a turnstile charity," she declared.[30] Only faithfulness to the gospel of love counted.

World War II was considered necessary and just by the majority of American Catholics, including the hierarchy and clergy, but Day was one of the few who risked arrest as she refused to cooperate with the war effort. She

---

26. For a more thorough analysis of Day's spirituality of nonviolence, see Klejment, "Spirituality of Pacifism," especially, 13–23.
27. Quoted in William D. Miller, *All Is Grace* (Garden City, NY: Doubleday, 1987), 108.
28. Quoted in Martha Hennessy, "Afghan Youth Sow Peace," *Catholic Worker* (June-July 2011), 4.
29. Day quoted in Ellsberg, ed., *By Little and By Little: The Selected Writings of Dorothy Day* (New York: Orbis Books, 1983), 64.
30. Dorothy Day, *House of Hospitality* (New York: Sheed and Ward, 1939), 189.

proposed that Catholics use only spiritual weapons as their shield against enemies. Conscientious objectors and war resisters, who refused to register for the draft or be inducted into the military, found succor from the Catholic Worker. In the *Catholic Worker*, she urged war workers to quit their jobs. She criticized as inhumane and immoral the Japanese internment and the bombing of civilians.[31] Furthermore, the voluntary poverty of the Catholic Worker movement aided her program of noncooperation with the war effort, since Day would pay no federal income tax, part of which would have subsidized the war.

These positions resulted in division and defection from the movement and the paper's dramatic loss of circulation.[32] Worried about her unconventional patriotism, authorities in the New York Archdiocese invited her to discuss her controversial resistance to war.[33] And, of course, the FBI fielded letters from concerned Catholics, read her paper, and watched her movements, ready to pounce should she make a misstep. During the turmoil, the movement continued its soup line and shelter ministry without interruption. But church authorities and the government—as well as private citizens—remained uneasy about the orthodoxy, integrity, and legitimacy of Christian nonviolence in wartime.

In 1952, at the height of the cold war, Ammon Hennacy, the self-proclaimed "one-man revolution" arrived at the Catholic Worker in New York City. A lifelong anarchist and war resister, Hennacy took an especially creative approach to engaging in nonviolent protest, a tendency that matched his colorful, outsized personality. Day admired how he memorialized the incineration of Japanese civilians in 1945 with picketing and fasting each August. His creative nonviolence brought Day and the Catholic Worker into partnership with secular pacifists before such alliances were common among Catholic activists. At the same time, Catholic Worker Robert Ludlow influenced the movement by advancing a strong theological argument for nonviolence.[34] Despite elevated alarm over the threat of communism that perme-

---

31. The Catholic Worker "sought legitimacy" for its Catholic pacifism by featuring papal statements on war and peace, a series on why Catholics could be conscientious objectors, and a pamphlet on gospel pacifism, both written by priest scholars. See Patrick G. Coy, "Conscription and the Catholic Conscience during World War II," in Klejment and Roberts, eds., *Catholic Pacifism*, 47–63.

32. Francis J. Sicius, "Prophecy Faces Tradition: The Pacifist Debate during World War II," in Klejment and Roberts, eds., *Catholic Pacifism*, 66–76; Nancy L. Roberts, *Dorothy Day and the "Catholic Worker"* (Albany: State University of New York Press, 1984), 179–182, provides circulation figures for the thirties through the early eighties.

33. See Thomas A. Lynch, "Dorothy Day & Cardinal McIntyre: Not Poles Apart," *Church* (Summer 1992): 10–15.

34. Patricia McNeal, *Harder Than War: Catholic Peacemaking in Twentieth-Century America* (New Brunswick, NJ: Rutgers University Press, 1992), 76–78.

ated the nation, Day stunned college students with her answer concerning the prospect of a Russian invasion: "I hope I could open my heart to them with love. . . . We are all children of the same Father."[35]

By 1955, when authorities required citizens to take cover during air-raid drills, Day and other members of New York City's Catholic Worker and war resistance communities joined in Hennacy's organized refusal to obey the law. Year after year, Day and other protesters sat in place as the sirens wailed, defying the law and subjecting themselves to arrest. These inspired acts of nonviolent civil disobedience, which resulted in jail for Day, effectively ended the compulsory drills in 1961 and brought greater attention to the Catholic Worker's opposition to war as the American public was beginning to question the wisdom of the arms race. With a global outlook in favor of social justice and peace originating with Pope John XXIII, plus publicity from Day's civil disobedience, a small but growing number of Catholics, were opening themselves to the possibility of social change through nonviolent direct action.

To support the civil rights movement, the *Catholic Worker* publicized nonviolent campaigns and reported on conditions in the South.[36] Concerned about the bombings and racist threats against Koinonia farm in Georgia, an interracial intentional community of evangelical Christians, Day supported the community during the crisis with her pen and with her presence there during Lent in 1957. Expecting to "suffer exceedingly" because of missing Lenten religious services, instead, she discovered: "It is more important to live the Passion. . . ." Later during her stay, as she sat on night watch for three hours, she and her companion were shot at by racists in an automobile. "It is what I came for," she insisted, "to share in fear and suffering."[37]

Day's influence on lay Catholics peaked during the 1960s and early 1970s. Day published powerful articles by Thomas Merton that challenged conventional thinking about modern war. Despite cold war rhetoric and action during the Kennedy administration, Day visited Cuba to observe the fruits of the revolution. Joining with international pacifists, she traveled to Rome during the Second Vatican Council to pray, fast, and lobby for more enlightened church teaching on war and conscience rights. As American involvement in Southeast Asia mushroomed, Day put herself at risk of jail by declaring her active support for draft resisters, some of whom were her followers. When Fathers Philip and Daniel Berrigan took their nonviolent protest to a new level with the draft board raid, Day confronted her own

---

35. Quoted in Forest, *All Is Grace*, 323.
36. Day had insisted on integrated living at the Catholic Worker and for a time had a branch in Harlem.
37. Dorothy Day, "On Pilgrimage," *Catholic Worker* (May 1957), 3, 6.

Dorothy Day and Eileen Egan walk behind the United Farm Workers flag in support of striking vineyard workers in the Delano, California area, August 1973. Day was later arrested and jailed with other picketers (Courtesy of the Department of Special Collections, Stanford Libraries, Fitch Gallery).

views on nonviolence as she considered whether the destruction of property constituted nonviolent action.[38]

In 1973, Dorothy Day's last arrest took place in solidarity with César Chávez and the United Farm Workers (UFW) movement. For decades, readers of *The Catholic Worker* were kept informed about conditions of farm laborers. The paper published articles about urban and rural working conditions and letters in support of strikes and boycotts.[39] And Day reminded readers, "We too shared a little in that poverty having fasted from grapes and

---

38. On Day and the Berrigans, see McNeal, *Harder Than War*, 173–210. For a somewhat different view, see Anne Klejment, "War Resistance and Property Destruction: The Catonsville Nine Draft Board Raid and Catholic Worker Pacifism," in Patrick G. Coy, ed., *A Revolution of the Heart: Essays on the Catholic Worker* (Philadelphia: Temple University Press, 1988), especially 284–300. An in depth study of the Catholic Worker and the Vietnam War is needed, but for an introduction to the topic, see Anne Klejment and Nancy L. Roberts, "The Catholic Worker and the Vietnam War," in Klejment and Roberts, eds., *American Catholic Pacifism*, 153–169.

39. According to a search of the name "César Chávez" in articles written by Day, the first mention of his name came in 1966 in an article published in *Ave Maria* and the first in the paper came in the March/April 1967 issue. Accessed at http://www.catholicworker.org/dorothyday/. César Chávez's first message in the paper was published in the June 1966 issue,

now from iceberg lettuce to assist in the boycott." It was small deeds such as boycotting that were helping the farm workers. Seventy-five years old, Day went to the vineyards in Delano, seated on her "folding chair-cane." Protesting a court injunction intended to curtail UFW picketing, Day refused to move and went to jail for the last time. Her picketing and presence in jail was accompanied by prayer, to which she attributed some modest progress in the union negotiations, not unlike César Chávez.[40]

The Early Life of César Chávez

Arizona native César Chávez, born in 1927, a generation after Dorothy Day, was the grandchild and son of immigrant Mexicans. Although Mexico had ended slavery decades before the United States, *Papa Chayo*, as his paternal grandfather Césario Chávez was known, fled the virtual slavery of a large Chihuahua *hacienda*. There, the babies of workers at birth had each received a demeaning identification tag. Once tagged, the expenses incurred by the infant were recorded so that at the start of employment, the child had a debt to repay. *Papa Chayo* crossed the border into Texas sometime in the 1880s.[41] The Chávez family appreciated this courageous act of resistance in the larger Mexican revolutionary drama. Having settled his large family near Yuma, Arizona, Césario Chávez managed to gain a toehold on the land.

Devoutly Catholic in a traditional Mexican way, despite the twenty mile distance from church, César's paternal grandmother, Dorotea (*Mama Tella*), anchored Catholicism in her home. Having instructed César and his sister Rita in the catechism, his convent-educated *abuelita* (grandmother) prevailed over an initially skeptical priest, who had intended to refuse them their First Holy Communion. Bible and miracle stories enlivened evenings as César heard about God's continuing presence, from ancient times to the present, in distant lands and in local mines where faith saved relatives from accidents.

---

according to the author index in Anne Klejment and Alice Klejment, *Dorothy Day and 'The Catholic Worker": A Bibliography and Index* (New York, Garland: 1986), 374, 270.

40. Dorothy Day, "Chavez, Workers Step Up Boycott," *Catholic Worker* (March–April 1973) accessed at: http://www.catholicworker.org/dorothyday/, and Dorothy Day, "On Pilgrimage," *Catholic Worker* (September 1973) accessed at: http://www.catholicworker.org/dorothyday/.

41. The family dates his arrival back to the 1880s. However, U.S. Federal censuses for 1900 and 1910, available through Ancestry.com are at odds with the oral and published record. A person who appears to be his grandfather is referred to as Isidro and his date of arrival in the U.S., often approximate in census returns, is given as 1890. Although a number of excellent volumes have been published on Chávez, to date scholarly works are riddled with error, as Luis Léon noted in "César Chávez in American Religious Politics: Mapping the New Global Spiritual Line," *American Quarterly* 59 (2007), 858. Léon, however, is overly optimistic about the accuracy of oral history in overcoming the problem. An authoritative biography has not yet been published.

Juana Chávez, César's mother, passed to her children traditional Mexican Catholic spirituality, including a "strong . . . belief in the saints and the Virgin of Guadalupe." As a *curandera* (healer), skilled in the use of herbs, "she couldn't bear to see anyone in pain."[42] From boyhood, César learned that violence offended God. Rather than automatically resorting to violence, his mother repeatedly chided César that "eyes and mind and tongue" were gifts of God to "get [you] out of anything." Violence, she insisted, sinned against God because it denied the goodness of the Creator and creation. In another of her *consejos* (advices), her son learned that an accomplice must shoulder a share of moral responsibility, so best to avoid troublemakers.[43] These *consejos* built a foundation for nonviolence. Helping rather than hurting others defined her moral legacy.

The family's modest economic stability was destroyed during the depression. A small-scale entrepreneur, Librado Chávez, César's father, farmed and ran a pool hall, garage, and grocery store. Having liberally extended credit, he could not pay property taxes and interest. At auction, his neighbor, an unscrupulous Anglo banker who had refused him a loan, snapped up the property for a fraction of its value. Dispossessed and without means of a legal challenge, the family took to the road in the late thirties. In California César's family joined other impoverished migrant fieldworkers eking out a meager existence and often living in conditions that were hardly fit for humans.

For the marginalized Chávez family, their early successes, such as increasing land holdings and owning small businesses, were followed by an extended period of virtually inescapable poverty. Poverty and destitution in the Mexican-American community, largely a consequence of racism, constituted an entrenched barrier to success. Often, home was a shack in a *barrio* or tent in a migrant camp, a drastic drop from the relative security of their Arizona ranch. Chávez recalled that "cabins were just empty shells surrounded by mud."[44] For Mexican-American migrant laborers, hard work was not rewarded with upward mobility. The moves cost children and parents deep and lasting friendships. "When we left our farm," Chávez observed, "our whole life was upset, turned upside down. We had been part of a very stable community. . . . We had been uprooted."[45]

---

42. Quoted in Jacques E. Levy, ed., *César Chávez: Autobiography of La Causa*, (Minneapolis: University of Minnesota Press, 2007 edn.), 11. For a brief analysis of *curanderismo*, see Luis Léon, "'Soy una Curandera y Soy una Catolica,'" in Timothy Matovina and Gary Riebe-Estrella, SVD, eds., *Horizons of the Sacred: Mexican Traditions in U.S. Catholicism* (Ithaca, NY: Cornell University Press, 2002), 100–102.

43. Susan Ferriss and Ricardo Sandoval, *The Fight in the Fields: César Chávez and the Farmworkers Movement* (New York: Harcourt Brace, 1997), 13.

44. Levy, ed., *Autobiography*, 69.

45. Ibid., 42.

The Chávez family did not allow their destitution to justify indifference toward the needs of others. The children, working alongside their parents, witnessed Christian ethics put to the test—and were required to imitate the values of their parents. Librado Chávez regularly defied the exploitation of not only his own family but other farm workers. Employing such tactics as quitting, convincing other workers to leave with the aggrieved party, and supporting union activity, his actions provided a clear message of where a person of principle must stand: join together with others to fight oppression. Self-identifying as the "strikingest family" around, the family aimed to better the lot of all farm laborers rather than seek their own advantage. César explained that his family was "constantly fighting against things that most people would probably accept because they didn't have that kind of life we had in the beginning, that strong family life. . . ." Even if the grievance against a grower involved other migrant workers, the family supported others by leaving their job if a wrong was not corrected. "We learned that when you felt something was wrong," Chávez recalled, "you stood up to it."[46]

When Librado Chávez challenged unfair labor practices, César learned an unforgettable lesson in human dignity and labor solidarity. "Our dignity," he commented, "meant more than money."[47] His father's example of principled solidarity with other migrant families later inspired his vocation as an organizer.

Never was Juana Chávez without humble means to provide food, a place to stay, and other services for the destitute. "On the road, no matter how badly off we were, she would never let us pass a guy or a family in trouble," her son noted. Disregarding the cost of gasoline, she ordered her children to chauffeur the unfortunate to seek emergency aid that she could not provide. Aid was given at a sacrifice, not from superfluous wealth. Husband and wife grasped the Christian message of the dignity of the most humble people and understood how the poor depended upon each other.[48] César's parents set an example for their children by regularly practicing generous works of charity and working for justice, tangible symbols of their faith.

As a teenager, César quit school after the eighth grade to contribute to the family income. Dutiful toward family, he rebelled against certain aspects of Mexican American culture. He disdained the folk remedies employed by his mother. He forsook Mexican music for the jazz of Duke Ellington and Billy Eckstine. Although he maintained his faith, he refused to accept

---

46. Ibid., 78–79, 33.
47. Ibid., 78–79.
48. Ibid., 70. See especially Ibid., 3–80, for one of the best overviews of parental influence.

"ask[ing] the favor of a saint (*manda*) and promis[ing] to visit the chapel of the saint's church (*promesa*)."[49]

César Chávez also began to challenge racism. During the Jim Crow era, when racism was embedded in culture, law, and custom throughout the United States, in states like California, the brown skin of the Chávez family, immigrant and native-born alike, guaranteed them outsider status and second-class citizenship in the Anglo-dominated world. At school, which César disliked, teachers forced the boy to speak English, punishing him when he spoke Spanish, and they Americanized his given name, Césario. Harboring a strong sense of indignation toward injustice, César flouted the racial ideals of the white middle class. Like some of his peers, César adopted the zoot suit style of 1940s *pachucos*, a silent but visible fashion protest that occasionally "provoked" Anglo violence. "[A]ll we did," he explained, "was wear some of the *pachuco* clothes, the pegged pants and the long coat . . . and we had to be rebellious to do it, because the police and a few of the older people would harass us."[50] During his teen years, César began challenging both "embarrassing" aspects of Mexican culture and oppressive bourgeois customs.

At age seventeen, Chávez joined the Navy during World War II, signing up because of the "awesome power" of the government, a desire to avoid being drafted into the army, and the ambition "to get away from farm labor."[51] Fighting to protect democracy in his homeland and overseas, he developed a heightened sense of the injustice of laws and customs that discriminated against Mexican Americans. Like other Americans of color during World War II, he believed that military service had earned him the right to equal citizenship. These demands for equality would revolutionize the lives of Americans of color within the next few decades.[52] Chávez endured his first arrest and brief jailing during the war, when the emboldened sailor flouted the segregation law that relegated Mexicans and others to a separate section of California movie theaters.[53]

Although Chávez had managed to obtain a grade school education, a miraculous achievement for a migrant child, limited opportunity ranked him below the educational norms of the white middle class of the 1940s.[54] Dis-

---

49. Ibid., 81.
50. Ibid., 82.
51. Ibid., 84.
52. For a discussion of the impact of the war on Latinos, see Ronald Takaki's *Double Victory: A Multicultural History of America in World War II* (Boston: Little, Brown and Co., 2000), 82–110 and especially 84, for Takaki's analysis of Chávez's wartime transformation.
53. Levy, ed., *Autobiography*, 84–85.
54. Authors differ on his educational level. He stated, "I left school in the seventh grade." César Chávez and Jerome Ernst, "Cesar Chavez Speaks," *Ave Maria* (July 2, 1966), 15.

crimination would continue to restrict work opportunities. Married to Helen Fabela shortly after the war's end, Chávez's organizing and activism, backed by his wife, began in earnest several years later when he befriended a priest dedicated to social justice.

Chávez's mentor was young Irish-American priest, Donald McDonnell, who had received special permission from Archbishop John Mitty for a ministry to Mexican Americans in the Spanish Mission Band.[55] Despite criticism from the Los Angeles archdiocese concerning the activities in San Francisco of the activist clergy, Mitty firmly supported his priests and their work.[56] After serving as a parish priest and as a professor at St. Patrick's Seminary in Menlo Park, McDonnell was appointed Director of the Rural Life Conference, the position he held when he first met Chávez.[57]

Rejecting a ministry to prosperous Catholics and life in a comfortable rectory, the Spanish Mission Band priests lived among the Mexican Americans. So appalling were the living and working conditions of the migrants, that the band justified activism as integral to their spiritual duties. "The priest is a man of Christ. . . . He is the agent of God, and his mission is to save men's souls. Yet his very care for souls will sometimes lead him among men whose physical, moral and economic conditions have become not only highly conducive to vice, but also offensive to Christian customs and religious practice."[58]

McDonnell cultivated Chávez as a lay assistant. Fluent in Spanish and devoted to the Mexican-American community, the priest won over the young husband and father as a friend by living modestly alongside Mexicans and with his desire to address the problem of poverty within the *barrios*, labor camps, and jails.[59] By 1957 the band advocated unionization of farm workers. "The main effort of the Church," McDonnell advised Mitty, "should be directed to

---

55. On the Spanish Mission Band, see Jeffrey Burns, "Prelude to Reform: The Church in San Francisco before the Council," *U.S. Catholic Historian* 23, no. 4 (Fall 2005), especially 3–5.
56. Jeffrey Burns, "The Mexican Catholic Community in California," in Jay P. Dolan and Gilberto M. Hinojosa, *Mexican Americans and the Catholic Church, 1900–1965* (Notre Dame, IN: University of Notre Dame Press, 1994), 208.
57. A search of *The Official Catholic Directory* for the years 1950 through 1966 provided the chronology of McDonnell's ministry. The 1952 through 1961 volumes document his tenure heading the archdiocesan Rural Life Conference. Apparently with the arrival of Archbishop Joseph T. McGucken in late 1961, McDonnell was sent to Cuernavaca, Mexico for "intercultural formation." By 1966, the directory placed him in Brazil. Mark Day, a priest who later worked with Chávez suggested that pressure from the growers "curtailed" the work of the band. Mark Day, *Forty Acres: Cesar Chavez and the Farm Workers* (New York: Praeger, 1971), 54.
58. First Bracero Priest Conference (1957) as quoted in Burns, "Prelude," 4.
59. Day, *Forty*, 18.

insisting on the human dignity of the men who labor in the fields. . . ."[60] When the priest asked Mexican Americans if they wanted their own parish in the San Jose *barrio* "*Sal Si Puedes*" ["Escape If You Can"], Chávez readily assented. A former *crucero* (altar boy), he offered his services to McDonnell whenever the priest would say Mass on a portable altar in the *bracero* camps or at the jail. While accompanying the priest on his circuit, helping with outfitting the parish, or going to strikes, Chávez began to read and discuss Catholic social teachings and economics with his priest friend.[61]

They discussed the same social encyclicals that had inspired Dorothy Day—*Rerum Novarum* and *Quadragesimo Anno*. Both documents provided spiritual justification for claiming rights for laboring people, including the right for workers to organize a union, but neither outlined a specific method for procuring these human rights.

McDonnell engaged Chávez in an informal lecture, reading, and discussion program that focused on their shared interest in social justice. Chávez would be influenced by many of the same historical figures and documents that had shaped the thought of Dorothy Day. After mastering the encyclicals, Chávez read a life of St. Francis of Assisi. As he learned of the saint's nonviolent encounters with a Muslim prince and a fierce wolf, he was "moved" by the saint's nonviolent faith and bravery, a brand of masculinity that, like Juana Chávez's *consejos*, rejected the violence of *machismo*.[62]

Since the unnamed St. Francis biography had referred to Gandhi, who he first encountered in newsreels, Chávez devoured Louis Fischer's admiring biography of Gandhi. Inspired by the Mahatma's practice of requiring others to do only what he himself was willing to do, Chávez grasped the authenticity of Gandhi's actions for Christians. The Mahatma's self-discipline, such as fasting, and accepting suffering oneself without inflicting it on another, likewise resonated with Chávez's faith.

Drawing from an ecumenical library, César Chávez's spirituality of nonviolence meshed with Catholic teaching, the values of his family, and the organizing approach that Fred Ross would teach him. The priest introduced his friend to Ross, a savvy community organizer, who could train him as an activist.[63] Chávez credited Gandhi for teaching him "quite a bit," but he felt

---

60. Burns, "Prelude," 4.
61. Ferriss and Sandoval, *Fight*, 46.
62. Levy, ed., *Autobiography*, 91.
63. Frederick John Dalton, *The Moral Vision of César Chávez* (Maryknoll, NY: Orbis Books, 2003), 48–49. In the Spanish Mission Band, McDonnell partnered with Thomas McCullough. Both supported CSO efforts. Through the priests and CSO, Chávez would meet his future collaborator, Dolores Huerta.

more indebted to Ross, who taught him how to conduct a house meeting, drawing Mexican Americans together in a socially comfortable environment. To start his union, Chávez would perfect Ross's technique.[64] Founder of the Community Service Organization (CSO), Ross recruited Chávez as a community organizer in the San Jose barrio. Community organizing involved arranging voter registration drives, citizenship education, and campaigns to support reform policies needed by the Mexican American community. Chávez's dream, however, was to organize a farm workers union. In 1962 after the CSO voted down the idea, he resigned his position to free himself to start organizing a farm workers union. To gain union recognition by the politically powerful growers, he would blend Gandhian nonviolence, Mexican-American religious practices, and the home meeting technique.

Chávez furthered his knowledge of nonviolent tactics and strategy by following the efforts of civil rights leader, Martin Luther King, Jr., who used crisis as a tool to open negotiation with his opponents. From Montgomery onward, King set precedents that Chávez could borrow and adapt, as in the use of economic boycotts, marches, and civil disobedience. He especially admired King's ability to capture public support, get results, and resonate with Christian rhetoric and symbolism. Chávez heard about Day while he was organizing for the CSO, but he did not explain how Day and her movement influenced him.[65] He believed, however, as did Day, Gandhi, and King, that "each . . . person can make a difference."[66]

To build the union Chávez planned to employ nonviolent means. His job required first convincing migrant workers of the need for a union and then teaching them the moral superiority and efficacy of nonviolent practice. If the union were to succeed, public support would be crucial for exerting more pressure on growers. The example of King's civil rights movement suggested the wisdom of remaining true to his religious roots while welcoming all willing to organize, publicize, and provide support for the fledgling union.[67] In calling for public support, remaining grounded in his Catholic faith, but open to volunteers from all backgrounds who subscribed to his nonviolent principles, Chávez's approach bore similarities to Day's.

Chávez faced tremendous odds. The mobility of migrant workers and their precarious economic situation presented one set of challenges. The response of the growers created another. Many of them Catholics and sons

---

64. Levy, ed., *Autobiography*, 91–93, 97–102.
65. Ibid., 500.
66. Chávez, "Lessons of Dr. Martin Luther King, Jr.," at http://www.ufw.org.
67. Chávez did not explain how King's difficulties, such as his failed attempt to seek racial justice in Chicago, influenced his nonviolent tactics.

of immigrants, growers financially supported many rural California parishes, which depended on their contributions. Insinuations of communist influence in the UFW and the Catholic bishops' dependence on the good will and largesse of growers and their allies meant that Chávez could not automatically count on Catholic support. UFW strikes and boycotts alienated some members of the hierarchy as well as some consumers.[68] As Chávez developed his union and its social vision, he advocated for a society transformed by the empowerment of the poor and marginalized.

The Spirituality of Nonviolence: César Chávez

Sacred and secular influences contributed to César Chávez's profoundly Catholic spirituality of nonviolence. Among the valued elements of his spirituality were: the dignity of all persons; nonviolent resistance to injustice; popular Mexican religious symbols; and Catholic practices. Drawing from many of the same sources used by Dorothy Day, Chávez relied on such spiritual weapons as prayer, attendance at Mass and reception of communion, self-sacrifice and penitence, including fasting, and pilgrimage. The teachings of Gandhi, Ross, and King enabled Chávez to incorporate practical experiences into his nonviolent spirituality.

Juana Chávez's teachings on nonviolence and human dignity enabled her son to view Moses and Jesus as precedent-setting leaders of successful nonviolent movements against tyranny. Writing to one of the UFW's opponents, he chided him about the dignity of the poor who "are not saints because we are poor but . . . neither are we immoral." In God's eyes farm workers were not "beasts of burden" or "rented slaves." Chávez's nonviolent thought distinguished between an opponent and an enemy. Hating an enemy amounted to violence. He faulted the agribusiness system, rather than a human enemy, and vowed to change it. To protect human dignity, the movement engaged in nonviolent struggle, without "destruction of human life and property."[69]

Besides the spiritual qualities of nonviolence, he valued its practical merits. By practicing nonviolence, he believed, activists developed skills required for participation in a democratic society. Because nonviolent tactics

---

68. For different perspectives on Catholic support for the UFW, see Marco G. Prouty, *Cesar Chavez, the Catholic Bishops, and the Farmworkers' Struggle for Social Justice* (Tucson: University of Arizona Press, 2006); Day, *Forty Acres*; Levy, ed., *Autobiography*; Dalton, *Moral Vision*; Léon, "Religious Politics;" Gerald M. Costello, "The Farm Labor Movement," *U.S. Catholic Historian* 19, no. 4 (Fall 2001), 33–40; and Jacobs, "Friends and Foes."

69. César Chávez, "Good Friday Letter, 1969," in Richard J. Jensen and John C. Hammerback, eds., *The Words of César Chávez* (College Station: Texas A&M University Press, 2002), 34–36.

César Chávez at the time of the Gallo Winery boycott, 1975 (Courtesy of the Department of Special Collections, Stanford Libraries, Fitch Gallery).

such as strikes and boycotts took the offensive, Chávez thought that they represented a certain advantage over the growers who had their operations to defend. A "clean victory," one won without resort to force, he believed, could prevent the escalation of violence and a cycle of retaliation.[70]

Chávez lived nonviolence to the best of his ability. It colored his views on a wide range of issues, including the Vietnam War. Friend of 1968 presidential candidate Robert F. Kennedy, he agreed with the senator that the war must end. At the time, however, he refrained from a public statement to preclude division during the strike. By 1971 Chávez was speaking out against the war. In a speech reminiscent of Martin Luther King, Jr., he expressed regret that "thousands of poor, brown, and black farm workers go off to war to kill other poor farm workers in Southeast Asia."[71] The war cost the United States—"by gutting the soul of our nation" and "destroy[ing] the moral fiber of the people."[72] By going to war, the United States showed weakness—a loss of authority—since it employed force.[73] War "is the worst type of violence," Chávez believed. It "has no place in our society . . . and it must

---

70. José-Antonio Orosco, *Cesar Chavez and the Common Sense of Nonviolence* (Albuquerque: University of New Mexico Press, 2008), 51, 43, and 61.

71. Jensen and Hammerback, *Words*, 63–65.

72. Steven W. Bender, *One Night in America: Robert Kennedy, César Chávez, and the Dream of Dignity* (Boulder: Paradigm Publishers, 2008), 79–80.

73. Orosco, *Common Sense*, 41.

be eradicated."[74] To prevent war, he proposed that people take responsibility to teach others "how to sacrifice for justice."[75] Chávez practiced what he preached. When his son Fernando stood trial for draft refusal, Chávez testified that he had taught his children to act nonviolently.[76] And he chided antiwar protesters that only "organized, disciplined nonviolent action" could defy powerful corporations and the military. Chávez and Day were of like mind concerning the Vietnam War.

The foundation of Chávez's nonviolence was spiritual.[77] Religious symbolism graced his surroundings and found an important role in his actions. Prior to organizing the union, in 1959 Chávez began using a banner of Our Lady of Guadalupe in public ceremonies, a symbol of the dignity of her "chosen" Mexican people, representing the dignity of the poor, patriotism, and resistance to injustice. "I set her marching up front," he recalled.[78] Dolores Huerta, who worked closely with him, considered his use of religious symbols "sincere" and important.[79] The Virgin, she believed, symbolized for the UFW "doing the impossible to win a victory. . . . [W]ith faith you can win."[80] Here again, Chávez's message resonated with Day's.

The pilgrimage, a public event involving a group walking with religious images for a spiritual purpose, likewise held meaning for Catholics, including converts like Dorothy Day as well as Mexican American farm workers.[81]

---

74. Chávez, "Introduction" in Day, *Forty Acres*, 12.
75. Jensen and Hammerback, *Words*, 64.
76. Bender, *One Night*, 80.
77. One of the more convincing sources on the spiritual aspects of Chávez's nonviolence is Stephen R. Lloyd-Moffett, "The Mysticism and Social Action of César Chávez," in Gaston Espinosa et al., eds. *Latino Religions and Civic Activism in the United States* (New York: Oxford University Press, 2005), 35–51.
78. He credited a woman protester for suggesting the use of the image. Quoted in Mario T. García, *The Gospel of César Chávez* (Lanham: Sheed & Ward, 2007), 121. Chávez's office displayed an image of the Virgin. And according to Huerta, he had intended to make a pilgrimage to her shrine at the basilica in Mexico City.
79. "Dolores Huerta on Spirituality" in Mario T. García, ed., *A Dolores Huerta Reader* (Albuquerque: University of New Mexico Press, 2008), 337–338.
80. Quoted in Claire E. Wolfteich, "Devotion and the Struggle for Justice in the Farm Worker Movement: A Practical Theological Approach to Research and Teaching in Spirituality," *Spiritus* 5 (Fall 2005), 162. Timothy Matovina has explored the multiple meanings of the Virgin in *Guadalupe and Her Faithful: Latino Catholics in San Antonio, from Colonial Origins to the Present* (Baltimore: Johns Hopkins University Press, 2005). The symbol of the Virgin sometimes alienated nonreligious supporters and traditional Catholics. One follower's car sported a bumper sticker reading: "I too was a virgin once." Ferriss and Sandoval, *Fight*, 119. Traditional Catholics were offended by the Virgin on the picket line, according to Huerta. Huerta quoted in Vincent Harding, "Interview with Dolores Huerta," in García, ed., *Huerta*, 184–185.
81. Day entitled her regular column "On Pilgrimage" from 1946 until her death in 1980. The change in title represented her understanding of daily life as a spiritual pilgrimage, seeking God in the ordinary.

Shortly after the onset of the grape boycott in 1965, Chávez and union leadership decided, upon recommendation by members, to launch a penitential pilgrimage from Delano to the state capital, since they intended to appeal to legislators.[82] The Lenten walk of approximately 300 miles involved some harassment from police, growers, and motorists. Despite the swollen and blistered feet, however, the pilgrims, including Chávez, experienced the generosity of supporters along the way. As planned, arrival in Sacramento on Easter Sunday reminded the marchers of a core Christian value—hope.[83]

Concerned with strikers' increasing pressure to engage in violence, Chávez undertook a penitential fast from solid food in 1968, a traditional spiritual practice of Catholics, especially during Lent, as well as an act of Gandhian nonviolence. Dolores Huerta commented that the fast represented an essential part of Mexican Catholic culture. Penance and "the whole idea of suffering for something, of self-inflicted punishment" gave meaning to the fast.[84] As he tried to make clear, the fast held multiple meanings for him. He hoped to arouse in strikers the need for the self-discipline required of nonviolent activists, including himself. Fasting meant sacrifice. And for Chávez self-sacrifice characterized true manliness: "To be a man is to suffer for others. God help us to be men!"[85] Fasting also drew attention to the involuntary poverty of farm workers. Every evening during the twenty-one day fast, Chávez and as many as 500 followers, some of whom carried gifts of crucifixes and religious statues, participated at Mass. To celebrate the end of the fast, an ecumenical Mass involved Jewish and Protestant lectors. After communion, blessed *semita*—"the bread of social justice"—was distributed to all in attendance by nuns.[86] Chávez's fast reflected traditional Catholic practices, such as fasting, a penitential act; participating at Mass; and receiving Holy Communion. The ecumenical liturgy, reflecting the openness of Vatican II, created a more inclusive spiritual presence in his movement. Consequently, the fast generated great support for Chávez and "la Causa."

Professing his love for the Church, Chávez, like Day, was scandalized by the Church's failure to grasp how to translate its social teachings into action. Privately, he told priests that Catholic farm workers "get offended" when the Church fails to address their material needs and that they "are tempted to

---

82. Léon, "Religious Politics," 871, claims that the march was inspired by MLK's "prayer pilgrimage" and Gandhi's Salt March, although Chávez mentioned the influence of an unnamed priest whose talk about Lent helped members to consider a pilgrimage, Levy, ed., *Autobiography*, 206.
83. Chávez discussed the pilgrimage at length. Ibid., 206–213.
84. Quoted in Wolfteich, "Devotion," 166.
85. Quoted in Jensen and Hammerback, *Words*, 166–167.
86. Day, *Forty Days*, 45–47.

lash out against it."[87] The Church's flaws left Chávez "depressed and pained" because the gospel required Christians to work toward a "revolution for social dignity."[88] Dorothy Day, too, had similar thoughts about the failures of the Church in transforming injustices in society without abandoning Catholicism.

As Dorothy Day had discovered earlier, César Chávez quickly learned that social movements dedicated to practicing the law of love and the works of mercy did not automatically ensure church support. Especially in the early years of the union, and again during strikes, meager Catholic support trickled into Chávez's movement. Certain church leaders expected priests to remain at the altar and not in the streets—and the wealth of the growers and their allies outweighed the financial contributions of the numerous, but impoverished, farm workers who filled the pews.[89]

At different stages in their social, religious, and ethical development, Day and Chávez concluded that nonviolent direct action best represented Christian means toward a just society. Each discovered that traditional Catholic practices supported their nonviolent witness. Yet these pioneer Catholic social activists journeyed beyond the rigid denominationalism of the era of the "Church triumphant." They partnered with non-Catholic activists who shared their values and occasionally borrowed their ideas. Lacking evidence of contemporary Catholic nonviolent activism, Day had turned to the witness of the Hindu Gandhi and his Protestant disciples in the United States. Chávez modeled his movement on the examples of Gandhi and King.

Conclusion

Dorothy Day and César Chávez embedded Catholic spiritual practices and teachings into their developing nonviolent thought and practice. They drew from many sources within their faith tradition. The catechism, the Bible, papal encyclicals, and the lives of such saints as Francis of Assisi fed them intellectually. Their preferred "weapons of the spirit" included prayer, fasting, attendance at Mass, and receiving Holy Communion. To rectify weaknesses in their religious training, Day and Chávez fortunately enjoyed a relationship with a mentor to help develop a social conscience informed by Catholic teaching. In each case, mentor and pupil bridged dramatic social differences in order to establish a relationship of trust.

---

87. Ibid., 58.
88. Ibid., 59
89. Ibid., 53.

Before it became common to do so, Day and Chávez bypassed denominational boundaries to inform themselves and to find supporters. Secular and non-Catholic influences enabled Day and Chávez to articulate a spirituality of nonviolence and to develop tactics that honored Christ's law of love in action. Crucial insights from the Hindu activist, Gandhi, and the witness of Protestant activists like Martin Luther King, Jr. or Richard Gregg, assisted their rejection of force as a necessity for the defense of human rights. Without inspiration from these non-Catholics sources, the nonviolent tactics, strategy, and spirituality of Day and Chávez might have been seriously retarded. The onset of American Catholic nonviolent activism, especially during the 1930s through the 1970s, benefitted from their efforts to address social issues.[90]

Through their pioneering efforts to engage in activism as lay Catholics, Dorothy Day and César Chávez negotiated uncharted waters in their quest to meet the basic needs of ordinary people through nonviolent direct action. Both practiced nonviolence in their daily lives. Their responses to crises reflected efforts to create a distinctly Catholic spirituality of nonviolence. As leaders of movements, Day and Chávez depended upon committed members and a larger group of supporters, socially progressive laity and non-Catholics who shared their goals of challenging war, racial discrimination, and economic injustice. During the Vietnam War, Catholic antiwar resistance became more visible than ever before, thanks to the decades of preparation of Day and Catholic Workers. By 1975 public opinion research claimed that 17 million Americans (12% of the adult population) were observing Chávez's grape boycott.[91] Their efforts energized the laity.

While this article focuses on their accomplishment of making nonviolence an authentically Catholic option for the laity, the nonviolent leadership and vision of Day and Chávez were subjected to criticism in their lifetime and posthumously.[92] Whatever their personal weaknesses, however,

---

90. Their movements welcomed not only the laity, but also women religious and clergy. Carol Frances Jegen, BVM, who was arrested in 1973 during UFW picketing described a single encounter with the imprisoned Dorothy Day, who said, "I'm so happy—now sisters can be everywhere!" Interview with Carol Frances Jegen, BVM, Chicago, June 2010.

91. The October 1975 Lou Harris poll concluded that a slightly smaller proportion was boycotting non-union lettuce, and 11 million boycotted Gallo wine. See http://media.the harrispoll.com/documents/Harris-Interactive-Poll-Research-BROAD-SUPPORT-FOR-CHAVEZ-UNION-1975-10.pdf.

92. Throughout Day's writings, she mentioned individuals who criticized her leadership and her policies. For the most critical views of Day and the *Catholic Worker* see Michele Teresa Aronica, RSM, *Beyond Charismatic Leadership: The New York Catholic Worker Movement* (New Brunswick: Transaction Books, 1987) and Carol Byrne, *The Catholic Worker Movement (1933–1980): A Critical Analysis* (Bloomington: Author House, 2010). Chávez's leadership, particularly during the 1980s and 1990s, has also received criticism. See Miriam Pawel, *The Union*

American Catholicism has had a richer heritage of social justice activism thanks to their labors. By the late 1960s, increasing numbers of the laity—not to speak of religious and clergy—would encounter a unique spirituality of nonviolence unknown in American Catholicism at the beginning of the twentieth century. The nonviolent direct action of Day and Chávez expanded lay activity beyond the confines of its 1930s Catholic Action mission. While Pope Pius XI had envisioned "the participation of the laity in the apostolate of the Church's hierarchy," Day and Chávez, inspired by their faith, initiated lay activity in areas neglected by the bishops. Furthermore, their example spread beyond progressive Catholicism as some antiabortion activists in the post *Roe v. Wade* era modeled their activism on the examples of these predecessors.

---

of Their Dreams: Power, Hope, and Struggle in Cesar Chavez's Farm Worker Movement (New York: Bloomsbury Press, 2010 edn.).

Black Power, Vatican II, and the Emergence of Black Catholic Liturgies

*Matthew J. Cressler**

To understand the ways U.S. black Catholics experienced the changes of the Second Vatican Council one must account for the Black Power movement. Starting in the late 1960s a growing number of black Catholics embraced the arguments for self-determination and black nationalism growing increasingly popular in the black freedom struggles. In this context, black Catholic activists interpreted Vatican II as an opportunity to integrate African and African American religious practices into the Mass. These liturgical innovations often occurred without the approval of ecclesial authorities and in the face of opposition from white and black Catholics alike. Resistance notwithstanding, black Catholic liturgies and the effort to produce "authentic black" Catholic worship transformed what it meant to be black and Catholic in the decades after the council.

Introduction

On December 1, 1968 Chicago's Knickerbocker hotel hosted a historic Catholic Mass, an event remembered as the city's first "African Mass." This service functioned as the culmination of a meeting of the Chicago Conference of Laymen, an organization dedicated to implementing the Second Vatican Council's teachings on the lay apostolate. When it came time for the presentation of the gifts at the beginning of the Liturgy of the Eucharist, a black man stripped to the waist processed to the altar with the chalice, along the way performing an interpretative dance "to the beat of jungle music." Musicians dressed in "African robes" provided the music and relied heavily on drums, leading some critics to label this the "Drum Mass."

---

*A version of this essay originally appeared in *U.S. Catholic Historian* 32, no. 4 (Fall 2014): 99–119. This contribution is part of a larger forthcoming work, *Authentically Black and Truly Catholic: The Rise of Black Catholicism in the Great Migration* (New York: New York University Press, 2017).

This innovative liturgy included a folk-music rendition of the Lord's Prayer sung by the congregation, the distribution of Eucharist in baskets "filled with small slices of French bread," and Scripture readings by women and men.

Father George H. Clements (1932–), a black priest and outspoken activist in Chicago, hailed the service as the future for U.S. black Catholics. "African masses as offered in the jungle village are in keeping with the renewal program of the Roman Catholic church as started by the second Vatican council," Clements argued. He went on to suggest that "African masses with jungle music" would soon be offered in Catholic churches throughout Chicago's black communities and that black saints like Martin de Porres and Benedict the Moor soon would populate Catholic sanctuaries. Chicago's Archbishop John Patrick Cody (1907–1982) strongly disagreed with black liturgies, rejecting Clements' claim that this represented a logical and legitimate consequence of Vatican II. To the contrary, he insisted that "permission has not been granted . . . nor will it be granted to conduct any services not in keeping with the devotional spirit of the liturgy. It is forbidden to introduce nonliturgical elements into the mass at any time."[1]

This exchange between Clements and Cody foreshadowed debates that would consume Catholic Chicago over the next few years, debates between black Catholics and the white archdiocesan establishment as well as among black Catholics themselves. This article explores the ways the Mass became politically and culturally charged for black Catholics in the years following the Second Vatican Council, arguing that, for black Catholics, the experience of Vatican II was inseparable from Black Power. An increasing number of black Catholic activists embraced the racial consciousness and political strategies growing more and more popular in the black freedom struggles of the late 1960s and early 1970s. Alongside many other objectives, these activists struggled to integrate African and African American religious practices into the liturgy in an effort to produce "authentic black" Catholic worship.[2] This arti-

---

1. Descriptions and quotes drawn from Richard Philbrick, "Jungle Drums Throb at Mass, Irk Cody," *Chicago Tribune*, December 6, 1968, 20; "African Masses Considered," *Chicago Daily Defender*, December 5, 1968, 1.

2. I consistently put quotation marks around the words "authentic black" and "authentically black" to indicate that these are historically contingent terms. Black Catholic scholars and activists began to use these phrases in the late 1960s, influenced by the black cultural nationalism of the Black Power era, and continue to use them today. The ten black bishops of the United States produced perhaps the most famous iteration of these words in 1984, when they declared that the black Catholics could finally be both "authentically black and truly Catholic." See "What We Have Seen and Heard: A Pastoral Letter on Evangelization from the Black Bishops of the United States" (September 9, 1984): http://www.usccb.org/issues-and-action/cultural-diversity/african-american/resources/upload/what-we-have-seen-and-heard.pdf.

cle first illustrates the relationship between Vatican II and Black Power, then focuses attention on Chicago, home to the nation's second largest black Catholic population by 1970,[3] with a discussion of the emergence of black Catholic liturgical innovations as part of a wider protest movement meeting resistance from both white and black Catholics. Finally, the article concludes with the national Black Catholic movement and the liturgical transformation the movement initiated.

What Does Vatican II Have to Do with Black Power?

Pope John XXIII surprised the world in 1959 when he announced his plan to convene an ecumenical council of the Catholic Church. Though it was not entirely clear at the outset why the pope had convened the council, one word quickly became the most prevalent way clergy and media described the council. "*Aggiornamento*" was the Italian word John XXIII regularly used to characterize his intentions for the council before his death in 1963. Defined variously as "bringing the church up to date," "adaptation," and "modernization," many Catholics understood *aggiornamento* to indicate the spirit of change and openness to the modern world they hoped the council might inaugurate. Over the course of the council's four sessions from 1962 to 1965, the bishops produced sixteen documents that introduced the most significant changes in the Catholic Church since the Protestant Reformation.[4]

Scholars continue to debate the extent to which the council represented a break with prevailing ways of being Catholic, or if instead it marked a culmination of shifting attitudes and practices among Catholics.[5] Regardless of which historiographical perspective one takes, the ways Catholics interpreted the council and applied its teachings extraordinarily shaped what it meant to be Catholic in the following decades. Timothy Kelly offers an insightful analysis of the unintended consequences of Vatican II. He argues that the council "dispersed authority away from the pope to the bishops (and perhaps beyond) . . . [and] defined the Church as the 'People of God' rather than the hierarchy." What is more, the "newly empowered and invigorated lay apostolate

---

3. George Shuster, SSJ and Robert M. Kearns, SSJ, *Statistical Profile of Black Catholics* (Washington, DC: Josephite Pastoral Center, 1976).
4. For more on the history of the Second Vatican Council, see Xavier Rynne, *Vatican Council II* (Maryknoll, NY: Orbis Press, 1999); David G. Schultenover ed., *Vatican II: Did Anything Happen?* (New York: Continuum, 2007); John W. O'Malley, *What Happened at Vatican II* (Cambridge, MA: Belknap Press of Harvard University, 2008); Massimo Faggioli, *Vatican II: The Battle for Meaning* (New York: Paulist Press, 2012).
5. The bishops in attendance at the Second Vatican Council debated whether the council represented a continuation of past teachings or an opportunity to transform the Church. This debate extends into current studies of Vatican II. See Schultenover, *Vatican II: Did Anything Happen?*

might move in directions unanticipated."[6] Here Kelly hints at the distinction between the council and its ever-elusive "spirit." Vatican II produced documents that instituted specific changes in the Church. But Catholic laypeople, women religious, and priests could (and did) draw their own conclusions from these documents, which sometimes brought them into conflict with other Catholics. Those who celebrated the council insisted that it had ushered in a "spirit" of renewal that extended beyond the formal proceedings of the event itself. Vatican II took on a life of its own in the hands of Catholics interpreting *aggiornamento* broadly. As a result, we must address the ways the council coincided with the changing circumstances in local communities to fully understand how Catholics experienced Vatican II.[7]

Black Catholics in the United States experienced the Second Vatican Council in a context defined by the rising prominence of Black Power. With the council's conclusion, changes in Catholic life were already underway across the world when Stokely Carmichael first called for "Black Power!" in 1966. With these two words Carmichael signaled a broad tactical and ideological shift in black freedom struggles, even though Black Power's components (black nationalism, community control, and self-defense) were not new.[8] Robert O. Self notes that from 1957 to 1967 movement precepts changed from "faith in law to faith in direct action; from faith in individualist remedies to faith in collective and community-based remedies; and from faith in American pluralism to faith in Black Nationalism and radicalism."[9] References to "Black Power" in this article presume not a singular, unified movement but rather to a constellation of social, political, and cultural practices and ideas embodied differently by various groups of organizers, activists, and intellectuals.[10] Across ideological and tactical divides, Black

---

6. Timothy Kelly, *The Transformation of American Catholicism: The Pittsburgh Laity and the Second Vatican Council, 1950–1972* (Notre Dame, IN: University of Notre Dame Press, 2009), 174–175.

7. Here I am influenced by "The Lived History of Vatican II" project and conference, sponsored by Northwestern University and the Cushwa Center for the Study of American Catholicism at the University of Notre Dame. The forthcoming book will be "the first comparative, international, lived history of Catholicism in the Vatican II era, which draws on close-grained local social histories of the immediate conciliar era and its aftermath in fifteen select dioceses spanning every continent." See http://cushwa.nd.edu/events/the-lived-history-of-vatican-ii/.

8. For one example of black nationalist traditions that predate Black Power, see Eddie S. Glaude, Jr., *Exodus!: Religion, Race, and Nation in Nineteenth-Century Black America* (Chicago: University of Chicago Press, 2000).

9. Robert O. Self, "The Black Panther Party in the Long Civil Rights Era" in *In Search of the Black Panther Party: New Perspectives on a Revolutionary Movement*, Jama Lazerow and Yohuru Williams, eds. (Durham, NC: Duke University Press, 2006), 36.

10. A lecture given by Thomas Sugrue at the "South Meets North" conference held at Northwestern University in 2010 inspired my definition of Black Power as a "constellation." It also draws on the reflections of scholar-activist Robert L. Allen who discusses the various

Power activists generally were united by their commitments to a critique of postwar racial liberalism and their embrace of black self-determination, cultural nationalism, and racial consciousness.[11]

Black Chicagoans contributed to this shift in black freedom struggles. One month after Vatican II closed, Martin Luther King, Jr., and the Southern Christian Leadership Conference (SCLC) announced plans for a Chicago Freedom Movement. In the summer of 1966, southern activists joined community organizers in an attempt to challenge racist real estate practices and alleviate poverty in Chicago. King and the SCLC hoped to extend the nonviolent direct action of southern civil rights struggles into the urban North. But the movement dramatized the extent to which strategies developed in the Jim Crow South were insufficient in the urban North. The movement failed to bring about substantive change and thus bolstered the arguments of local activists already skeptical about the effectiveness of nonviolence and integration for achieving equality. Chicago activist organizations increasingly committed themselves to black nationalism and self-determination throughout the 1960s. The assassination of King on April 4, 1968 and the riots that erupted in the wake of his death accelerated this process. Young black Chicagoans on the West and South Sides founded the Illinois chapter of the Black Panther Party in the months that followed. Led by charismatic leaders Fred Hampton and Bobby Rush, the Panthers became famous across the city for combatting police harassment and brutality, providing free meals and social services for those who needed them, and forging an interracial coalition of black, white, and Latino radical activists known as the "Rainbow Coalition."[12]

---

ideological persuasions of "Black Power" in *Black Awakening in Capitalist America* (New York: Anchor Books, 1970).

11. Thomas J. Sugrue and Martha Biondi offer two of the best recent definitions of Black Power. Sugrue identifies Black Power as "a series of experiments, attempts to envision a political alternative to the racial liberalism" prevalent in the postwar era that shared broad ideological commitments to thinking globally and acting locally, to a psychological understanding of racism, and to a cultural politics of blackness. Sugrue, *Sweet Land of Liberty: The Forgotten Struggle for Civil Rights in the North* (New York: Random House, 2008), 354–355. Biondi argues that Black Power emphasized "the creation of Black-controlled institutions and racial solidarity and entailed a vigorous emphasis on culture—both in celebrating African American culture and in seeing it as a catalyst for political action and the forging of a new Black consciousness." They "saw themselves as unmasking U.S. institutions...and exposing the whiteness disguised as universalism." Martha Biondi, *The Black Revolution on Campus* (Berkeley, CA: University of California Press, 2012), 4.

12. See Jakobi Williams, *From the Bullet to the Ballot: The Illinois Chapter of the Black Panther Party and Racial Coalition Politics in Chicago* (Chapel Hill, NC: The University of North Carolina Press, 2013), 15–51; Taylor Branch, *At Canaan's Edge: America in the King Years, 1965–1968* (New York: Simon and Schuster, 2006), 501–561. This period also witnessed the rise of black student protests on Chicago's college campuses; see Biondi, *The Black Revolution on Campus*, 79–113.

When black Catholics in Chicago engaged the *aggiornamento* of Vatican II, they did so in an urban environment influenced by the racial and political consciousness of Black Power. How they understood and engaged the Second Vatican Council became inseparable from debates about Black Power. Starting in 1968 a number of black Catholic activists began to interpret Vatican II as an opportunity to incorporate Black Power in Catholic life. They soon set the terms of the discussions that developed among African American Catholics generally. With the council intimately connected with Black Power, Catholic practice and identity in the wake of Vatican II became bound up with ideas about what it meant to be black. African American Catholics who struggled with conciliar change often objected to the political strategies and cultural aesthetics of Black Power in the same breath. This made disagreements among African American Catholics in the late 1960s and early 1970s especially bitter. What it meant to be black and Catholic was hotly contested.

John T. McGreevy's classic essay "Racial Justice and the People of God" helps further analyze the interconnectedness of the council with the black freedom struggles in the mid-twentieth century. McGreevy illustrates how Vatican II promoted new theological conceptions of religious authority and church community that were particularly important for Catholics interested in racial issues. The council replaced hierarchical and institutional definitions of "the Church" with the biblical image of "the people of God" and emphasized the need for the laity to actively work for social justice. It gestured toward "the formation of a global church" with regard to worship, by abandoning Latin and introducing an "unprecedented tolerance of new liturgical forms." McGreevy goes on to discuss how, compelled by the spirit of renewal, many Catholic liberals rushed to enter struggles for racial justice.[13] New conceptions of authority and community impacted black Catholics in the wake of the council as well. But for black Catholics in Chicago, Black Power rather than civil rights shaped their reception of Vatican II. As we will see, the experience of the council for Chicago's black Catholics became virtually inseparable from ongoing debates about Black Power.[14]

---

13. John T. McGreevy, "Racial Justice and the People of God: The Second Vatican Council, the Civil Rights Movement, and American Catholics," *Religion and American Culture* 4, no. 2 (Summer 1994): 221–254.

14. My thinking about the inseparability of Black Power and Vatican II has been shaped by conversations with Mary Henold who argues that for many Catholic women debates about the council were unintelligible outside of contemporaneous debates about feminism. Henold, Comments at "Presidential Roundtable: The Place of Gender in Catholic Studies," American Catholic Historical Association, Washington, D.C., January 4, 2014. My emphasis on Black Power (rather than the Civil Rights movement) has interesting parallels with Bryan N. Massingale's current project, which calls on Catholic theologians to engage Malcolm X and black nationalism as theological sources to recover critical black theological challenges to white

Black Catholic Protest in Chicago, 1968–1969

Vatican II and Black Power converged in dramatic fashion in late 1968 Chicago. On December 18, a little over two weeks after the "African Mass," Father Gerald Scanlan retired from his pastorate at St. Dorothy Church in the Chatham neighborhood on Chicago's South Side. Scanlan, nearly 800 parishioners, and twenty-one "inner-city priests" all urged Cardinal Cody to name Father George Clements the new pastor. Clements had served as an assistant at St. Dorothy since 1962 and had become popular for his increasing involvement in black freedom struggles. But rather than promote Clements, Cody transferred Father Rollins Lambert (1923–2009) from St. James Church, a parish on the near South Side. Lambert, the first African American priest ordained by the Archdiocese of Chicago (ordained in 1949) had served briefly as an assistant priest at St. Dorothy and had been assigned to the pastorate at St. James not ten months prior.[15] When Cody refused to promote Clements and effectively placed one black priest in supervision over another, a movement rose up in defiance of the archbishop. This movement grew from alliances between black Catholics, white Catholic allies (including the Catholic Interracial Council), and secular Black Power organizations including the Black Panther Party and the Afro-American Patrolmen's League. The coalition demanded black control of Catholic institutions in black neighborhoods and more specifically that Cody appoint black priests to positions of power throughout the archdiocese. In the midst of this larger protest movement, the Mass became an important site of struggle. Black Catholic liturgical innovation in Chicago emerged quite literally out of protest.

One of the first public acts of protest occurred on January 4, 1969 as parishioners at St. James parish celebrated Sunday morning Mass.[16] Protestors organized as the Concerned Black Catholics (CBC) gathered in the pews for what they called a "pray-in." Black Panthers stood guard in the

---

supremacy. See Massingale, "Malcolm X as Neglected 'Classic' for Catholic Theological Reflection," *Origins: CNS Documentary Service* 40, no. 9 (July 8, 2010): 130–144; and Massingale, "Malcolm X and the Limits of 'Authentically Black and Truly Catholic': A Research Project on Black Radicalism and Black Catholic Faith," *Journal of the Black Catholic Theological Symposium* 5 (2011): 7–25.

15. Rollins Lambert not only became heavily involved in this protest movement in Chicago but also assumed key leadership positions in both the Black Catholic Clergy Caucus and the National Office for Black Catholics in the late 1960s and 1970s.

16. Liturgical protest also came alive in less public settings. In 1969 the Concerned Black Catholics gathered together in the rectories of supportive inner-city priests each Friday night for their own special black liturgies that experimented with the incorporation of black religious practices. These home Masses were followed by "Dissent Centers," wherein black Catholics and their allies discussed strategies for their ongoing struggles with the Catholic establishment. "Rebels Hold Black Home Mass Friday," *Chicago Daily Defender (Big Weekend Edition)*, February 22, 1969, 29.

vestibule as more than fifty black Catholics and white allies sang and prayed. One prayer in particular illustrated the protestors' intersecting of Vatican II and Black Power:

> That we as Black people may never stop striving for Our place in the sun.
> [*Those gathered for the pray-in responded to each intention: "Hear us, Lord.*]
> That we might recognize Our blackness as a thing of pride and beauty.
> That more of Our Black Brothers and Sisters might be brought into the One Black Fold.
> That we might always have the courage to carry out OUR THING—whatever it may be.
> That the Lord may strengthen Our faith in each other and love for one another.
> That Archbishop Cody might soon come to understand OUR BLACK THING.
> That Father Rollins Lambert might soon return to St. James as pastor.
> That Father George Clements be brought back to St. Dorothy as pastor.
> That ALL of Our Black priests might be put in leadership positions in Our Church.
> That the churches in the Black community might be run by Black people.
> That we might never have dissension among Our Black People.
> That Rev. Dr. Martin Luther King Jr. might be recognized as a saint by all Black People.[17]

The CBC had adapted a version of the general intercessions (the "prayer of the faithful") to fit their needs. The revival of these intercessions was one element of liturgical reform the Second Vatican Council had instituted in its 1963 "Constitution on the Sacred Liturgy" (*Sacrosanctum Concilium*). The prayer of the faithful encouraged lay people to actively engage in the liturgy by praying for the intentions of the church community. The council intended it to include not only prayers for the Catholic Church but also "for the civil authorities, for those oppressed by various needs, for all mankind, and for the salvation of the entire world."[18] The St. James pray-in exemplified the conciliar call for more participatory lay people committed to addressing the needs of the oppressed.

---

17. Quoted in Williams, *From the Bullet to the Ballot*, 109–110. Williams discovered the text of the prayer in the records of the Chicago Police Department's surveillance of the Black Panther Party, collected in "Information report: 'Pray In,'" January 5, 1969, box 229, folder 2, items 3, 3–1, Red Squad papers, Chicago History Museum.

18. *Sacrosanctum Concilium*, Constitution on the Sacred Liturgy, Paul VI, December 4, 1963. See http://www.vatican.va/archive/hist_councils/ii_vatican_council/documents/vat-ii_const_19631204_sacrosanctum-concilium_en.html.

At the same time the pray-in directly confronted the leadership of the Archdiocese of Chicago and drew explicitly on black cultural nationalism and self-determination. The first and final intentions echoed cultural nationalist calls for black self-love, pride, and, unity. The prayer described African Americans as "Black people," celebrated the beauty of "Our blackness," and hoped that "more of Our Black Brothers and Sisters might be brought into the One Black Fold." The middle intentions made specific demands of the archbishop and articulated their underlying political philosophy. They prayed that Cody might have a change of heart and called for the immediate installation of Fathers Rollins Lambert and Clements as pastors. Protestors also yearned for black Catholic self-determination, "that the churches in the Black community might be run by Black people." This prayer of the faithful illustrated the mutual influences of Black Power and Vatican II on Concerned Black Catholics in Chicago.

Black liturgical innovation and political expression were publicly displayed again one week later when thousands crammed into St. Dorothy Church for a service, called the "Black Unity Mass," that stretched over nearly three hours. The service featured eleven black priests in "African-style vestments." Protestant, Jewish, Muslim, and nonreligious African Americans joined black Catholics in worship. White allies, such as members of the Catholic Interracial Council, attended. Black Panthers provided security, "strung out all over the sanctuary."[19] Rev. Jesse Jackson was present and his civil rights organization, Operation Breadbasket, provided the music with an eight-piece band and eighty-voice choir.[20]

The *Los Angeles Times* described the event as "an old-fashioned hymn-singing religious rally and Mass of a kind never seen in a Catholic Church in the city."[21] The homilist insisted on the immediate appointment of Father George Clements as pastor and called on the congregation to "be proud of their blackness and to defy the tactics of racists by affirming themselves in black unity." Statements of pride and power were met with roars of applause. Two different descriptions of the Black Unity Mass, one from skeptical *Chicago Tribune* reporter Anne Getz and the other from the sympathetic black priest and activist Father Lawrence Lucas (1933–), provide a multidimensional view of the liturgy. Getz offered a vivid account of the Mass, though her disapproval rung clear. The musicians were "a rock-and-roll band

---

19. Lawrence Lucas, *Black Priest/White Church: Catholics and Racism* (New York: Random House, 1970), 121–122.
20. "St. Dorothy Church Commemorative: 75th Anniversary" (1991), 22, Archives of the Archdiocese of Chicago.
21. D.J.R. Bruckner, "Race, Authority Issues Peril Chicago Diocese," *Los Angeles Times*, February 3, 1969, 17.

which played Negro spirituals," she wrote, and the experience was participatory, as "members clapped vigorously and priests and church members swayed to the beat of drums." Getz went on to say the service was "barely recognizable as a traditional Catholic ceremony" because "Father Clements and Father Lambert were dressed in multi-colored robes," "altar boys wore zebra-striped robes; the altar was adorned with African symbols and a picture of the late Rev. Martin Luther King, Jr.; and the ceremony rose to a fever pitch as a priest proclaimed 'unity before God.'" Getz further noted the militancy of Jesse Jackson who spoke at a press conference after Mass, where he challenged Cardinal Cody to fight Catholic racism by putting "Catholic money into black banks," employing "black laborers in Catholic schools," and using "products made by black persons."[22]

Father Lucas, on the other hand, described the Mass as a celebration unlike any he had experienced before: "this, after all, is what Mass is supposed to be—a celebration." Lucas connected this celebration with the politics of protest. "Black Catholics had come together for a cause, a cause worthy of celebration," he wrote. "They came to tell Cardinal Cody and the entire American Catholic Church that they disagreed that the Church in Chicago had no room in it for a relevant black man in a position of power." Lucas hoped the liturgy might spur other black Catholics to action, that black Catholics would wake up and shout out "'you can't continue to use one of us to shoot another down; you can't continue to misuse and abuse black people; you can't continue to make Uncle Toms of black folks.'"[23] The Black Unity Mass reveled in the inseparability of religion and politics. It embodied the argument growing among black Catholics who embraced Black Power that the Church could only be truly Catholic if it allowed for the authentic cultural and political self-expression of black people.

The Black Unity Mass displayed the ways the Mass could serve as a site of black Catholic protest. Protest politics, in the more conventional sense of the word, was on display throughout the service. A portrait of the late Martin Luther King, Jr. watched the congregation from the altar, Black Panthers stood guard over the service, the homily directly challenged the archdiocesan leadership, and local activist leader Rev. Jesse Jackson joined in these criticisms after the liturgy. What is more, the liturgy performed a cultural protest of sorts by insisting on an emergent understanding of black Catholic identity and practice. Influenced by black cultural nationalism, some black Catholics were beginning to understand themselves as rooted in the Black Church tra-

---

22. Anne Getz, "Rev. Jesse Jackson Joins Black Priest Fight, Challenges Cody," *Chicago Tribune*, January 13, 1969, 6.
23. Lucas, *Black Priest/White Church*, 121.

Father Lawrence Lucas wearing vestments inspired by the Black Liberation Flag, colored red, black, and green, 1970 (Courtesy of the editor, *U.S. Catholic Historian*).

dition and inheritors of African religious legacies. When priests celebrated the Mass in "African robes" and parishioners sang "spirituals" they were making profound statements about the relationship between cultural particularity and the Catholic liturgy.

Black Critics of the Black Unity Mass

By most accounts, the experience deeply moved those present for the Black Unity Mass. Yet if the Black Unity Mass expressed the aspirations of some black Catholics, it embodied the worst fears of others who remained uncertain about Vatican II and Black Power. Catholics across racial, ethnic, and class spectrums were deeply divided over the changes in Catholic life after Vatican II, a conflict compounded among black Catholics when protestors connected liturgical and theological changes with ideas about racial authenticity. Black Catholic activists in Chicago embraced Black Power and worked to integrate ritual and symbolic representations of "blackness" into religious life. Enthusiastic about the Vatican II changes and the political and cultural strategies of Black Power, they hoped to transform what it looked like, felt like, sounded like, and meant to be black and Catholic. On the other hand, many black Catholics strongly objected to the idea that the Mass could (or should) include distinctively black practices or address political concerns, fearing that black Catholic activists had embraced racial particularism over and against "real" universal Catholicism. Black Catholic critics of Black Power grew increasingly distressed as they witnessed statues of white saints painted black and as Sunday Mass began to include African drums. The conflict within Chicago's black Catholic communities exploded after the Black Unity Mass.[24]

The bitterness of this divide was displayed in the archdiocesan newspaper *The New World* in the weeks following the Black Unity Mass. One writer thought it unfair to assume that all of St. Dorothy Church is "black." This black Catholic had converted to Catholicism for a variety of reasons, prominent among them the devotional style of Catholic worship prior to Vatican II. "The Mass was held as a dignified, reverent, solemn service," the reader reflected. It had been a "time to retreat, if necessary, to meditate, and hear a lesson sermon that would enlighten, encourage, and inspire one by quoting the words of God." The anonymous writer rejected outright all this "black this or the other" that now seemed to invade Catholic sermons, pointing out that "I do not need it repeated for me or to me over and over again to make me know it or to feel proud. Everyone knew I was black the minute I was born."[25]

One black Catholic woman, writing to the *Chicago Defender*, accused Catholics who embraced Black Power of being outsiders not representative of real Catholicism. "It was not the parishioners of the church that made the [Black Unity] mass a success," she said. "We hated it," she exclaimed. She challenged the legitimacy of those opposed to the archdiocese, arguing "Cardinal Cody has been good to black people and these crazy black priests aren't helping us any."[26] Another disgruntled black Catholic wrote, "I am a Catholic and have been all my life . . . [and] I am a Negro and cannot see why we have to have a Baptist minister to be on our altar to tell us how to run our church." "We do not need those black militants to have any part of our religion," this reader lamented. "We always had such a solemn and quiet church, you could meditate, but not any more."[27]

Not long after, the letters adopted a conspiratorial tone. One reader was convinced that black Catholics had only remained silent in the face of rising

---

24. John McGreevy discusses this conflict among Catholics over race in *Parish Boundaries: The Catholic Encounter with Race in the Twentieth-Century Urban North* (Chicago: University of Chicago Press, 1996), 209–247.

25. P. Armour, "'Quiet' Voice from St. Dorothy," *The New World*, January 31, 1969.

26. Elizabeth Johnson, "Views and Opinions: St. Dorothy Member Speaks," *Chicago Defender*, February 8, 1969, 12.

27. L.P., "Mass 'Shocking,'" *The New World*, February 14, 1969.

The Black Unity Mass at St. Dorothy Church was the first of many celebrated in Chicago. Pictured here is a Mass for "black unity" at St. Agatha Church, Chicago, February 2, 1969 (Courtesy of the editor, *U.S. Catholic Historian*).

Black Power militancy because they had not fully comprehended the implications of the protest movement surrounding Father Clements. It finally had become clear that the Church faced nothing short of its complete "take-over" by militants, many of them "non-Catholic." The silent black Catholic majority must be spurred to action, another reader admonished. Otherwise, the results would be cataclysmic: "I foresee the day when the bunch of little Hitlers, not content with telling us how, when, and where Holy Mass should be celebrated, will be dictating our manner of dress, of wearing our hair, and choosing our friends lest we be declared 'traitors to the cause.'"[28] Another reader similarly drew on Nazi imagery to characterize Black Power activists, charging them with having "every characteristic of and use every tactic of Hitler storm troopers." This concerned critic wondered whether Father Clements was "first a racist and second a Christian? For a racist is one who subordinates all judgments to the racial issue, and fails to see any point of view but his own."[29]

The accusation that black Catholics who embraced Black Power were racists first and Christians second highlighted a profound tension within the black

---

28. Mattie Cross, "Reader Says 'No' to Militants," *The New World*, January 31, 1969.
29. E.F.H., "Church Has Different Role to Play," *The New World*, January 31, 1969.

Catholic community. Should black Catholics be distinctively Catholic, offering their own unique contributions to the broader Church as *black* people? Or, was distinctiveness antithetical to what it meant to be *Catholic*? Many black Catholics debated these two perspectives in the 1960s and 1970s.[30] On the one hand, the embrace of "blackness" as a celebrated identity and "race" as a critical analytical lens for challenging social, political, and religious white supremacy was foundational for Black Power.[31] On the other hand, many African Americans in the first half of the twentieth century had converted to Catholicism, the "One True Church," and adopted bodily disciplines and distinctive practices that set them apart from other black religious traditions.

It is impossible to understand just how inseparable Vatican II and Black Power had become for most black Catholics without accounting for the forceful critics of both. Black Catholic activists celebrated Vatican II as an opportunity to integrate black cultural traditions into the liturgy and actively engage in the black freedom struggles. Black Catholics skeptical of Black Power, on the other hand, scoffed at the seeming infiltration of "blackness" into their churches and lamented the diminishing quiet of once-reverent worship. They feared that the traditional Latin Mass was being replaced by a "Protestantized" one, reminding them of the churches some of them had left through conversion. And they were increasingly anxious about connecting religious life with political action. Anxieties shared by many U.S. Catholics became particularly potent in black Catholic debates when linked with ideas about racial authenticity.

The Black Catholic Movement and the Emergence of Black Liturgies

The African Mass, the pray-in, and the Black Unity Mass sparked vigorous debates among black Catholics in Chicago. And while they formed part

---

30. Albert Raboteau notes that black Catholics have confronted the tension between the Catholic ideal of universalism and the demands of racial particularism throughout their history. Albert J. Raboteau, "Minority within a Minority: The History of Black Catholics in America" in *A Fire in the Bones: Reflections on African-American Religious History* (Boston: Beacon Press, 1995), 136.

31. Nikhil Pal Singh persuasively suggests that the emergence of the category of race as a "political space" may be the most enduring contribution of the long civil rights era. "What may be most remarkable about the long civil rights era is the emergence of black people as a distinct people and a public—and the concomitant development of race as a political space.... In doing so, [black social struggles] not only mounted a definitive challenge to white supremacy at home, but also established race as a framework from which to enlarge upon the public meanings of words like 'freedom' and 'democracy' within the wider world." Singh, *Black is a Country: Race and the Unfinished Struggle for Democracy* (Cambridge, MA: Harvard University Press: 2004), 214.

of a local protest movement, they also exemplified the goals of a nascent national movement. Over sixty black Catholic priests gathered for the foundational meeting of the Black Catholic Clergy Caucus (BCCC) in Detroit not two weeks after Martin Luther King's assassination in April 1968. The BCCC produced a statement at this meeting that voiced the frustrations and aspirations of many black priests. It boldly began "the Catholic Church in the United States, primarily a white racist institution, has addressed itself primarily to white society and is definitely a part of that society."[32] According to the BCCC, the Church was "not cognizant of changing attitudes in the black community and is not making the necessary, realistic adjustments."[33] Black women religious founded their own organization later that same year.[34] The National Black Sisters' Conference (NBSC) pledged "to work unceasingly for the liberation of black people." The sisters proclaimed that "expressions of individual and institutional racism found in our society and within our Church are declared by us to be categorically evil and inimical to the freedom of all men everywhere, and particularly destructive of black people in America."[35] In 1970 these vocational associations, soon joined by lay people, brothers, and seminarians, established the National Office for Black Catholics (NOBC) that centralized their collective efforts.

Together, these organizations initiated more than a decade of advocacy that became known as the Black Catholic movement.[36] This movement included a wide array of activists and scholars who promoted a number of arguments about black Catholic identity, practice, and participation in the U.S. Church. At the heart of the matter were claims about material and spiritual power. Leaders in the Black Catholic movement insisted that black Catholics had been denied not only positions of power in the institutional Church, but also the freedom to fully express their true spiritual selves. In other words, black Catholics had not just been marginalized in the social and political realms of the Church. They had been forced to adopt essentially

---

32. "A Statement of the Black Catholic Clergy Caucus, 1968" collected in *"Stamped with the Image of God": African Americans as God's Image in Black*, Cyprian Davis, OSB, and Jamie Phelps, OP, ed. (Maryknoll, NY: Orbis, 2003), 111.

33. Ibid., 112.

34. For more on the activism of black Catholic sisters, see Shannen Dee Williams, "Subversive Habits: Black Nuns and the Struggle to Desegregate Catholic America after World War I" (Ph.D. dissertation, Rutgers University, 2013).

35. "The Survival of Soul: National Black Sisters' Conference Position Paper, 1969" collected in *"Stamped with the Image of God,"* 114.

36. Since the Afro-American Catholic Congresses and Federated Colored Catholics had mobilized black Catholics before 1968, some referred to this moment as the "second," "third," or "contemporary" Black Catholic movement. For more on black Catholic protest in the early twentieth century, see Marilyn Wenzke Nickels, *Black Catholic Protest and the Federated Colored Catholics, 1917–1933: Three Perspectives on Racial Justice* (New York: Garland Publishing, 1988).

white ways of being religious in order to be Catholic; they had been forced to convert to whiteness. The Black Catholic movement advocated for black control of Catholic institutions and for the inclusion of "authentic black" ways of being religious. Though the full range of issues the Black Catholic movement directly addressed is beyond this article's scope, the remainder of the article will focus on the development of black Catholic liturgies, a critical objective for the Black Catholic movement in the 1970s.[37]

The idea that black people should worship in distinctively black liturgies was a consequence of the convergence of Vatican II and Black Power. Scholar-activists such as Sister Martin de Porres Grey, RSM (Patricia Grey Tyree) (1943–) and Brother Joseph M. Davis, SM, (1927–1992), the founder of the NBSC and the executive director of the NOBC, respectively, drew heavily on the black cultural nationalist traditions circulating of the late 1960s and 1970s. They asserted that African Americans shared ways of knowing and living in the world with black peoples across Africa and the Americas. Speaking to a conference of mostly white Josephite priests in 1971, Sister Grey said "black people understand blackness as that unique manner of speaking, writing, dancing, singing, cooking, dressing, drawing, acting and behaving, which is innate to black people in American [sic] and characteristic of people of African descent living anywhere in the West." "Blackness," Grey concluded, "is the sum total of all the ideas, attitudes, actions and creations that stem from the African's attempt to accommodate himself to, dig this, to integrate into, co-exist with, and separate from the West."[38] A few years later Brother Davis elaborated on the religious content of "blackness," arguing that African Americans possessed a special attunement to the sacred passed on by their African ancestors, which he called "SOUL." This one word served as "a concise description of [the] fundamental world-view and life style of Black people, as it has been retained from our African heritage."[39] Juxtaposed with "cerebral" white religion, black spirituality was lived "with the fullness of

---

37. What is offered here is necessarily a selective history of the movement focusing on a specific question. For more on the development of the Black Catholic movement, see Joseph M. Davis and Cyprian Lamar Rowe, "The Development of the National Office for Black Catholics," *U.S. Catholic Historian* 7, nos. 2–3 (Spring–Summer 1988): 265–289; M. Shawn Copeland, "African American Catholics and Black Theology: An Interpretation," in *African American Religious Studies: An Interdisciplinary Anthology*, ed. Gayraud S. Wilmore (Durham, NC: Duke University Press, 1989), 228–248; Cyprian Davis, OSB, *The History of Black Catholics in the United States* (New York: Crossroad Publishing Company, 1995), 255–259.

38. "Josephite Conference, July 1971—Transcript," Joseph M. Davis Papers, Box 1, Folder 28, University of Notre Dame Archives, Notre Dame, Indiana (hereafter UNDA).

39. Joseph M. Davis, "The Undying Struggle: Restoring Greatness" (1975), Davis Papers, Box 1, Folder 11, UNDA; "Religion And Race / Testimony Presented by the National Office for Black Catholics Before the Bicentennial Hearings of the National Conference of Catholic Bishops" (1975), Davis Papers, Box 1, Folder 14, UNDA; and "Religious Education in the Black Community" (1976), Davis Papers, Box 1, Folder 4, UNDA.

one's being: the head, the heart, the body, the hands, the feet, the SOUL."[40] Scholars and activists in the Black Catholic movement such as Grey and Davis laid claim to a distinctive black heritage and insisted that black Catholic religious life be situated firmly in that tradition.

Conciliar documents including *Sacrosanctum Concilium* and *Ad Gentes* (Decree on the Mission Activity of the Church) contributed to the growth of black liturgies by emphasizing the ways universal faith was situated in particular cultural contexts. Those in the Black Catholic movement took this teaching as an opportunity to reinterpret practices long understood to be emblematic of "true" Catholicism as, instead, representative of various European-American Catholicisms. Black Catholics should root their religious identities and practices in their particular cultural and historical heritage, much as other Catholic communities had done for millennia. Sister Jamie Phelps, OP, a black Catholic theologian, has spoken and written at length on this process of "inculturation"—though the term itself was not used until later.[41] Just as Irish, Italian, German, and Polish Catholics had incorporated their own unique devotional practices into the religious life of their churches, so too black Catholics should be free to express their Catholicism in ways that resonated with their black and African cultural traditions.

The Black Catholic movement thus operated on the principle, inspired by Vatican II and Black Power, that black Catholics had inherited distinctive religious-cultural traditions and that the council had opened spaces for black Catholics to incorporate those traditions in religious life. But a question quickly emerged. How, then, could the liturgy of the Mass become "black"? The National Office for Black Catholics set about answering this question by actively evangelizing in black Catholic communities. The NOBC hoped to convince black Catholics that their distinctive black religious roots did not contradict Catholic universality. In order to accomplish this goal, the NOBC founded a Department of Culture and Worship. Directed by famed black liturgist Father Clarence J. Rivers (1931–2004), this department served as a center for the transformation of black Catholic liturgies across the country throughout the 1970s. One major element in this effort was the publication of *Freeing the Spirit: The Magazine of Black Liturgy Published by the National Office for Black Catholics*. The first issue, published in 1971, was dedicated to "those Blacks who still have not found themselves; who have not discov-

---

40. Davis, "Religious Education in the Black Community," UNDA.
41. Jamie T. Phelps, OP, interview with the author, March 12, 2012. See also Phelps, "Inculturating Jesus: A Search for Dynamic Images for the Mission of the Church among African Americans," in *Taking Down Our Harps: Black Catholics in the United States*, Diana L. Hayes and Cyprian Davis, OSB, eds. (Maryknoll, NY: Orbis Books, 1998), 68–101.

Freeing the Spirit, magazine of black Catholic liturgy published from 1971-1981 by the National Office for Black Catholics, Washington, D.C. (Courtesy of the editor, *U.S. Catholic Historian*).

ered their *Beautiful Black Self.*"[42] Over the next decade *Freeing the Spirit* offered academic articles on the history of African religions and the Black Church as well as sample "black liturgies" and practical tips for introducing them into parishes.

Beyond its written publications, the Department of Culture and Worship provided direct liturgical consultation by prominent black Catholic liturgists including Father Rivers and jazz pianist Mary Lou Williams (1910–1981), who trained choirs and congregations in black musical idioms and worship practices.[43] The department forged relationships across the black Catholic

---

42. *Freeing the Spirit: The Magazine of Black Liturgy Published by the National Office for Black Catholics* 1, no. 1 (August, 1971) [emphasis in original].
43. I should note that Clarence Rivers, Mary Lou Williams, Eddie Bonnemere, and a few other composers had already begun experimenting with the incorporation of black musical idioms into the Catholic liturgy by the early 1960s. But, as Mary E. McGann and Eva Marie Lumas note, a full-fledged "Black Catholic liturgical movement" did not emerge until the 1970s, launched in large part by Rivers' directorship of the NOBC Department of Culture and

diaspora with those involved in attempts to "Africanize" churches in Africa and the Caribbean. The department also developed a sophisticated system for inculcating these practices in black Catholic communities across the country. It hosted workshops like "White Priest: Black Church," dedicated to producing "black-thinking" white priests and sisters, as well as summer courses that equipped black Catholic lay people with the tools to introduce black liturgies in their own communities.[44] These efforts culminated in the conference on "Worship and Spirituality in the Black Community" in 1977, when theologians, liturgists, and activists argued for the inclusion of "black cultural considerations" in Catholic worship.[45] The impact of these efforts increasingly legitimized these practices in black Catholic churches and effected a shift of black Catholic identity and practice.

Conclusion

In his 1974 book *Soulfull Worship*, Father Rivers recalled that "unauthorized" black liturgies began to appear following the inaugural publication of *Freeing the Spirit* and how "this upset some of the bishops." Rivers' response was telling. "Of course, if we were going to do anything about black Liturgy in the Roman Catholic Church in the United States it had to be 'unauthorized' presently," he pointed out, "since nobody in authority was black."[46] Rivers elaborated on this point later in an answer to his rhetorical question "Where, indeed, does true authority lie in the matter of authentic Afro-American Catholic worship?" While acknowledging that first authority in matters of worship lies with bishops, Rivers repeated the blunt fact that "no present group of bishops with ordinary authority in the United States are competent judges of what is authentically Afro-American." Rivers hoped that when bishops realize "that blacks themselves must ultimately decide on their own authenticity as blacks, the bishops must find a way of sharing their Catholic authority with blacks."[47] In the meantime, he and other members

---

Worship. See McGann and Lumas, "The Emergence of African American Catholic Worship," *U.S. Catholic Historian* 19, no. 2 (Spring 2001): 27–65. For a précis of Father Clarence Rivers' perspective on black Catholic liturgy, see Clarence Jos. Rivers, "Thank God We Ain't What We Was: The State of Liturgy in the Black Catholic Community," *Freeing the Spirit* 6, no. 2 (Spring 1979): 28–32; also reprinted in *U.S. Catholic Historian* 5, no. 1 (1986): 81–89. Vaughn A. Booker, Jr. discusses Mary Lou Williams at length in "'Is That Religion?' The Jazz Profession and Afro-Protestant Cultural Representation" (Ph.D. dissertation, Princeton University, 2016).

44. National Federation of Priests Council Papers, Box 18, Folder 39, UNDA; and National Office for Black Catholics Papers (microfilm), UNDA.

45. *This Far By Faith: American Black Worship and Its African Roots* (Washington, DC: National Office for Black Catholics, 1977).

46. Clarence R. J. Rivers, *Soulfull Worship* (Washington, DC: National Office for Black Catholics, 1974), 6.

47. Ibid., 23.

of the Black Catholic movement produced distinctively black liturgies and worked to convince both ecclesial authorities and fellow black Catholics of their legitimacy.

Black Catholic liturgies were among the most enduring contributions black Catholics made to U.S. Catholicism in the decades following the Second Vatican Council. U.S. Catholics experienced the changes of Vatican II on a deeply personal level in the Mass. Many of these changes were instituted from above. Liturgical reforms may not have been easily or evenly accepted, but in most cases they were enforced with the full weight of ecclesiastical authority. Some Catholics hoped to expand on these reforms, however, beyond what the hierarchy authorized. They interpreted what they took to be Vatican II's spirit of renewal as an impetus for the development of new liturgical forms that might give fuller expression to Catholicity in the modern world. Often initiated by lay people, this experimentation could conflict with the official implementation of conciliar reform. When it did, the very act of worship could become a site of protest.

The liturgy became a central site of struggle for black Catholics in particular in the 1960s and 1970s. What it meant to be black and Catholic changed in the wake of Vatican II and in the midst of Black Power. Sisters, lay people, brothers, and priests in the Black Catholic movement increasingly insisted that to be black and Catholic meant to be Catholic differently. Though they remained members of a predominantly white U.S. Church, these scholars and activists identified black Catholics as part of the Black Church tradition. Black Catholics had inherited distinctive ways of praying, singing, and preaching that set them apart from other U.S. Catholics, legacies that scholars traced back before slavery to the African continent.[48] The National Office for Black Catholics characterized black spirituality as a holis-

---

48. Here scholars and activists in the Black Catholic movement were influenced by black historians, theologians, and ministers who argued that Africans had distinctive ways of being religious which they brought with them across the Middle Passage and into the Americas, religious practices that survived the holocaust of slavery and gave black people their unique styles of song, preaching, and prayer. The idea that "the Black Church" was rooted in Africa was, of course, not new. W.E.B. Du Bois famously stated that this distinctive black religiosity was "sprung from the African Forests"; Du Bois, "Of the Faith of the Fathers," in *The Souls of Black Folk* (New York: Signet Classic, 1995 [1903]), 212. This argument was resurgent in the black cultural nationalism of Black Power. Black nationalist activists and scholars contributed to a flourishing of theological and historical studies about the nature of the Black Church, black religion, and their relationship to Africa and African slavery in the Americas. For examples see Eugene D. Genovese, *Roll, Jordan, Roll: The World the Slaves Made* (New York: Vintage Press, 1976); Lawrence W. Levine, *Black Culture and Black Consciousness: Afro-American Folk Thought from Slavery to Freedom* (New York: Oxford University Press, 1978); Albert J. Raboteau, *Slave Religion: The "Invisible Institution" in the Antebellum South* (New York: Oxford University Press, 1978).

tic tradition that involved the mind, body, and soul in joy-filled and exuberant worship. As a result, liturgists in the Black Catholic movement developed "black liturgies" that could express the black and African heritage of black Catholics. What is more, they strove to convince the wider Church that black liturgies were an authentic—if not the only authentic—expression of black Catholic faith. And, as events in Chicago illustrated, black Catholics who embraced Black Power and celebrated Vatican II brought these black liturgies to life with or without their bishops' approval.

The Cold War, the Council, and American Catholicism in a Global World

*Joseph P. Chinnici, OFM**

With the end of World War II and the beginning of the Cold War, American Catholicism entered into a new phase. As the Church in the U.S. grew and developed, it was linked to a nation recognized as a global superpower, playing a major role in the formation of the Catholic Church throughout the world. As a result, the history of American Catholicism cannot be understood outside of the long trajectory of Cold War periodization from 1945 to 1989. This opening to a greater role in the worldwide Church is most manifest in the episcopal participation in the Second Vatican Council (1962–1965). The American bishops' change in awareness is traced to the first period of the council when they made significant contributions to debates over the liturgy, bolstered the ecumenical emphasis of Pope John XXIII, and through their participation in the council were exposed to the experiences of the Church in other countries. An even more intensified commitment to internationality occurred during the council's later sessions as the horizontal relationship between bishops found expression in the concept and practice of collegiality. Many post-conciliar developments in catechetics, pastoral practice, religious life, and priesthood, cannot be understood without placing them within this context of an "American Church" gone global and the Vatican's awareness of the outsized influence of the U.S. Church because of its attachment to a global superpower.

Early in the spring of 1986, Monsignor William Murphy, representing the Pontifical Commission Justice and Peace, wrote to Archbishop Rembert Weakland with observations about the second draft of the pastoral on economics of the National Conference of Catholic Bishops. The Roman commentator called particular attention to the questions which the proposed pastoral raised on the relationship between one bishops' confer-

---

*This essay originally appeared in *U.S. Catholic Historian* 30, no. 2 (Spring 2012): 1–24.

ence and another and between the multiple bishops' conferences and the Holy See. If the bishops released the pastoral on economics, could there not be "the possible confusion of their teaching authority with some prudential economic and social judgments?" Did not the teaching of the U.S. bishops "have direct and indirect real repercussions on the bishops in other countries and on the role of the Holy Father in the social domain"? Seen from a global perspective, Murphy asked,

> Is it not important to maintain the principle that the bishops speak with one voice regarding values, principles and social teaching? In a world grown small does not a Church that is Catholic have all the more reason to protect itself in such a way that its social teaching is clear and clearly seen as consistent and coherent?[1]

Murphy's observations were followed in April 1986 by a consultative meeting between selected U.S. bishops, their Latin American counterparts, and representatives from France and Germany. Just as the pastoral on war and peace had been discussed with the Europeans, so the Holy See requested that economic principles articulated in the northern hemisphere be discussed with those representing the southern hemisphere. The meeting took place under the vertical aegis of the Holy See and was comprised of the horizontal relationships existing between east and west, north and south. It situated the Church in the United States within a global context and placed it squarely within the dynamics of international history. What happened in the United States and the approach that the American bishops took to the relationship between the Gospel and society carried "international repercussions" affecting the whole Church.[2] The local realization of the Church in North America needed to be coordinated with other local realizations; both had to be structured so as to reflect Catholicism's universality.

This 1986 meeting, one among many which occurred during that decade, symbolized the culmination of a long process of transformation which had been occurring in the American Catholic community since the close of World War II. I would describe the development in its broadest

---

1. Msgr. W. Murphy to Rembert Weakland [April 1986], "Some Observations on the Second Draft, Catholic Social Teaching and the U.S. Economy," Collection on the Economics Pastoral, Weakland Papers, Archives of the Archdiocese of Milwaukee (hereafter WP/AAM).

2. Confer the series of letters related to the consultation with the Latin Americans, April 16–17, 1986: Msgr. Hoye to Weakland, February 6, 1986; Pontifical Commission Justitia et Pax, February 10, 1986; Malone to Cardinal Etchegaray, March 12, 1986; William M. Levers, CSC, to Weakland, March 17, 1986; handwritten notes, Latin American Consultation, April 16–17, 1986, Collection on the Economics Pastoral, WP/AAM.

terms as initially a process of internationalization—some might call it "globalization," others, "trans-nationalization," or still others, the "creation of a world culture."[3] The phenomenon itself reflects two fundamentally connected trajectories: (1) The changing fortunes of the United States and its ascendancy to the status of a political, social, economic, and cultural superpower. American historians largely frame this development as a movement away from a history rooted in the nation-state towards a history shaped by the vast "networks of worldwide interconnectivity."[4] (2) The corresponding development within our country and elsewhere of a "world Church."[5] This latter development has since been referred to by theologians as the movement towards a polycentric Church whose unity is determined not only by creedal statements and authoritative vertical structures centered in Rome, but also by pathways of reciprocity between local churches.[6] What is important for the purposes of this essay is the fact that the American Catholic story is now situated within a global context and simultaneously attached to the multi-dimensional world outreach of the United States of America. Within American history the preoccupation with "exceptionalism" has lost some of its valiancy; within Catholic history, the predominantly immigrant and European-American axis of interpretation has passed. Interconnections, reciproc-

---

3. See Frank J. Lechner and John Boli, *World Culture, Origins and Consequences* (Malden, MA: Blackwell Publishing, 2005), for a broad survey of developments; Edward S. Herman and Robert W. McChesney, *The Global Media, The New Missionaries of Corporate Capitalism* (New York: Continuum, 1997), for reflections on the phenomenon in the light of global media.

4. Charles Bright and Michael Geyer, "Where in the World is America? The History of the United States in a Global Age," in Thomas Binder, ed., *Rethinking American History in a Global Age* (Berkeley: University of California, 2002), 63–99, with citation from 67. In addition to this collection of articles see the fundamental approaches of Ian Tyrrell, "Making Nations/Making States: American Historians in the Context of Empire," *The Journal of American History* 86 (December 1999): 1015–1044; Thomas Binder, *A Nation Among Nations, America's Place in World History* (New York: Hill and Wang, 2006). For the relationship with imperial reaches, see Robert J. McMahon, "The Republic as Empire: American Foreign Policy in the 'American Century,'" in Harvard Sitkoff, ed., *Perspectives on Modern America, Making Sense of the Twentieth Century* (New York: Oxford University Press, 2001), 80–100; Charles S. Maier, *Among Empires, American Ascendancy and Its Predecessors* (Cambridge, MA: Harvard University Press, 2006).

5. Karl Rahner, "Towards a Fundamental Theological Interpretation of Vatican II," *Theological Studies* 40 (1979): 716–727. For more recent reflections tracing this development see Robert Schreiter, *The New Catholicity, Theology Between the Global and the Local* (Maryknoll, NY: Orbis Books, 2007); Stephen Schloesser, "Against Forgetting: Memory, History, Vatican II," in John W. O'Malley, Joseph A. Komonchak, Stephen Schloesser, and Neil J. Ormerod, *Vatican II, Did Anything Happen* (New York: Continuum, 2007).

6. For reflections along these lines, see the entire issue of George Kilcourse, ed., *The Catholic Theological Society of America, Proceedings of the Thirty-Ninth Annual Convention, Washington, D.C., June 13–16, 1984,* Vol. 39; Richard R. Gaillardetz, *Ecclesiology for a Global Church, A People Called and* Sent (Maryknoll, NY: Orbis Books, 2008); William R. Burrows, "From a Roman Catholic 'Mission Church' to a Catholic 'World Christianity' Paradigm: A Personal Pilgrimage," *U.S. Catholic Historian* 24, no. 3 (Summer 2006): 165–179.

ities, interchanges, intersections, the border lands of exchange, a global ecology of movements, ideas, and influences: these are the categories which more and more structure contemporary thinking, creating a new horizon for the historical imagination.

Whatever name we would want to give to it, this historical transformation of the last seventy years has placed the American Catholic community within a larger relational context. Internationalization has changed the basis from which social and ecclesial identity is shaped. It has forced upon the Catholic community in the United States the twin questions: How does our religious practice, tied as it is to the cultural influence of a global power, impact the rest of the world? How is being an American Catholic shaped by the forces of a globalized world and a world Church? Affecting as it does almost every segment of life, this international relational structure must also change the community's self-narration, the way we write our own history.

In this essay I would like to explore some dimensions of how "American Catholicism in a world made small" came about. Many themes could be explicated, as for examples, the international networking that intensified the scholarly exchanges, patterns of travel, and global meetings of the post-war era; the worldwide spread of the religious reform movements of the same era (Family Rosary Crusade, The Christophers, Christian Family Movement, Catholic Students' Mission Crusade); the international moral and religious discourse spread through the growth of the modern media; the intensification of the forces of globalization both in the Church and in the world in the 1970s.[7] All of these dimensions make for a new horizon for the writing and understanding of American Catholic history.

For the purposes of illustration and clarity, this essay will concentrate on locating the American Catholic story within the periodization established by the Cold War and on the American participation in the council during its first and second sessions. It is in the convergence of these two developments that the Catholic community began to make the turn towards the self-awareness of a world Church. The essay will conclude by suggesting how this approach might illuminate developments within the Catholic community in the post-conciliar period.

---

7. For the post-conciliar period, see Niall Ferguson, Charles S. Maier, Erez Manela, Daniel J. Sargent, eds., *The Shock of the Global, the 1970s in Perspective* (Cambridge, MA: Harvard University Press, 2010); Ian Linden, *Global Catholicism, Diversity and Change since Vatican II* (New York: Columbia University Press, 2009).

Periodization: An Overview of Developments, 1945–1989

It is certainly possible to write the story of post-war American Catholicism within a periodization created by our national history. Here the early Cold War, the "long sixties" or the "long seventies," create the chronology that shapes an interpretive strategy based on internal economic, political, and cultural patterns. In this framework, suburbanization, the civil rights, antiwar, and feminist movements provide substantial lines of development. Another scenario could be created by focusing directly on the impact of Vatican II, its "declension" or "event" within the history of the Church in this country. Great insights have been achieved using these temporal structures. Yet, I have not found these approaches completely satisfactory. They help but do not quite explain the archival records. I think we also need to consider a more international presentation of the material as has been shown most recently in Andrew Preston's *Sword of the Spirit, Shield of Faith*.[8]

In his seminal study on the Vatican and the American hierarchy, Gerald Fogarty describes the watershed impact of World War II on the Church in the United States in its relationship with the universal Church. He notes four major developments: a) the Vatican's recognition of the importance of the American Church "because of the political and military influence of the United States in world affairs"; b) the recognition that the conference of bishops, then known as the National Catholic Welfare Conference (NCWC), functioned as the "official voice of the American hierarchy," thus paving the way for Vatican II's "concept of collegiality"; c) the way in which the war solidified the patriotism of American Catholics and demonstrated that, despite their ethnic diversity, "Catholics constituted one Church" in this country; and, lastly, d) with World War II came the proof to the "cultural majority" that Catholics had achieved "truly American status."[9] These insightful remarks indicate how the war experience catapulted the Catholic community in the United States unto the stage of the Church as a transnational actor with which to be reckoned. Three distinct pathways were here intersecting: a) the faith community's unified public presence as expressed in the National Catholic Welfare Conference; b) its commitment to American political and cultural values; and c) its coupling with the global outreach of the United States.

A good illustration of this very new development can be seen in the exchange of correspondence between the official representatives of the

---

8. Andrew Prestron, *Sword of the Spirit, Shield of Faith: Religion in American War and Diplomacy* (New York: Alfred A. Knopf, 2012).
9. Gerald Fogarty, *The Vatican and the American Hierarchy from 1870 to 1965* (Wilmington, DE: Michael Glazier, 1985), 311.

National Catholic Welfare Conference and the under-secretary of state for Pius XII, Giovanni Montini (1897–1978). In 1947 the bishops had published a pastoral letter on "secularism" and wished to follow it up the next year with one "regarding the inroads which secularism is making in the fields of education, economic life, and civil polity." The draft pastoral was sent to Rome for a preview in order to discover if the authors (Cardinals Edward Mooney and Samuel Stritch) had correctly interpreted the teaching of the papal encyclicals in two key areas: economic life and political settlement. A two-page response came back within a month. Some caveats were expressed as to how the bishops were applying *Quadragesimo Anno* (1931) in the economic sphere and, with respect to Church-state relationships, specific wording was suggested that would uphold Church teaching while acknowledging the validity of the First Amendment settlement.[10] In a private communication it was noted that the draft had received the "most careful consideration and was given well deserved approval. Montini further expressed the conviction that the statement would be the source of great good for Catholics not only of the United States but of many other countries as well."[11] The expectation on the part of the Holy See was clearly one which was beginning to see the implications of American interpretations for a universal Church—and the fundamental areas were central realities of the post-war world, economic life, and Church-state-society relationships.

This post-war American world into which the Catholic community was thrust was one shaped by the adversarial but undulating relationships between the United States and the Soviet Union. From the time of the Yalta and Potsdam Conferences (February, July 1945) to the collapse of Soviet hegemony over Eastern Europe (October-November 1989), Cold War relationships shaped the foreign policy, political rhetoric, and many of the domestic cultural realities of the United States.[12] The intensities and relaxations in super-power relationships, from the Korean War through détente to renewed regional confrontations, were paralleled by the developing geo-

---

10. Rev. Walter Carroll to Monsignor J.B. Montini, October 13, 1948; Domenico Tardini to Monsignor Walter Carroll, November 3, 1948, file 1, box 65, collection 10, NCWC Administrative Board: Statements, 1944–1948, Archives of The Catholic University of America (hereafter ACUA).

11. NJC to Your Eminence, November 8, 1948, 010–65–1, NCWC, ACUA.

12. General overviews of the timeframe may be found in John Lewis Gaddis, *The Cold War* (New York: Penguin Books, 2005); Mike Sewell, *The Cold War* (New York: Cambridge University Press, 2002); Odd Arne Westad, *The Global Cold War* (New York: Cambridge University Press, 2007). For two examples of impact on domestic cultural realities, see Elaine Tyler May, *Homeward Bound: American Families in the Cold War Era* (New York: Basic Books, 1988, 1999); Richard Lingeman, "Domestic Containment: The Downfall of Postwar Idealism and Left Dissent, 1945–1950," in Mark C. Carnes, ed., *The Columbia History of Post-World War II America* (New York: Columbia University Press, 2007), 201–225.

political strategies of the papacy. This general timeframe connected with the Cold War is well accepted and it bears consideration when examining the historical narrative of American Catholicism. Thus a person cannot understand the development of internal Church policies without reference to the intense Cold War anti-communist era of Pius XII (1939–1958).[13] The same would be true of developments in the emerging countries in Africa and Asia as they touched questions of civil rights, sovereignty, anti-communism, and liberation.[14] Many events in the 1960s need to be framed within the international opening to "men of good will" represented by John XXIII's *Mater et Magistra* (1961) and *Pacem in Terris* (1963). In turn, the cultural opening created by détente encouraged the reception of the new social teaching of the Second Vatican Council and Paul VI on peace, the dignity of the person, solidarity, human development, and "dialogue."[15] While the issue of dissent is often interpreted in the light of internal Church issues, it is becoming clearer that the 1960s witnessed a worldwide turn towards social critique and ecclesial protest in rejection of Cold War political and cultural accommodations.[16] As détente ended, from 1973 onwards the conflictual political constellations in Central America became a neuralgic area for theological, political, and economic differences within the Catholic community.[17] Lastly the escalating tensions of the second phase of the Cold War, 1977–1989, coupled with the struggle against both communist and neo-liberal hegemonies, impacted the geo-political strategy of the papacy of John Paul II. This in turn shifted how the Church interpreted and applied the teachings of *Gaudium et Spes* and *Dignitatis Humanae Personae* to questions of social and ecclesial order.[18] Given the reality of the Church as a transnational actor and the world status

---

13. Étienne Fouillouix, ""L'église catholique en 'guerre froide' (1945–1958)," *Cristianesimo nella Storia* 22 (2001): 687–715; Dianne Kirby, ed., *Religion and the Cold War* (New York: Palgrave, 2003).

14. Thomas P. Melady, "Understanding New Nations," *Social Order* 11 (February 1961): 81–84; John H. Hicks, "Negroes and African Nationalism," *Social Order* 11 (April 1961): 151–155; Quentin L. Quade, "American Catholicism and International Affairs," *Social Order* 12 (June 1962): 257–266; Thomas Borstelmann, *The Cold War and the Color Line: American Race Relations in the Global Arena* (Cambridge, MA: Harvard University Press, 2001).

15. John T. Donovan, *Crusader in the Cold War: A Biography of Fr. John F. Cronin, S.S. (1908–1994)* (New York: Peter Lang, 2005), chapter 7.

16. Jeremi Suri, *Power and Protest: Global Revolution and the Rise of Détente* (Cambridge, MA: Harvard University Press, 2003); Martin Klimke, *The Other Alliance: Student Protest in West Germany and the United States in the Global Sixties* (Princeton, NJ: Princeton University Press, 2010); Preston, *Sword of the Spirit, Shield of Faith*, 501–519.

17. See, for different perspectives, Van Gosse, "Active Engagement, The Legacy of Central America Solidarity," *NACLA Report on the Americas* XXVIII (March/April 1995), 22–29; James Hitchcock, *The Pope and the Jesuits* (New York: The National Committee of Laymen, 1984); George Weigel, *Tranquilitas Ordinis, the Present Failure and Future Promise of American Catholic Thought on War and Peace* (New York: Oxford University Press, 1987).

18. See Herminio Rico, SJ, *John Paul II and the Legacy of* Dignitatis Humanae (Washington DC: Georgetown University Press, 2002).

of the United States, how can developments within the Church in the United States be understood outside of this global context?

A few examples will suffice to indicate some of the connections which emerge when developments in this country are placed within the broader chronological framework shaped by the Cold War. Certainly, if the statements of the American hierarchy are any indication, the changing relationship between the major superpowers framed developments in the international Catholic community in Eastern Europe and, of a consequence, the Church in this country in the 1950s. Cold War ideology and a focus on the family unit with the father at the head went hand in hand.[19] The devotional style associated with the 1950s mirrored an international struggle against communism.[20] The debates between the "rightists" and "leftists" in the Church in the United States on the eve of the council and the popular and elite splits in the American Catholic community over the social and theological thaw of John XXIII, Vatican II, and Paul VI were deeply related to fundamental differences over international relations.[21] More than likely the roots of the 1980s "culture wars" began sprouting in these divisions.[22] At the council itself, during its last session, the American hierarchy divided on issues of war, peace, and nuclear disarmament depending on the bishops' relative assessments of the dangers of Soviet aggression.[23] In the first phase of the post-conciliar era, 1965–1978, an "open moment" witnessed the convergence between the international language of rights, the Church's ministry of human rights, and, during the Carter administration, international policies. Clearly, the appropriation of "rights" language into the Church in the United States during this same era occurred against a large international

---

19. See Raphael M. Huber, ed., *Our Bishops Speak: National Pastorals and Annual Statements of the Hierarchy of the United States: 1919–1951* (Milwaukee: Bruce Publishing Company, 1952); Hugh J. Nolan, ed., *Pastoral Letters of the United States Catholic Bishops II, 1941–1961* (Washington DC: National Conference of Catholic Bishops, United States Catholic Conference, 1984). For family ideology see Elaine Tyler May, "Cold War—Warm Hearth: Politics and the Family in Postwar America," in Steve Fraser and Gary Gerstle, *The Rise and Fall of the New Deal Order, 1930–1980* (Princeton, NJ: Princeton University Press, 1989), 153–181.

20. Joseph P. Chinnici, OFM, "The Catholic Community at Prayer, 1926–1976," in James M. O'Toole, ed., *Habits of Devotion: Catholic Religious Practice in Twentieth-Century America* (Ithaca, NY: Cornell University Press, 2004), 52–70.

21. See for examples the materials related to the Washington Catholic Roundtable: Msgr. Clarence D. White to Msgr. Tanner, May 17, 1962, in Organizations: Secular, 1962–1963, NCWC 10/78, ACUA; George G. Higgins to Paul F. Tanner, June 8, 1964, in Social Action: General 1959–1966, NCWC 84, ACUA; Joseph H. Fichter, "Liberal and Conservative Catholics," in *Priest and People* (New York: Sheed and Ward, 1965), 123–139; Garry Wills, *Politics and Catholic Freedom* (Chicago, IL: Henry Regnery Company, 1964).

22. Joseph P. Chinnici, OFM, "An Historian's Creed and the Emergence of Postconciliar Culture Wars," *Catholic Historical Review* 94 (April 2008): 219–244.

23. Vincent A. Yzermans, ed., *American Participation in the Second Vatican Council* (New York: Sheed and Ward, 1967), 216–221.

backdrop.[24] How the internal application of rights into the body of the Church in the United States would affect pastoral practice in other parts of the world now became a burning question in a new era of global Catholicism, particularly in the areas of the role of women and sexual identity.[25]

This broad outline of a Cold-war time frame is complex, for certain. But it is illuminating. Any historical consideration of the developments in the American Catholic community needs to recognize the intersecting and divergent geo-political interests on the part of the United States, the Soviet Union, the papacy representing the universal Church, the local Church in this country, and the other local churches throughout the world.

The American Conciliar Experience as an Opening to a Global Church

At a very fundamental level the battle with communism opened up the Church in America to the reciprocities inherent in a global world. Vatican Council II, formally taking place between 1962 and 1965, occurred precisely in the middle of this Cold War experience and furthered among its American participants on both an experiential and structural level the transition to a world Church. Joseph Gremillion (1919–1994) was the southern pastor who had toured Latin America in the early 1960s. At the council he worked with James J. Norris (1907–1976), president of the International Catholic Migration Committee, to address world poverty, and became secretary for the Pontifical Commission Justice and Peace, 1967–1974. He probably best identified the change that the council inaugurated.[26] He identified three

---

24. See for an illuminating reflection, J. Bryan Hehir, "Religious Activism for Human Rights: A Christian Case Study," in John Witte Jr., ed., *Religious Human Rights in Global Perspective, Religious Perspectives* (The Hague: Martinus Nijhoff, 1991), 97–119; and for the political background, Elizabeth Borgwardt, *A New Deal for the World: America's Vision for Human Rights* (Cambridge, MA: Harvard University Press, 2005); Kenneth Cmiel, "The Emergence of Human Rights Politics in the United States," *Journal of American History* 86 (December 1999): 1231–1250; David F. Schmitz, *The United States and Right-Wing Dictatorships, 1965–1989* (Cambridge/New York: Cambridge University Press, 2006); John A. Soares, Jr., "Strategy, Ideology and Human Rights: Jimmy Carter Confronts the Left in Central America, 1979–1981," *Journal of Cold War Studies* 8, no. 4 (2006): 57–91.
25. See Mary Ann Glendon, "Women's Identity, Women's Rights and the Civilization of Life," in Alphonsus López Trujillo, Julianus Herranz, and Aelius Sgreccia, *"Evangelium Vitae" e Diritto, "Evangelium Vitae" and Law: Acta Symposii Internationalis in Civitate Vaticana celebrati 23–25 maii 1996* (Roma: Liberia Editrice Vaticana, 1997), 63–75.
26. For Gremillion's relationships with James Norris and Barbara Ward at the council, see Jean Gartlan, *Barbara Ward: Her Life and Letters* (New York: Continuum, 2010), 142–151; Raymond J. Kupke, "An American Intervention at Rome, Father Judge and James Norris at Vatican II," in Joseph C. Linck, CO, and Raymond J. Kupke, eds., *Building the Church in America* (Washington, DC: The Catholic University of America, 1999), 230–251.

levels of "network information, influence and action" which now marked the global face of Catholicism:

1) From the center (Rome) outward to the national church bodies (the periphery), i.e. church headquarters in Washington, Seoul, Manila, Salisbury, etc.
2) From the periphery (national churches) to the center.
3) From periphery to periphery, from one national body to another; or from one region to another, e.g. Washington to Latin America, or to southern Africa, or to the Mideast.[27]

Gremillion's remarks situated the Church in the United States no longer within a European-American context but now within a global network of horizontal exchanges between local churches. It was an awareness that many other American participants in the council shared; and their change in viewpoint can only be described as one of the "conversion" outcomes of the conciliar experience.[28] As Bishop Ernest Primeau (1909–1989) of Manchester, New Hampshire noted in his memoir: "The changes that came about in the direction of the Council and in the attitude of the participants were, as it might be expected, generally gradual. For better or for worse no one of us is quite the same. Yet few of us could accurately trace every step of the path that we have travelled."[29] A short tracing of the trajectory undertaken towards a global church as early as session one (October 1–December 8, 1962) provides one illustration of this gradual change.[30]

Although the National Catholic Welfare Conference had been an effective instrument for collective action in the pre-conciliar period, the 241 bishops from the United States who came to the first session of Vatican II had

---

27. Joseph Gremillion, "The Structures of the Roman Catholic Church as a Transnational Actor for Peace and Justice," in Gremillion, ed., *Harvard Seminar on Muslim Jewish Christian Faith Communities as Transnational Actors for Peace and Justice, March 10–11, 1979* (Washington, DC: Interreligious Peace Colloquium, 1979), 20–29, with citation from 29. See also "North American Ecclesial Consciousness in Its Global Context," *CTSA Proceedings* 36 (1982), 113–129. Perhaps the earliest interpreter was Ivan Vallier, "The Roman Catholic Church: A Transnational Actor," in Robert O. Keohane, Joseph S. Nye, Jr., eds., *Transnational Relations and World Politics* (Cambridge, MA: Harvard University Press, 1971), 129–152.

28. Any stress on the "experience" of the council can unnecessarily feed into the current debates over the council as "event," but the purpose here is not to enter into the questions of continuity and discontinuity but simply to narrate what some of the American participants acknowledge, a real change in awareness and mode of operation. For the current debates see Massimo Faggioli, *Vatican II, The Battle for Meaning* (New York/Mahwah, NJ: Paulist Press, 2012); Joseph Komonchak, "Vatican II as an 'Event,'" *Theology Digest* 46 (Winter 1999): 337–352.

29. Memoir enclosed in letter to P. Alain Dominique Tirot, OP, February 4, 1966, in Primeau Papers, 316/6/32, ACUA.

30. For the purposes of length, I am concentrating on session one and using it as an example, but the argument here could be expanded a hundred fold if the other three sessions were included.

A grouping of American bishops converse in front of St. Peter's Basilica, Vatican City, during the first session of the council, October 1962: Bishop Thomas H. Gorman of Dallas, Texas; Bishop Philip M. Hannan, an auxiliary of Washington, D.C.; Bishop Albert R. Zuroweste of Belleville, Illinois; Bishop James H. Griffith, an auxiliary of New York City; and Bishop John J. Wright of Pittsburgh, Pennsylvania (Courtesy of the Associated Press).

little experience of collateral open discussion either amongst themselves or between bishops of different countries.[31] Shortly after the council began on October 11, 1962, Bishop Primeau, who was clearly one of the Americans most steeped in negotiating Roman ways, addressed his fellow American bishops and proposed some internal organizational structure for work during the sessions: "The body of the American bishops seems to me at the moment floundering because the individual bishop does not understand fully the procedure to be employed in the Council or hesitates to make vocal his own thoughts on a particular matter lest he repeat what one of his brother bishops

---

31. See comments of Bishop Charles A. Buswell in Michael R. Prendergast, M.D. Ridge, eds., *Voices form the Council* (Portland, OR: Pastoral Press, 2004), 9–15. For global profile of bishops at the first session of the council see Vincent A. Yzermans, "Bishops at Vatican II," *Homiletic and Pastoral Review* 63 (March 1963): 491–497. Buswell's view is supported by Pierre Fortin, "The American Hierarchy at the Eve of Vatican II," in *Le Deuxième Concile du Vatican (1959–1965)* (Palais Farnese: École Francaise de Rome, 1989), 155–164; Joseph A. Komonchak, "U.S. Bishops' Suggestions for Vatican II," *Cristianesimo nella Storia* 15 (1994): 313–371, especially 322–325.

intends to say unknown to him."[32] The hierarchy met at the North American College on October 18, appointed a commission to study Primeau's suggestions, and on October 21 adopted an overall structure by which they might engage the council.[33] The first collective meeting was held on October 28, at which the bishops heard addresses by Archbishop John Krol (1910–1996) on the procedures of the council, Archbishop Paul Hallinan (1911–1968) on the Liturgical Commission, and the *peritus* Frederick McManus (1923–2005) who spoke on "Papal Directives on the Liturgy."[34] Archbishop Hallinan of Atlanta was aware very early in the council of the importance of the process of collective consultation and attempted to make the bishops aware of it. Late in session one he argued for a collective demonstration of support for chapter I of the liturgy schema; 132 bishops signed the petition.[35] Primeau, acting as an intermediary between the Americans and other episcopal conferences, regularly joined an international fraternity of some of the bishops at Domus Mariae. The location became a gathering place for this "conference of twenty-two" which was one of the council's more important interest groups. Primeau met with them five times during the first session and subsequently throughout the council. "This gathering," as one person described it, "had its beginning almost spontaneously from the desire of the conciliar Fathers of different nations to have a means of inter communication between nations on subjects being treated in the Council."[36]

Despite these actions, and although the bishops were holding regular Monday meetings, progress in mutual communication amongst themselves and action with the other bishops was slow. On November 26, as the first

---

32. E. Primeau, dictation of October 16, 1962, Ernest Primeau Papers, 316/2/3, typed manuscript, ACUA. For background on this leader of the American hierarchy, see Douglas J. Roche, "Life of a Council Father," *The Sign* 43 (December 1963): 11–17, 71, 72.

33. For information on the process, see Primeau Papers, 316/7/3, ACUA. The commission was composed of Lawrence Shehan (1898–1984) of Baltimore, Francis Reh of Charleston (1911–1994), and Primeau. Primeau's suggestion of American commissions paralleling the conciliar commissions was adopted. The working groups are listed with their names in Floyd Anderson, *Council Daybook Vatican II, Session 1, October 11 to December 8, 1962, Session 2, September 29 to December 4, 1963* (Washington DC: National Catholic Welfare Conference, 1965), 60.

34. See "Presidency of General Committee of the USA Bishops for the II Vatican Council," Primeau Papers, 316/7/3, ACUA; for McManus's important address see "Papal Directives on the Liturgy," George Higgins Papers, 129/305/2, ACUA. For background see Yzermans, *American Participation*, 133.

35. Hallinan, "Report of Commission," George Higgins Papers, 129/305/2, ACUA; Hallian to Your Excellencies, November 22, 1962, Ibid. See Thomas J. Shelley, *Paul J. Hallinan: First Archbishop of Atlanta* (Wilmington, DE: M. Glazier, 1989), 173.

36. For meetings see "Secretariat of the International Bishops Committee 1962–1964," Primeau Papers, 316/7/3, 316/7/3; 316/6/38–39, ACUA. For the importance of the Domus Mariae grouping see J. Grootaers, "Une Concertation Épiscopale au Concile: la Conférence s des Vingt-Deux (1962–1963) in Grootaers, *Actes et Acteurs à Vatican II* (Leuven: University Press, 1998), 132–165.

session wound down, Primeau pled for more open communication: "Rather than insisting on serving secrecy," he noted, the American bishops should move towards objective and robust information sharing, not about what each of them would say but on those things and opinions the council was considering. All of this would be important preparation for the second session of September, 1963.[37] After the first session was over, Luigi Ligutti (1895–1994), a consultant to the conciliar commission on the laity, clearly frustrated with the lack of collective action, wrote to Primeau throughout the spring of 1963 urging him to galvanize the bishops: "push—push—push for greater US active participation."[38] Assessing the inability of the American contingent to get other bishops to join them in supporting a vernacular breviary in session two, McManus opined:

> The failure of the American episcopal conference to enter into regular contacts, formal and informal, with the other hierarchies, makes it difficult to secure support on an issue of this kind, where other groups do not feel deeply involved. If there had been concerted action with other groups, they could be approached on the basis that the conciliar commission should be for the broadest advantage sought by any substantial body in the Church.[39]

Compared to members of the other conferences, for example, Chile, Germany, France, Holland, and Indonesia, the American effort seemed diffuse, its internal diversities evident on the council floor.[40]

Yet, generally short of the collective action which some hoped for, something was happening to some of the American participants. A few of them had been deeply impressed with John XXIII's opening address, *Gaudet Mater Ecclesia*, and recognized that a new opening to the world and to separated brethren was being called for. A "new era" was dawning.[41] Several bishops,

---

37. Primeau, original in Latin, "Oratio su concio habenda et non habita," distributed to the American bishops November 26, 1962, George Higgins Papers, 129/305/2, ACUA.
38. Ligutti to Primeau, February 10, 1963; confer also letters of January 14, 1963; March 24, 1963, April 5, 1963, Primeau Papers, 316/6/5, ACUA.
39. "Modi concerning the Vernacular to be Proposed for Vota," [1963], Frederick McManus Papers, unprocessed, 117/ 4, ACUA. For background see Hallinan to Arcadio Cardinal Larrona, September 4, 1963, McManus Papers, ACUA.
40. Joseph M. Marling, *The Second Vatican* Council, address delivered at St. Charles Seminary, Carthagena, Ohio, May 19, 1963, privately printed, 4, describing the first session; Yzermans, *American Participation*, 137–138, where he details the disagreements over the vernacular in the liturgy expressed by McIntyre of Los Angeles, Meyer of Chicago, and Hallinan of Atlanta.
41. Lawrence Shehan, *A Blessing of Years, The Memoirs of Lawrence Cardinal Shehan* (Notre Dame, IN: University of Notre Dame, 1982), 141–144; Buswell in *Voices from the Council*, 9; Gerald M. Costello, *Without Fear or Favor: George Higgins on the Record* (Mystic, CT: Twenty-third Publications, 1984), 125; Steven M. Avella, *This Confident Church: Catholic*

whose views would be highly influential, were serving in significant positions, most notably, Archbishop John J. Krol of Philadelphia (1910–1996) as an undersecretary, Bishop John Wright of Pittsburgh (1909–1979) and Archbishop John Dearden of Detroit on the Theological Commission, and Archbishop Hallinan on the Liturgical Commission.[42] The leadership from the Midwest in the persons of Cardinals Albert Meyer of Chicago (1902–1965) and Joseph Ritter of St. Louis (1892–1967) was replacing that of Cardinals Francis Spellman (1889–1967) and James McIntyre of Los Angeles (1886–1979).[43] In their memoirs and recollections several participants refer to being impressed with the "freedom" that was being exercised by the bishops in the council.[44] Archbishop Patrick O'Boyle (1896–1987) of Washington, D.C., claimed that the first session was "one of the most democratic meetings he had ever attended."[45] Douglas Horton, the representative of the International Congregational Council, likened the assembly to being present at "the General Synod of the United Church of Christ or some other Protestant body."[46] Krol in his summary penned after the second session of the council, echoed similar sentiments: "There has never been a council in which the participants

---

Leadership and Life in Chicago, 1940–1965 (Notre Dame, IN: University of Notre Dame Press, 1992), 331; notes of Mark J. Hurley, Fresno Retreat, May 16, 1966, in Hurley Papers, Archives of the Archdiocese of San Francisco (AASF); note the comments of Bishop Robert Dwyer of Reno, Nevada, in describing the reaction to John XXIII's *aggiornamento* in Yzermans, *American Participation*, 641.

42. For Krol see Thomas W. Spalding, CFX, "Dissimilitude: The Careers of Cardinals Lawrence J. Shehan and John J. Krol," *U.S. Catholic Historian* 17, no. 4 (Fall 1999): 50–63; for Wright see Adolph Schalk, "At The Council with Bishop Wright," *U.S. Catholic* 30 (February 1965): 6–14.

43. On change of leadership from Spellman to Meyer, see Yzeremans, *American Participation*, 7–8. For Meyer see Steven M Avella, "Albert Meyer: Preparation for Greatness," and "The Crucible of Chicago Catholicism: Albert Meyer Prepares for Vatican II," *Chicago Studies* 48 (Summer 2009): 118–137, 138–158; on Ritter, Robert Donner, "Cardinal Ritter, Welcoming the Future," *The Sign* 42 (March 1963): 14–17, 74–75;

44. Shehan, *The Memoirs*, 148, notes the effective criticism of the schema on the Church by Montini, Suenens, and Lecaro; Raymond Hunthausen refers to the opening assertion by the council of the right to elect the members of its own commissions, *Voices from the Council*, 48; Marling, *The Second Vatican Council*, 3–4, does the same; Victor Reed of Oklahoma noted that he "learned a greater appreciation of the idea of freedom within the Church from his time in Rome" as cited in Jeremy Bonner, *The Road to Renewal, Victor Joseph Reed and Oklahoma Catholicism 1905–1971* (Washington DC: The Catholic University of America Press, 2008), 80–86; Krol mentions freedom and the diversity of the American bishops in his preface to Yzermans, *American Participation*, xi; Yzermans, "U.S. Bishops wanted freedom of Religion," singles out the trend towards freedom as one of the four major developments at the council.

45. As noted in Morris J. Macgregor, *Steadfast in the Faith, The Life of Patrick Cardinal O'Boyle* (Washington DC: The Catholic University of America Press, 2006), 262. Buswell, page 9, uses the same phrase. Confer remarks of John Noonan who compared the workings of the council to a "legislature in action" in *The Lustre of Our Country: The American Experience of Religious Freedom* (Berkeley, CA: University of California Press, 1998), 338.

46. Douglas Horton, *Vatican Diary 1962* (Philadelphia, PA: United Church Press, 1964), 38, also notes a "democratic way of doing things."

had as much opportunity to propose topics, to express their views and to direct the actual trend of conciliar decisions."[47] In addition to this experienced opening in terms of shared authority and conversation, numerous other avenues encouraged an exchange of opinions between the American bishops and *periti*, bishops and non-Catholic observers, bishops and the press corps.[48] One priest described the behind-the-scenes work of the American scripture scholars, their education of the bishops, and dinner conversations.[49] Vincent Yzermans, one of the most astute members of the press corps, took as one sign of freedom observers and bishops "rubbing shoulders in the coffee bar," and carrying on "a religious dialogue the likes of which had not been witnessed in Rome or elsewhere in many a century."[50]

All of these developing relationships taken together seemed to be moving the bulk of the American group forward towards more collegial work and self-understanding. Debates during the first session on the principles governing liturgical reform and on the sources of revelation confirmed a general move away from a juridical approach to the Church towards John XXIII's vision of a "pastoral" *aggiornamento* on all levels.[51] At first quite divided on the issue of a vernacular liturgy, the bishops as a group would move by the end of the first session to support its extensive use.[52] Even more significantly, when the debate over the sources of revelation occurred in November 1962, the American bish-

---

47. Address of John J. Krol to Jewish leaders, March 10, 1964, printed in NCWC News Service, March 16, 1964, 9.

48. Notable instances of these exchanges may be found in the Frederick McManus Papers 177/3 unprocessed, ACUA; George Higgins Papers, 129/305/2, ACUA. At the first session of the council there were nineteen American Protestant observers. A listing of observer delegates at the first two sessions may be found in Floyd Anderson, ed., *Council Daybook Vatican II*, 17, 138–140. The most thorough presentation of the council from this perspective is Douglas Horton, *Vatican Diary*. See "The Observers, Friendly Guests, Keen Critics," *The Sign* 43 (October 1963): 24–31. A listing of American *periti* may be found in Floyd Anderson, ed., *Council Daybook*, 76.

49. Sully to Dear Father McDonald, November 23, 1962, Mark Hurley Papers, AASF. The scholars were Ray Brown, Eugene Maly, and Barnabas Ahern; the others, Bishop Leo Maher and Archbishop Joseph T. McGucken. For the "Human Side of the Council" see Anderson, *Council Daybook*, 85.

50. "U.S. Bishops wanted freedom of Religion." As one example, see Douglas Horton to Bishop Primeau, February 4, 1963, in which Horton requests Primeau to review his diary of the first session, Primeau Papers, 316-6-3, ACUA.

51. This is evident in the developments in the areas of the schema on the Church, revelation, and ministry and life of priests. See Yzermans, *American Participation*, 29–31, 106–111, 469–487.

52. Yzermans, *American Participation*, 4, 142–143, refers to a "development" and by the end of the second session a "metamorphosis" in the body, a fact confirmed by the archival evidence in Higgins and McManus Papers, ACUA. Confer pages 146–147 for the statement of the bishops issued on December 4, 1963, the same day the *Constitution on the Sacred Liturgy* was passed. It is notable that when Paul Hallinan spoke on the liturgy, October 31, 1962, he was commended by Krol, Ritter, Griffiths, Reed, and McDevitt. See Shelley, *Paul J. Hallinan*, 168.

ops became well exposed to the issues. November 13, as critiques of the initial draft circulated among the conciliar bishops, Dearden attended the Theological Commission meeting and witnessed the contentious debate between Cardinal Alfredo Ottaviani (1890–1979) and Cardinal Paul-Émile Léger (1904–1991). The Archbishop of Detroit made a cautious option for Léger's side of free discussion.[53] On November 14, Dearden followed the debates in the Council Hall with great attention, closely summarizing the arguments of Léger, König, Alfrink, Suenens, Ritter, Bea, and Maximos.[54] Ritter spoke that same day and gave a severe critique of the initial schema. Horton wrote in his diary of the day's exchange: "Then the dam broke. At last the council fathers in public assembly had the opportunity to say what they felt about the proposals."[55] Two days later, November 16, McIntyre spoke in favor of the initial schema. The next day, the German theologian Otto Semmelroth (1912–1979) noted in his diary that the American contingent had requested innumerable copies of Karl Rahner's (1904–1984) critique of the proposed schema.[56] On November 19, Meyer, following Cardinal Augustin Bea (1881–1968) and echoing Bishop Emile de Smedt (1909–1995), called for a reconsideration of the method employed in the schema—a clear opening to the ecumenical and pastoral style advocated by John XIII. James Griffiths (1903–1964), auxiliary bishop of New York, more conciliatory towards the initial schema, still argued for a change of style.[57] Bishop Lawrence Shehan would later call de Smedt's speech "eloquent."[58] Bishop Joseph Marling in his memoirs noted the importance of the debate and showed a moderate openness to scripture scholar-

---

53. Dearden's notes of this most important meeting may be found in "Notes on Meeting of Theological Commission, November 13, 1962," Dearden Papers (CDRD), 1/06, Archives of the University of Notre Dame (AUND). See also his notes on the mixed commission meeting of November 25, Ibid. For importance of the debate, Riccardo Burigana, *La Bibbia nel concilio, La redazione della constituzione "Dei verbum" del Vaticano II* (Società Editrice Il Mulino, 1998), 128–130; Karim Schelkens, "Cardinal Paul-Émile Léger and the Establishment of the Mixed Commission on Revelation," in Michael Attridge, Catherine E. Clifford, Gilles Routhier, eds., *Vatican II, Expériences canadiennes, Canadian experiences* (Ottawa: University of Ottawa Press 2011), 184–208.

54. His extensive notes may be found in "De Revelatione Divina," CDRD 3/12, AUND.

55. Horton, *Vatican Diary 1962*, 111; cf. 122–123.

56. Giuseppe Alberigo, Joseph A. Komonchak, eds., *History of Vatican II, The Formation of the Council's Identity, First Period and Intersession October 1962-September 1963* (Maryknoll, NY: Orbis Books, 1997), II: 261, fn 75.

57. The debates and interventions are covered in Yzermans, *American Participation*, 105–111; de Smedt's speech is printed in Vincent Yzermans, *A New Pentecost, Vatican Council II: Session I* (Westminster, MD: The Newman Press, 1963), 204–207. On Bea, see Jerome-Michael Vereb, CP, *"Because He Was a German!" Cardinal Bea and the Origins of the Roman Catholic Engagement in the Ecumenical Movement* (Grand Rapids, MI: William B. Eerdmans Publishing Company, 2006).

58. Shehan, *A Blessing of Years*, 148; Shehan notes the ecumenical importance of this debate in his public address of October 23, 1963, United States Bishops Press Panel, George Higgins Papers, 129/305/3, ACUA.

ship.⁵⁹ Primeau referred to the "crucial debate on Divine Revelation."⁶⁰ That afternoon, the scripture scholar Barnabas Ahern, CP, spoke to the assembled hierarchy at North American College on modern exegesis. He successfully defended the new scholarship against the Apostolic Delegate's remarks "with devastating effect."⁶¹

On November 21, John XXIII intervened in the council's debate and announced the establishment of a "mixed commission" led by Ottavanni and Bea to try to resolve the differences expressed on the council floor. Cardinal Meyer was named a member, and later on Dearden, Wright, and Griffiths joined him.⁶² As the council was making this great turn towards an ecumenical and pastoral opening to the world, Yves Congar, OP (1904–1995) recorded in his diary a visit from the American scripture scholar Raymond Brown, SS (1928–1998). The latter informed him that the Americans along with the other English speaking bishops had changed their ideas in the last few days.⁶³ The private intervention days later by the supporters of those who argued primarily for the affirmation of "doctrinal principles in order to defend the Catholic faith against errors and deviations that today are scattered about almost everywhere," among whom was Cardinal McIntyre, did not succeed.⁶⁴ The debates, the educational experiences, the interventions of the *periti*, the dinner conversations, had all served to open many of the Americans, especially the leadership, to new initiatives.

This development during the debates on the sources of revelation paralleled that of the debates on the liturgy. As the council closed its first session the American bishops along with the others overwhelmingly approved the first chapter of the schema on the liturgy on December 7, 1962. Its passage, as Hallinan and others explained later in their reports, contained important

---

59. Marling, *The Second Vatican Council*, 14–17.
60. Primeau memoir in letter to Tirot, February 4, 1966, Primeau Papers 316/6/32, p.2, ACUA.
61. Yzermans, *American Participation*, 104. The heart of Ahern's thinking may be found in his articles "The Gospels in the Light of Modern Research," *Chicago Studies* 1 (Spring 1962): 5–16; Barnabas M. Ahern, CP, "Sacred Scripture," *The Critic* XXI (August-September 1962): 27–30; "The Biblical Way of Life," *The Critic* XXIV (August-September 1965), 38–47; "Lasting Impact in Revelation Document," in Floyd Anderson, ed., *Council Daybook, Vatican II, Session 3* (Washington, DC: National Catholic Welfare Conference, 1965), 139–140. See also the notes of Mark J. Hurley in file marked "Revelation Resource" where he has notes taken in November 1962 and other materials related to the controversy, Hurley Papers, AASF.
62. Floyd Anderson, ed., *Council Daybook Vatican II, Session 1, October 11 to December 8, 1962, Session 2, September 29 to December 4, 1963*, 83–84, 117–118 for background. A succinct description of the importance may be found in John W. O'Malley, *What Happened at Vatican II* (Cambridge, MA: Harvard University Press, 2008), 150–151.
63. Yves Congar, *Mon Journal du Concile* I (Paris: Les Éditions du Cerf, 2002), 252.
64. As cited in Giuseppe Alberigo and Joseph Komonchak, eds., *History of Vatican II*, II: 347.

ecclesiological and ecumenical principles: "through the eucharist the Church is formed"; wider use of the vernacular; wider use of Scripture; norms of adaptation; full and active participation of the faithful; the authority of regional conferences of bishops; diversity of application.[65] Frederick McManus noted the importance: "For our entire Constitution on the Sacred Liturgy has as its hinge the concept that the liturgical restoration in great part shall be handed over to execution by the bishops in different ways according to the various conditions of their region."[66] The *peritus* Godfrey Diekmann, OSB, present at the second session in 1963, would later remark: "the general direction of the council was assured in the first session."[67] On December 6, the council participants had received "Norms for the Work During the Interval Between the First Session of the Council and the Beginning of the Second."[68] More and more were becoming convinced that Vatican Council II was a call to develop a pastoral outreach of openness, dialogue, ecumenical relations, and engagement with modern scholarship, even perhaps a different way of thinking about the Church and practicing the faith.

At first glance this examination of developments in the first session of Vatican II might not seem connected to the American Church's globalization. However, what was happening at all levels was an opening to other people, cultures, and viewpoints. Formally, the preparatory work, liturgical studies, and debates on revelation had occasioned some exposure to the positions of other national groupings of bishops.[69] Informally, the general congregations, coffee houses, dinner parties, and mix of people created a certain

---

65. Citation from Hallinan, Supplement to the Report on the Work of the Commission on the Sacred Liturgy, October 4, 1963, p. 3, CDRD 12/17, AUND. See also Paul J. Hallinan to Your Excellencies, November 22, 1962, George Higgins Papers, 129/305/2, ACUA; Hallinan, Report on the Work of the Commission on the Sacred Liturgy for the Meeting of the Bishops of the United States, Chicago, August 6–7, 1963, CDRD 3/17, AUND. See the important commentary, published on December 8, 1962, by Ciprano Vagaggini, OSB and contained in Anderson, *Council Daybook*, 123–127, also published in Yzermans, *A New Pentecost*, 171–182. The evidence supports the general argument of Massimo Faggioli, "Sacrosanctum concilium and the Meaning of Vatican II," *Theological Studies* 71 (June 2010): 437–452.

66. McManus, "Excerpts from the Reports of the Conciliar Commission on the Sacred Liturgy," 22 pages [1963] in McManus Papers, 117/3, unprocessed, ACUA. He is referring to article 22 of Chapter I. See also Bishops' Commission on the Liturgical Apostolate, CDRD 12/19, AUND.

67. As cited from his diary in Kathleen Hughes, RSCJ, *The Monk's Tale, A Biography of Godfrey Diekmann, OSB* (Collegeville, MN: The Liturgical Press, 1991), 224.

68. *Council Daybook, Sessions 1 & 2*, 114.

69. For examples, see "Enmiendos al Proemio y il capitulo primero del esquema de Constitution sobre la Sagrada Liturgia propuestas por la Conferencia de los Obispos de Chile," distributed to American prelates at instruction of Bishop Waters, four pages in Latin, George Higgins Papers, 129/305/2, ACUA; "Observations of the Italian Bishops Presented by Archbishop," Ibid.; Archbishop Garrone of Toulouse, "The Collective Responsibility of the Episcopate," translated from French original and completed at N.C.W.C. News Service, February 2, 1961, Mark Hurley Papers, AASF.

impression of universality among both the bishops and *periti*.⁷⁰ The intensity of the atmosphere is perhaps best captured by Mark Hurley, one of the *periti*, in a letter to a friend:

> Here at this Hotel called the Mondial, we are known as the seat of revolution because here all sorts of opinions are expressed. Bishops and Archbishops and even one Cardinal has asked to come over to listen. We have a Common Room where many of the experts, some ten or twelve anyway, speak very freely. We've had Hans Kung, Gustave Weigel, Father Baum from Canada, members of the Congregations of the Holy Office of the Council, and of the Secretariat of State, members from the Biblical Institute, Butch Fenton and all sorts of people here expressing, in very violent terms sometimes, what they think.⁷¹

Edward Duff, the Jesuit editor of *Social Order*, wrote in *La Civiltà Cattolica* that one of the clear outcomes of the first session on the part of the American bishops was a sense of the universal church and their responsibility in it.⁷² Diverse participants reacted in the same way. Even while the first session was still in progress Archbishop McGucken of San Francisco commented in the local Catholic paper:

> If I understand your question, I would answer that one major result has been the knowledge and understanding by the Bishops of each other's needs and problems around the world. We in the U.S. knew something of Latin America but now we have learned first hand of the problems of Japanese Catholics, Indonesians, Africans, and Polynesians; the prelates from all over the globe who have spoken have helped us all to distinguish better what is essential in the Church and what is non-essential.⁷³

The same prelate would identify the "great consensus on the part of the episcopacy of the world" as the "most significant accomplishment" of the first session.⁷⁴ Primeau in his 1966 recollections described a more personal reaction: "How can I evaluate what I have learned from the hundreds of interventions given in the Aula, many of them of great theological moment;

---

70. This comes through in almost all the archival evidence, but a clear example is provided by the general comments of George Higgins, especially on the gatherings at Villanova House for the second third and fourth sessions of the council. See Gerald M. Costello, *Without Fear or Favor*, 121 on gatherings at Hotel Mondial during the first session, and 127 for those at Villanova House.

71. Mark J. Hurley to Reverend Joseph O'Connell, CM, November 20, 1962, Hurley Papers, AASF.

72. Edward Duff, "Echi del Concilio, negli Stati Uniti," in *Il Concilio Vaticano II, Il Primo Periodo 1962–1963* (Roma: Edizioni "La Civiltà Cattolica"), 489.

73. "Archbishop McGucken on Council," *San Francisco Monitor* (December 7, 1962).

74. Questionnaire attached to letter, Frank Morris (*The National Register*) to Most Rev. J.T. McGucken, August 19, 1963, "Ecumenical Council," McGucken Papers, AASF.

from the private conversations in the refreshment bars or elsewhere in Rome; from the many friendships that I have made and the others that I have strengthened; from the examples of heroic fortitude of our brothers living in persecution, or in the case of a few, those who have died martyrs' death since the Council began."[75] In its summary to be used by the bishops for their press conferences upon returning to the United States in December 1962, the U.S. Press Panel Service noted that the "accomplishments of this first session lie in elements actually outside the Council itself, but which can and will have a very direct impact on subsequent phases." Mentioning the numerous face to face contacts and the plenary sessions, the authors called particular attention to the impact of the council on American participants. Local problems "assumed a quite different aspect when viewed in a global background. Bishops the world over have gained a new insight into their Church-wide responsibilities." "They go home with a new group consciousness, with a more penetrating insight into the needs of the Church today than if there had been no Council."[76] Vincent Yzermans, trying to capture the whole experience, noted that a new "internationalization" of the Church was taking place.[77]

Over the course of the next few months other bishops would confirm this opening to the world. Bishop Marling of Jefferson City, Missouri, in his reflections in May illustrated for his seminarians the wide range of issues covered and the movement towards a collegial understanding that the first session occasioned.[78] Cardinal Ritter, clearly more progressive but nonetheless affirming the same point, noted: "No bishop can go back to his own little diocese—or his big diocese—and forget about the rest of the world's people, whether they be Catholic or non-Catholic. . . . The Bishops have learned from this one session that we are all brothers, and members of the human family."[79] The progressive Cardinal from St. Louis was more explicit in an interview before the second session:

> There is a new mood and direction in the Church, almost everyone senses it. And the Council is a part of it. Perhaps it would be best to say that the Council and the spirit it reflects is a combination of trends in

---

75. Attached to Primeau to Tirot, February 4, 1966, Primeau Papers, 316/6/32, ACUA.
76. "Notes on the First Session of Vatican Council II," George Higgins Papers, 129/305/2, ACUA.
77. NCWC News Service, "U.S. Bishops wanted freedom of Religion in Pluralistic Society Defined at Council," February 11, 1963, citing Yzermans, in Primeau Papers, 317/7/8, ACUA.
78. Marling, "The Second Vatican Council," *passim*, and "one of the golden results of the Council to date has been the awakening of bishops" to their place in the "episcopal college" (19–20).
79. N.C.W.C. News Service, "New Definition of Church Needed to Spur Christian Unity, Cardinal Declares," February 18, 1963, Primeau Papers, 316/7/16, ACUA.

religion, culture and education that have been going on for some time. The jet and space age have focused man's attention on his relationship to every other man and have forced him to ask questions that might not have occurred to him in his insular past. This has had its effect on the development of the ecumenical movement as well.

Then you can't overlook the experience we have had in this century with major wars and the ever-present threat of nuclear warfare—these have made men conscious of the perils of the time and their need for guidance.[80]

Calling the council the "grace of a lifetime," one of the key leaders of the American hierarchy spoke for many who were there. Later, in their 1964 and 1965 recollections John Wright and John Krol would agree.[81]

Recent commentaries on the American experience at the council have referred to this experience which began to be delineated at the first session as an "effervescence."[82] The participants did not speak of "effervescence," but rather, hard work. They understood the experience as a movement of the Holy Spirit, a "new Pentecost."[83] In the context of the contemporary interpretations arguments have centered on continuity and discontinuity, spirit and letter, style and form.[84] Little attention has been paid to the American participation, usually confined to questions of religious liberty or ecumenism. What is clear, even for the first session, is that prelates as diverse in generation and outlook as John Krol, Joseph Ritter, Joseph Marling, Patrick O'Boyle, James McIntyre, Ernest Primeau, Albert Meyer, Francis Spellman, James Griffiths, Stephen Leven, Lawrence Shehan, Victor Reed, Joseph McGucken, and Paul Hallinan; experts from different places with different trainings and background as Frederick McManus, Thomas Stransky, Luigi

---

80. Daniel Moore, "Return to Rome," *Ave Maria* 98 (September 14, 1963): 5–9, quote at 6.

81. Krol, NCWC News Service, March 16, 1964, Primeau Papers, 316/7/12, ACUA; "Most Rev. John J. Wright," *America* 112 (March 27, 1965): 418–420.

82. In making this argument Andrew Greeley relies upon the sociological study of Melissa Wilde who applies the concepts of Emile Durkheim and the social theory of change developed by William Sewell, Jr. See Greeley, *The Catholic Revolution: New Wine, Old Wineskins, and the Second Vatican Council* (Berkeley: University of California Press, 2004), 41–70; Melissa J. Wilde, *Vatican II: A Sociological Analysis of Religious Change* (Princeton, NJ: Princeton University Press, 2007). See also John A. Coleman, "Vatican II as a Social Movement," in D. Donnelly, J. Famerée, M. Lamberigts, K. Schelkens, eds., *The Belgian Contribution to the Second Vatican Council* (Leuven: Uitgeveru Peeters, 2008), 5–28.

83. "Most Rev. John. J. Wright," certainly not given to enthusiasms identifies it as such.

84. See Neill Ormerod, "Vatican II—Continuity or Discontinuity? Toward an Ontology of Meaning," *Theological Studies* 71 (September 2010): 609–636; Gerard Whelan, SJ, "Interpreting Vatican II, Questions of Style, Meaning, Truth," *Gregorianum* 92 (2011): 606–616; Kristin Colberg, "The Hermeneutics of Vatican II: Reception, Authority, and the Debate over the Council's Interpretation," *Horizons* 38, no. 2 (2011): 230–252.

Ligutti, Eugene Maly, Barnabas Ahern, Joseph Fenton, George Higgins, John S. Quinn, and others scattered throughout Rome—all testified that something different was happening.[85] None of these people seem to have framed the experience in terms of "continuity" or "discontinuity." Many recognized that a turn had been taken towards the "pastoral," "ecumenical," and "worldwide" dimensions of the Church. The term "pastoral" carried not simply rhetorical connotations but theological, social, and anthropological meaning. Bishop James Griffiths, commenting during the debate on the sources of revelation, captured the connection in his comments on the council floor, November 19, 1962:

> Still we have not found clear examples of that ecumenical style, as it is called. Perhaps it is intended that the Constitutions and decrees should be written with the utmost charity and with concern for the mind of the great number of good non-Catholics spread throughout the world, who anxiously await solace for the soul from this ecumenical assembly. If this is the way in which it is understood, then we gladly and sincerely approve and recommend the proposal.[86]

Still searching certainly, yet bishops, *periti*, and commentators felt that the council experience had generated a new conciliar and worldwide awareness with considerable ramifications.

Clarifying words, concepts, structures, and an intensified collegial experience would come during the next sessions of the council (II: September 29–December 4, 1963; III: September 14–November 21, 1964; IV: September 14–December 8, 1965).[87] The dynamics of interchanges between American bishops and *periti*, the worldwide consultation between regions of bishops, and the pressure and counter pressure between the council, the press, and the world would only grow in intensity. Each session would have its own integrity, but in terms of internationalism, they would all move in the same general direction, a cumulative reinforcement of global solidarity. For purposes of this article, a glance at the second session of the council will suffice to confirm this movement.

---

85. See "Theologians Available in Rome for 'Consultation,'" Keeler Papers, Archives of the Archdiocese of Baltimore (hereafter AAB). I am grateful to archivist Tricia Pyne for this reference.

86. Yzermans, *American Participation*, 110. For further references in 1962 to the "pastoral" turn see comments of Meyer, Ritter, Shehan, Hallinan, Connare, Reed, in Yzermans, *American Participation*, 107, 105, 152, 157, 162, 169.

87. See "Notes on the Second Session of Vatican Council II," Mark Hurley Papers, AASF; Floyd Anderson, *Council Daybook, Vatican II, Session 3* (Washington DC: National Catholic Welfare Conference, 1965); "Notes on Session IV of Vatican II," George Higgins Papers, 129/305/6, ACUA.

Discussion on the nature of the Church began during the second session on October 1 and continued intermittently until the culminating vote on October 30 that overwhelmingly affirmed episcopal collegiality.[88] The intense exchange that followed on November 8 between Cardinal Joseph Frings (1887–1978), critiquing the Roman curia, and Cardinal Ottaviani, asserting curial rights, did not go unnoticed amongst the American bishops.[89] They were clearly well informed about the debates.[90] On November 10, 1963, Bishop Hallinan sent the bishops a memorandum advocating adoption of the entire liturgical constitution and pushing for as wide as possible use of English in the liturgy. The action would show collegiality in practice and shape the role of national conferences in the Church.[91] Despite the disagreements over the juridical authority of national conferences, which would remain a bone of contention in the post-conciliar Church, the American bishops' support for collegiality and assertion of the rights of the local ordinary in governance came through strongly in public and private comments.[92] At the end of the session, on December 4, the bishops issued a

---

88. During this session there were fourteen public interventions into the debate on the Church, five into the debate on ecumenism, and eight into the discussion of the pastoral office of bishops. While disagreement was expressed on the reinstitution of the permanent diaconate and the teaching authority of conferences, there was greater consensus on collegiality, the role of the laity, and the Church as the people of God. Note the public interventions into the debates on the Church in 1963 by Primeau, Ritter, Marling, Spellman, Meyer, Shehan, Wright, Hannan, Tracy, Russell, in Yzermans, *American Participation*, 53–72; *Council Daybook, Sessions I & II*, 225. For background and importance, O'Malley, *What Happened at Vatican II*, 178–185.

89. *Council Daybook, Sessions 1 & 2*, November 8, 1963, 246–249. For just one example of reaction to the Frings-Ottavanni debate see Shehan, *A Blessing of Years*, 157–159. For importance see O'Malley, *What Happened at Vatican II*, 192–193; Joseph Ratzinger, "Cardinal Frings's Speeches During the Second Vatican Council: Some Reflections Apropos of Muggeridge's *The Desolate City*," in Pope Benedict XVI, *The Unity of the Church* (Grand Rapids, MI: William B. Eerdmans, 2010), 85–105.

90. As examples of what the bishops were receiving, see *News Bulletin* No. 4, October 3, 1963, on the Church; October 16, 1963, on chapter 3 of the schema, "The Church as people of God," *Concilio Ecumenico Vaticano II, Documentation*, Mark Hurley Papers, AASF. For collegiality see Archbishop Garrone of Toulouse, "The Collective Responsibility of the Episcopate"; R. Martelet, K. Rahner, J. Ratzinger, "De Primatu et Collegio-Episcoporumn in Regimine Totius Ecclesiae,"[October 1963], Mark Hurley Papers, AASF; *Council Digest*, Appendices 5–6, "Synthesis of the Conciliar Discussion 'De Episcopis'", CDRD 1/11, AUND. T.W. Coyle, C.SS.R., "Episcopal Collegiality in Tradition and Theology," U.S.A., C #2, B; and Barnabas Ahern, C.P., "Witness of Sacred Scripture to Collegiality of the Apostles and Bishops," in CDRD 3/08, AUND.

91. Hallinan, "Memorandum on the Use of the Vernacular," CDRD 1/11, AUND.

92. On November 12–13, the American cardinals displayed their open disagreements on the juridical authority of national conferences of bishops (McIntyre and Spellman in opposition, Ritter in favor, Meyer both/and). See Yzermans, *American Participation*, 366–373, 379–389; *Council Daybook, Sessions 1 & 2*, 255–260. For the "animadversions" on these subjects see CDRD 3/07, AUND, with two representative examples being those of Helmsing and Krol, pp. 68, 69, 93.

formal statement "wholeheartedly" welcoming the *Constitution on the Sacred Liturgy* and agreeing to make "full use of the vernacular."[93] The implications for collegiality and governance were clear.

On November 18, 1963, the council began discussion of the proposed decree on ecumenism. While the first three chapters considered ecumenical relationships between the various churches, Chapter IV examined attitudes towards non-Christians, especially the Jews, and Chapter V, religious liberty. It was the last two chapters that carried implications for every human being on the planet. On November 19, Cardinal Bea introduced Chapter IV and Bishop de Smedt presented the chapter on religious liberty.[94] Two days later the American bishops drafted a unanimous petition urging the necessity of a declaration on the human person in the matter of religious liberty and calling for its treatment as soon as possible.[95] But as this conciliar session ended, the council failed to address both chapters. Cardinal Joseph Ritter submitted a written intervention on December 3, 1963, and then in late January 1964, wrote to the American bishops asking them to intervene.[96] The galvanizing effect was extraordinary. Letters from American bishops flooded the Secretariat for Christian Unity, all of them arguing for a declaration on religious liberty that would affect all non-Christians, the Jews in particular.[97] The communication from Edward A. Fitzgerald, Bishop of Winona, captures the general attitude:

> I heartily endorse the statement made by His Eminence Joseph Cardinal Ritter of St. Louis on the question "De Oecumenismo Quintum de Libertate Religiosa." In this concurrence I am speaking in the name of my priests, religious and laity in the Diocese of Winona and, I am sure, in agreement with almost unanimity with the Council Fathers of the United States. We sincerely hope that these subjects will be included for thorough discussion and vote in the next session of the Council.[98]

---

93. For their robust declaration see Yzermans, *American Participation*, 146–147. For another recognition of the relationship between collegiality, the role of conferences, and the liturgical reform, see Dearden to Francis Simons, D.D., [Bishop of Indore, India], January 8, 1964, CDRD 7/02, AUND.

94. *Council Daybook, Sessions 1 & 2*, 282–284; for de Smedt's address see "De Oecumenismo," U.S. Bishops' Press Panel, Primeau Papers, 316/3/16, ACUA.

95. Cf. Primeau Papers 316/8/11 and 316/6/34, ACUA.

96. See "Confidential Memorandum," January 27, 1964, CDRD 5/13, AUND.

97. See the flood of letters in January-March 1964, Primeau Papers, 316/4/3, ACUA. I have counted thirty in addition to Archbishop Karl J. Alter's (G-114) which were submitted on behalf of ninety bishops; confer also 316/8/11, ACUA.

98. "De Capite V in Genere," G-51, Primeau Papers, 316/4/3, ACUA. See also John Krol to Primeau, February 19, 1964, Primeau Papers 316/8/11, ACUA; "Observations on the Schema de Oecumenismo," [Helmsing], 316/3/16, Ibid.

The long journey that would lead eventually to *Nostra Aetate* and *Dignitatis Humanae Personae* is fairly well known.[99] But in getting there other important things happened. A theory and a practice had been established which would reshape the Church in the coming years. On November 13, in the middle of the debates of session two, American bishops and *periti* gathered to listen to a paper by Piet Fransen (1913–1983), a Belgian Jesuit, on "episcopal conferences."[100] The theologian argued that collegiality was not primarily a juridical reality but an ontological, personal one:

> This profound unity in origin and scope brings it about that the bishops can never be completely separated from one another in an atomic view of the Episcopate of sorts, only externally related to one another through the power of jurisdiction of the Pope. The very nature of the one body of bishops is to represent, as a corporate entity, the priestly Presence of Christ amid his Church.

There exists, he noted, a "common responsibility in the government of the whole Church." The theologian then went on to name two institutional forms in which collegiality might be expressed: an Ecumenical Council and episcopal conferences. "Common responsibility," "fellowship," "mutual obligation of fraternal love" were meant to be the underlying realities reshaping old structures and occasioning new ones. As another *peritus* put it at the time:

> So viewed, Catholicity no longer meant merely looking toward Rome; it also meant looking toward one's neighbors. This "horizontal" element included orientation toward the neighbor and the joint assuming of Christian responsibility. Finally such thoughts must lead to a search for practical ways of realizing collegiality—i.e., to the question of the bishops' common ministry. An outline of this was attempted in this session's debate of the draft schema on bishops and the governance of dioceses.[101]

Not envisioned at the time, this opening to a "horizontal element" in the international context established by the Cold War and in a fast emerging

---

99. See for background Piertro Pavan, "Declaration on Religious Freedom," in Herbert Vorgrimler, ed., *Commentary on the Documents of Vatican II* (New York: Herder and Herder, 1969), 49–62; George H. Tavard, "American Contributions to Vatican II's Documents on Ecumenism and on Religious Liberty," *Chicago Studies* 42 (Spring 2003): 17–30; Silvia Scatena, "Emiel-Jozef de Smedt, John Courtney Murray and Religious Freedom," in *The Belgian Contribution to the Second Vatican Council*, 633–645.

100. "Episcopal Conferences," November 13, 1963, given at Graduate Department of the American College, Shehan Papers, Box 1, Series 1–7, "Decree on the Bishops' Pastoral Office," AAB. See Piet Fransen, "Episcopal Conferences: Crucial Problem of the Council," *Cross Currents* 13 (Summer 1963): 349–371.

101. Joseph Ratzinger, *Theological Highlights of Vatican II* (Mahwah, NJ: Paulist Press, 1966, 2009), 83.

Pope Paul VI with Council Fathers presiding over the proclamation of five conciliar decrees, including *Nostra Aetate* (Declaration on the Relation of the Church to Non-Christian Religions) and *Dignitatis Humanae* (Declaration on Religious Freedom), October 28, 1965 (Courtesy of the Associated Press).

global world would place the Church on a new trajectory, and reposition the story of American Catholicism into the larger narrative of a world Church.

In summary, the discussion on the Church as the "people of God," the emphasis on the mission of the laity, the debate on collegiality, the assertion of the role of the bishop in the governance of the Church, the function of national episcopal conferences—all of these issues converged in the second session with the adoption of the *Constitution on the Sacred Liturgy* and the debate on ecumenism. A new awareness of collegiality and authority and the possibility of its functioning in concrete situations had now emerged. The consolidated response to the question of religious liberty and the relationship with the Jews served as a flash point to congeal a vision of the Church. What was clearly implied in all of this was a change not in the hierarchical constitution of the Church, but in the functional operation of authority as it touched not only the local church but also the relationship between the bishops and the Roman curia and, most importantly for this essay, the relationship of the bishops amongst themselves and between their national bodies. In the near future, the issue of collegiality in vision and practice would structure the initial implementation of the council. This new awareness developed in the second session would only be strengthened in sessions three and four as the ecumenical question opened up to touch world religions, the issue of religious liberty shifted the axis of church-state relationships towards the dignity of the person and constitutionalism, and the global challenges of poverty and war pushed for a common human response.[102]

The course of the council had been established in the first two sessions and reinforced in the next two. For the pragmatic and organized American contingent, these ideas as they touched the world Church would eventually take concrete institutional shape in the post-conciliar world in multiple ways: (1) the establishment of their own national conference; (2) their horizontal relationships with other conferences; (3) the world wide creation of secretariats of justice and peace and ecumenical relationships; (4) the Synod of Bishops established by Paul VI, September 15, 1965; and (5) the substantive relationship with the Roman curia and papal teaching office. In the post-conciliar Church it is these institutional developments that would first carry and then occasion an awareness of the Catholic Church in America becoming global.

Conclusion: Awareness of an American Church Gone Global

The convergence between the long arc of the Cold War and the Second Vatican Council created a new map for both thinking about the American Catholic story and writing its history. The story of the Church in this country has gone global. Examining the sources for the post-conciliar period the historian can see this new world reality playing itself out in the exposure given to the Church in the United States by the worldwide media, in the participation by the American bishops and *periti* in the series of Roman Synods, in the impact of the American interpretation of justice through the Pontifical Commission Justice and Peace, and in the increasing attention given to pastoral developments in the Church in the United States by other conferences of bishops and by the Roman curia. Reciprocities, networks of exchange, pressures and counter-pressures, advocacies and resistances have marked the relationships between the local churches. The Church in the United States because of its size, infrastructure, and attachment to a global power, has often been the key catalyst for action and reaction. While the general awareness of such a new development emerged only gradually, the terrain of this global map was becoming increasingly clear by the mid-1970s. It is at that point that one can discern its impact on how the post-conciliar world developed. I would like to conclude with just a few references which convey the general change.

---

102. Only in this light can one interpret John Wright's very synthetic article "Vatican II in '24 Seed Ideas,'" *Homiletic and Pastoral Review* 67 (October 1966): 23–30.

From the mid-1970s onwards the recognition that the role of the Church in the United States within the universal Church had changed since World War II surfaces repeatedly in the remarks of the Apostolic Delegate Jean Jadot (1909–2009). Other knowledgeable commentators follow suit.[103] Archbishop Joseph Bernardin (1928–1996), upon the completion of his three year term as president of the National Conference in November 1977, explicitly noted: "The Holy Father has often told me that the Church in many parts of the world looks to the U.S. Episcopal conference to play a leadership role—to be a pace-setter in a number of respects—and he shared this view. He has high expectations for the conference and counts on it to make major contributions to Catholic life not only in the United States but universally."[104] By 1977 decisions made within the American context were being perceived by many as having world-wide impact. For example, when the *National Catechetical Directory* for the United States was reviewed in Rome in 1978 the text received close attention. As Cardinal John Wright remarked at the time, "I am not sure that all our hierarchy appreciates the impact and normative power of an American pronouncement of this kind, and so words will be weighed beyond doubt."[105] And lastly, the internationalist implications of American pastoral practices permeate the sources connected to events of the 1980s. The study of the American seminaries, the investigation into religious life, and examination of the pastoral practices within the Archdiocese of Seattle, all have international repercussions and in some measure are engendered not simply by forces within the local Church but by the concern of other local churches for the impact of the American implementation of Vatican II. Once the long arc of the Cold War is identified from 1945–1989, these local events become questions of international import. As John R. Roach (1921–2003), the Archbishop of Minneapolis–St. Paul, remarked to the American bishops after returning from an *ad limina* visit to the Holy See: One of the chief concerns of the pope

> is the fact that the Church in the United States, because of its size, wealth, and access to the media, has an exceptional influence—a ripple effect—on the Church in other countries. Having just returned from

---

103. For Jadot see "Signs of Hope for the Future of the Church," address at the Centenary Celebration of the Cathedral of the Holy Name, Chicago, September 19, 1974, in *Selected Addresses of Archbishop Jean Jadot*, 1–4, in Apostolic Delegate, Varia, AASF; see also his address "A View Toward Religious Priorities" at Reception of the Pax Christi Award, St. John's University, Collegeville, Minnesota, Ibid., 11–13. Confer also Archbishop John Quinn, "Invitation to Assess the U.S. Church," at the annual meeting of the National Conference of Catholic Bishops, May 1, 1979, *Origins* 8, no. 47 (May 10, 1979).

104. "NC Documentary: Interview with Archbishop Bernardin," November 8, 1977, AASF.

105. John Cardinal Wright to Most Rev. John R. Quinn, March 20, 1978, AASF.

the Synod in Rome, where I mingled with bishops from all over the world, I have no doubt of that.[106]

For the historian, what is happening in the United States in this era can no longer be interpreted as simply a conflict along a Roman-American axis, but needs to be framed in terms of the role of American Catholicism within a world Church and the concerns in the world Church of an outsized American religious hegemony. The interpretive question then remains: Has the reaction to elements of national hegemony bequeathed to the present generation a deficiency with respect to the council's vision of collegiality, national diversities, the dignity of the person, religious liberty, and the people of God? Perhaps this is the setting that has occasioned the current historiographical debates over the council's interpretation.

---

106. John R. Roach, "Presidential Address," November 14, 1983, AASF.

www.ingramcontent.com/pod-product-compliance
Lightning Source LLC
Chambersburg PA
CBHW080346300426
44110CB00019B/2521